PROGRAM BUDGETING:

THEORY AND PRACTICE with

particular reference to the U. S.
Department of the Army

By **FREDERICK C. MOSHER**
Associate Professor of Political Science
Syracuse University

PUBLIC ADMINISTRATION SERVICE

TO MY MOTHER

*who also has had long experience
and concern in matters
budgetary*

foreword

by W. O. Reeder

From August 15, 1946 to January 31, 1953, I was in the Pentagon and concerned with the Army's budget. During the last four and a half years of that period I was intimately and importantly connected with the programming and budgeting process for the Army. As a member of the Budget Advisory Committee, I helped to formulate budgets; later in the process as the representative of my chief, I assisted in the explanation and justification of the budget before the Department of Defense, the Bureau of the Budget, and the Congress. Because of this experience, my impression of this book may be of some weight.

The study which preceded the writing of this book must have been very arduous and very thorough. In reading it, I found no error or lacuna of importance. The conclusions drawn are well based and in nearly every case coincide with my own. I should be very proud to have written it myself.

The book itself deals with the subject in a way that may have been thought of by many but certainly had never been reduced to writing. It cannot fail to be instructive even to those who have been daily engaged in budget work, for it clearly presents thought which they may have only partly formulated. To those who are ignorant of the full implications of the programming and budget process, and that will include many who are now dealing with the budget, a perusal of this book should be most enlightening. I heartily recommend this book to any who deal with the budget and fiscal processes of government and to any citizen who wishes to learn why it is not a simple matter to cut the budget at will.

W. O. REEDER
Major General, U. S. Army (Retired)

iv

foreword

by Paul H. Appleby

The professional study of public budgeting is inappropriate, I think, to undergraduate education. It belongs at the graduate level where it may be added to broad educational preparation and posed in terms going far beyond the confines of a single textbook. The first appeal I find in Professor Mosher's book, therefore, is in the fact that he has not attempted a textbook. Its second appeal, however, seems contradictory; this is in the fact that in a single volume, except for legislative handling, he has covered almost the whole range of budgeting, from technique to statesmanship.

General Reeder has testified convincingly to the accuracy and the understanding characterizing the treatment of the Army's budgeting processes and problems contained in this volume. I consider the same pages from the standpoint of one who had to do for eleven years with the budget of another—but civilian—department of government, for three years was Assistant Director of the U. S. Bureau of the Budget, and for seven years has been participating in a program of academic training for the public service. I find this book as useful and as stimulating for my purposes as General Reeder finds it for his.

Budgeting is not the only function which may provide a vantage point for the consideration of administration in the broad sense, nor the only means of controlling, directing, and coordinating the programs of government which are the valid focus of public administration. But budgeting is central and crucial, and up to now it is the most advanced, systematized, and consolidated of all the functions which might well compete with it in these respects.

The power of the purse is fundamental to organizational control. This basic power, in our government, is properly lodged in the Congress. The manageability of it for Congress is dependent upon preliminary executive powers, and these powers flow from the President downward through budget offices. These are the centers of highly competitive drives for shares in public funds, drives which reflect preoccupations with specialized responsibilities which in their turn reflect and represent popular concerns and drives. In successive levels of treatment these drives must be equated, related, and deflated. In this treatment is involved not economy alone, but program, high policy, and the transformation of democratic aspiration for order, security, and well-being into whatever practical reality appears then attainable.

Budgeting is importantly influenced by structure—governmental and societal. Structure itself is also influenced by budgeting. Good budgeting requires deep understanding of structure and skill in organizational performance. Good public budgeting requires also deep understanding of the nation and its people. The whole effectiveness and acceptability of diversified activities and the development and utilization of lines of responsibility essential to popular control are involved in budgetary considerations.

Many may get confused in the stress of the budgetary process, and pedestrian pursuit of technique can conceal or thwart purpose. Mr. Mosher's book moves solidly along the ground of budgetary reality, but it lifts the eyes of any who read it with understanding to the high issues and the great values to which technical budgeting is incidental. This is an important book for students and practitioners of public administration, whether or not they have any special concern with Army budgeting.

PAUL H. APPLEBY
Dean, Maxwell Graduate School
Syracuse University

preface

This work is an effort to merge two areas of inquiry—public budgeting and military administration—that have traditionally been treated quite distinctly. The need for such a merger today is not without significance. It is probably now true, as never before, that a true understanding of the governmental budget must include acquaintance with its largest segment. Conversely, our military plans, programs, and institutions have never depended more directly and more apparently upon the budgeting process.

The study of a department is a fruitful means of learning at least part of the budget process. Equally, the study of the budget process is a convenient means to the understanding of the organization and administrative characteristics of a department. Exploration of one without reference to the other is certain to produce an incomplete picture. The department without its budget is an organization without its well-springs and without one of its principal channels of social, economic, and political influence. The budget without the content and context of its agency is a circulatory system without the blood which it carries and the flesh for which it exists. It is process and technique, formal and to a considerable extent mythical.

My explorations within the Department of Defense have impressed me, perhaps more than anything else, with the interrelatedness of budgeting with virtually everything else that affects policy and administration. A primary significance of the budget process seems to me the bringing together of an almost infinite variety of factors and perspectives—in fact virtually the totality of government and its administration. Its study has led me into fields that are sometimes but not usually treated in studies of budgeting—military planning, unit equipment requirements, manpower control, procurement, personnel systems, and others. My focus on the central budget process itself has prevented more than brief reference to most of these, but the importance of their relation to budgeting is, I think, emphasized.

I have also concentrated upon the activities within administrative departments. The organization and processes of the Executive Office of the President, of Congress, and of other agencies outside the departments themselves are not covered in a systematic way. Likewise, I have omitted any treatment of the budgeting of nonmilitary functions within the military departments, such as the civil program of the Corps of Engineers.

My study has been directed to the Department of Defense, and the greatest concentration has been placed upon the Department of the Army. The Air Force receives somewhat less attention. I have made no careful study of Navy budgetary practice, but have referred occasionally to developments which appear pertinent to the experience in the other military departments.

For many obvious reasons, the Department of Defense and its Department of the Army are not "typical" agencies in the field of Federal budgeting. Their extremity in size, complexity, and institutionalization may nonetheless bring out, in profile, aspects and problems that might be more obscure in smaller organizations. The current, and probably the future, predominance of the military departments in terms of dollars has its own significance. In one sense at least, they are more "representative" of Federal budgeting than all the other agencies together.

The Defense Department and the Army are significant areas for an exploration of this kind for other reasons. For the last several years, they have been a seed-bed of activity and experiment in the field of budgeting and in other areas directly pertinent to budgeting. Among those in which important changes have been made, are being made, or are being planned, may be mentioned: the entire area of unification of the armed forces; the reform of procurement and supply organization and procedures; the reform of accounting systems; manpower controls; revolving funds of various types; new systems for planning and programming; performance budgeting; and the development of comptrollership. Many of these developments are, of course, significant beyond the purely military agencies, and in some respects the military departments are moving faster and farther than their civilian brethren.

My own interest in this subject was perhaps most importantly stimulated during the spring of 1952 when, as a Ford Foundation faculty fellow at Harvard, I participated in a graduate seminar given by Professor Arthur Smithies, Chairman of the Harvard Department of Economics. A number of the sessions of this course were directed to the problems of the Federal budget and particularly to those arising in connection with the Department of Defense.

Subsequently, Professor Smithies engaged me to study the systems and problems of military budgeting with particular reference to the Army and the Air Force. This research was for the purpose of providing materials to be used in a general study on Federal budgeting that he was then undertaking for the Committee for Economic Development. I spent the summer months of 1952 in and around Washington for these dual purposes. In this work I was intellectually and materially aided by the research office and staff of the Committee for Economic Development, headed by Howard B. Myers.

Early in 1952, the College of Business and the Maxwell School of Citizenship and Public Affairs of Syracuse University entered into an agreement with the Department of the Army for the training of selected officers in Army comptrollership. In preparation for this program, now in its second year, both colleges sent a number of faculty members to Washington in 1952 for the development of teaching materials. I was privileged to participate in a number of the conferences and interviews set up by the Army for this purpose. I am thus indebted to the comptroller training program both for information and ideas brought out in these meetings and, later, for the opportunity to discuss Army budgeting problems with the comptroller students themselves, experienced Army practitioners.

In preparing this study, I have relied heavily upon documentary sources, published and unpublished, that appeared pertinent to the subject matter. But the core of my research was a program of interviews with officials and employees, civilian and military, within the Department of Defense and all three of its subdepartments, and with a number of persons outside the military establishment. I talked with principal officers in the budgetary field as well as from operational agencies, and, particularly in the case of the Army, with some at all echelons down to the installation level. In these interviews, the officials were encouraged to express their views and observations about the process as they saw it—the problems, the principal considerations and factors affecting it, the key issues expressed in it. It was a search primarily for thoughts, attitudes, and perceptions.

It would be impracticable to list all those, in the Pentagon and out, who contributed to my understanding of this problem in the past eighteen months. I should like, however, to make special note of my gratitude to Professor Smithies and Mr. Myers who, in a very real sense, made this study possible; to Frederick W. Lawton, then the

Director of the Budget, and Arnold Miles, Edgar J. Owens, Henry
Puppa, William F. Schaub, and Wells Thompson, all then of the staff
of the Bureau of the Budget; to W. J. McNeil, Assistant Secretary of
Defense (Comptroller), Daniel Borth, Joseph Corie, Howard K. Hyde,
Robert C. MacClinchie, Charles A. Phillips, and Melvin K. Zucker, all
then on the Defense Comptroller's staff; to Don K. Price, then Deputy
Chairman, Research and Development Board; to John W. Macy, then
Special Assistant to the Under Secretary of the Army; to Lt. Gen.
George H. Decker, Comptroller of the Army and Leonard W. Hoel-
scher, Deputy Comptroller; to Col. Charles B. Duff, Lt. Col. Chester
E. Glassen, and Lt. Col. James B. Via, all of the Plans Branch of the
Office of the Army Comptroller; to virtually the entire staff of the Es-
timates and Funding Branch and particularly Frank Watters and Lt.
Col. D. W. Benedict; to Dr. W. J. Garvin, then of Army's G-4; to Lt.
Col. William L. Thorkelson of G-3; to Lt. Col. W. H. Van Atta, Comp-
troller at Fort Belvoir; to Col. Robert E. Benjamin and K. G. Fallon
of the Comptroller's Office at First Army Headquarters.

In the Air Force, I am particularly indebted to Brig. Gen. F. J. Dau,
Brig. Gen. W. I. Miller, Col. B. J. Webster, Lt. Col. A. C. Reid, and F.
A. Karu, all then of the Comptroller's Office; to W. T. Ellis, Jr.. and
Elmo A. Jensen in the office of the Deputy Chief of Staff, Operations.

Others who contributed greatly included: John F. Floberg, then Assistant Secretary of the Navy for Air and Comptroller of the Navy;
Rear Admiral E. A. Solomons, Deputy Comptroller; William M. Cap-
ron, Matthew Cullen, William A. Gill, Robert Jacobs, Bertram Klein,
Robert Lenhart, and Harold Stein; and my colleagues at Syracuse,
Dean Paul H. Appleby, Professors Jesse Burkhead, Howard F. Miller,
and Roscoe C. Martin, Chairman of the Department of Political Science, and Maj. Gen. W. O. Reeder (Retired). To these and the many
others who gave of their knowledge, wisdom, and time I am deeply
grateful.

Finally, I should note that most of the research on which this study
is based was conducted in 1952 and had reference to the budget work
then underway. The changes brought about in 1953 under the Republican Administration have not been treated systematically. But it does
not now appear that the basic systems and problems have been fundamentally modified to date. All responsibility for the pages that follow, of course, remains my own.

FREDERICK C. MOSHER

Syracuse University, December, 1953

contents

figures

the study of budgeting

The understanding of budgeting in its totality presents difficult problems to the student. It is a field in which several different social science disciplines are concerned and have made their contributions. But the disciplines do not quite come together. Bringing them into a meaningful context is no simple job. It involves mastering and relating their different approaches and interests, their differing degrees of abstraction and specificity, their varieties of technique, and their jargons. Few persons if any have accomplished the task to their satisfaction.

Political scientists, among the first in the field, have long been concerned with the problems involved in control of fiscal affairs, the relations of the legislature and the executive in this field, the constitutional and legal bases of fiscal activities generally and of budgeting in particular. They have given much attention to the organization of the Executive as it relates to budgeting among other things, to the Bureau of the Budget, and particularly to the organization and processes of Congress for appropriations and revenues. There have also been scattered discussions of substantive issues in the budget incident to studies of various fields of public policy such as foreign aid and social welfare.

Modern public administration, an outgrowth and still, by most definitions, a part of political science, has since its birth about half a century ago concentrated its attention in the field of budgeting upon formal organizational arrangements and procedures. Its accent has been upon the mechanism, the calendar, the forms and justifications, the classification of accounts, and the system of responsibilities. It has pushed the development of program planning, work measurement, cost accounting, and reporting. Probably more than any other field, it is responsible for the rationalist concept in budgeting and for the model form now generally accepted for the budget process on the administrative side.

1

The economists and their ancestors, the political economists, were involved in one phase of public fiscal affairs for many, many decades and even centuries. Most of the classical economists from Adam Smith on studied public finance, but their primary concern was its effect upon the nonpublic economy. Their major field of interest was upon revenues and taxation with accent upon the incidence of taxes. It was not until relatively recently, about two decades ago, that much attention was directed to the expenditure side of the budget or to the application of economic principles and techniques to public financial management. The tremendous acceleration of economists' activity in the public sphere was, of course, stimulated by the recovery experiments of the New Deal and later the problems of economic and financial management of the war economy and the efforts toward postwar planning. Specific concern with the Federal budget as an economic problem was stimulated by the development of the Fiscal Division of the Bureau of the Budget and, later, of the Council of Economic Advisers, and by the invention of such new devices as the national economic budget and the consolidated cash budget. Probably more than any other group, the economists are contributing to the understanding of, and policy relating to, the Federal budget as a totality, the interrelationships of Federal fiscal activity with the private sector of the economy, and the implications and impact of various major budgetary programs and policies. Their concern is more with substance and economic policy in the budget, less with procedural and political power aspects.

The fourth professional field which has been importantly concerned in public budgeting is that of accounting, vaguely related on one side with economics and on the other with public administration. Although accounting has served governments since time immemorial, it is probably safe to say that current emphasis in accounting thought and practice is in the area of business rather than public finance. There are intrinsic differences between the two, and the Federal accounting system, developed on foundations laid down by Alexander Hamilton, is in many ways unique unto itself. Much of the current ferment about reforms of the Federal financial system is being stimulated and led by the accounting fraternity, and part of it at least is characterized by the effort to adapt private accounting practice to the Federal system. Accounting concern extends well beyond the forms and techniques of keeping books, the classifications of accounts, the financial reports and controls. The accounts are the basis of budget estimates, in large part the informational base for evaluation and decision on budgetary questions, and the source of authority for budgetary expenditures. The classifications of accounts and the way they are related to programs, functions, and organizations, are highly significant in decision-making and management generally. The current drive in the direction of accrual accounting, costing, revolving funds, and consumer budgeting importantly affect organization, program, and the entire system of responsibility.

Other disciplines have contributed only fragmentarily to our understanding of budgeting. It is particularly unfortunate that those social sciences in the general field of social relations, such as anthropology, sociology, and social psychology, have not used the budget process as a laboratory for some of their approaches and hypotheses. There is a conspicuous need for exploration of the significance of institutional arrangements and of interpersonal relationships in budgeting.

The obvious disparity in the aspects of the various approaches is particularly significant in the study of budgeting, because the very essence of this activity is in bringing aspects together, in providing links between program and action, between policy and administration, and between an infinite multiplicity of detail and a few understandable and generalized issues. It is two movements, following each other in sequence but going in opposite directions: a movement of synthesizing and generalizing, and a reverse movement of particularizing. The concentration upon the generalized issues at one end or upon the specific details at the other misses the vital character of the phenomenon as a whole.

BUDGETING AS COMMUNICATION

Another way of expressing this is that budgeting is a device whereby the same phenomena and the same ideas are progressively translated into differing levels of meaning. If one were to ask a carpenter who is at work on a house what he is doing, he might reply, "I am pounding these nails into these boards," or, "I am helping to build this house." It is vastly improbable that he would say "I am expending these nails and these boards and depreciating this hammer," though such an answer would be correct from the accounting standpoint. If he had a broader frame of reference, he might answer, "I am part of an industry which provides the places where people can live and work and thus build the future prosperity and happiness for all of us." These do not exhaust his possible correct answers. He might say that he was simply carrying out the blueprint provided him by the contractor; or that he was only practicing his trade; or that he was abiding by the policies and regulations of his union; or that he was earning the where-withal to provide his family with food, clothing, and shelter.

Obviously, all these answers, while technically accurate, would not be equally appropriate or useful. Their propriety would depend heav-ily upon the source of, and reason for, the inquiry. It is also probable that the nature of the reply would depend upon the carpenter himself —his own view of his activity and his trade and particularly his per-ception of the inquirer and the latter's motivations.

The budget process permits, and to some extent compels, objectivity in the perception of information. This it does by formalization, by standardizing the categories of information that will be considered and the form of their presentation, and by prescribing specifically against the introduction of certain kinds of personal and institutional consid-erations. In reference to our carpenter analogy, the attempt is made to minimize the carpenter's subjective considerations—as well as those of the inquirer—in framing the answer to the question.

The budget process also serves as a device whereby the carpenter's answer may be translated into a level of meaning useful and significant to consideration and decision by the inquirers at successively broader levels of cognizance. Thus it may be put together with the answers of a great many other carpenters, plumbers, electricians, and other build-ers. The kind of meaning appropriate to each successive level may well be, and to some extent probably should be, different from the ones below and above it. In more specific terms, we might imagine the information having to do with a carpenter's activities and the plans for his future work in the Army Corps of Engineers. Does the budget process provide the information necessary for planning and decision at the level of his foreman? the project director? the District Engineer? the Division Engineer? the Chief of Engineers? the Chief of Staff? the Secretary of the Army? the Bureau of the Budget? the President? the Congress? It is evident that the information necessary and appropriate to the kinds of decisions at many of these levels differs not only in its extent and in its detail, but also in kind. This applies to the accumu-lating or estimating part of the process and also to the reverse part of the process, the allocation and allotment of resources into increasingly specific purposes and accounts.

There are, of course, a variety of ways to translate information in both the synthesizing and the "spreading" processes. The ways in which it is done importantly affect the kinds of treatment and kinds of decisions that can be made at various levels. Furthermore, it can and usually must be done in various different ways at the same time for the same items of information. This is why budgetary classification has always assumed an important role; in one sense, it is the essence of the rationale of the recent strivings toward "performance budgeting."

The importance of the two-way movement approach to budgeting is directly related to the factor of organizational size and functional heterogeneity. The greater the size and complexity, the greater is the factor of organizational distance, the more difficult is the communication, and the greater are the disparities in points of view and kinds of considerations brought to bear upon the same information at different levels. Furthermore, in large organizations, the possibility of effective consideration of details progressively declines as the information moves up the levels of hierarchy. A significant factor in our present budgetary problems is that we have inherited from the past budgetary practices and philosophy which were originally developed for organizations of far less size and complexity. For example, it may be perfectly appropriate for a town council in a small town to consider the job of an individual carpenter, his wage and his habits of economy or profligacy in the use of boards and nails. But for the President or the Congress to give similar attention to the Corps of Engineers carpenter at Camp Drum would be inappropriate, useless, and in fact impossible on any systematic basis. Budgetary information and budgetary classifications must be tailored to the needs, the scope, and the areas of effective decision at various levels in large organizations.

Purposes and Principles of Budgeting

The budget process thus presented is primarily a system of communications, regularized and cyclical. Its purposes fall into two logical categories: first, the bringing of information to the proper level for the making of decisions—a category in governmental policies, programs, and objectives, which we may roughly classify as policy; and, second, the providing of information both upward and downward so that those decisions will be properly carried out—a category we may roughly classify as administrative.

Its potential value in the first connection is tremendous and unique. It is the only device invented in democratic governments which does, or can do, all of the following things:

1. Bring about a regular, periodic reconsideration and re-evaluation of government purposes and objectives.
2. Facilitate a comparative evaluation of different purposes and programs in relation to each other and in relation to their relative costs.
3. Provide a basis for examining the total role of the government and its

cost, in relation to the private sector of the economy, and thus for tailoring the governmental program to the society and the economy as a whole.
4. Provide a periodic link among the administrative organizations, the Executive, the Congress, and segments of the public, and thus an important basis of democratic information and discussion and of democratic control of governmental activities.

The second category of budgetary purposes involves its use as an instrument for carrying out public policy legally, honestly, and efficiently. In this function it:

1. Provides the legal basis for the expenditure of funds.
2. Provides the framework for public accounts and fiscal accountability.
3. Makes possible systematic re-examination of internal operations from the standpoint of efficiency and economy.
4. Facilitates delegation of operating as well as financial authority and responsibility, while providing the basis for central controls.

It is probable that the greater part of budgetary theory and of budgetary principles have been dedicated to the second, or administrative, type of purpose. In fact there appears to be fairly widespread agreement on what these principles are. Many of them are expressed in the literature on budgeting. Presented below, for yardstick purposes and without any attempt to develop new, or criticize old, principles of budgeting, is a synthesis of some of the "doctrines" of budgetary administration that are most pertinent to large governmental organizations.

A first principle is the principle of responsibility: that officials be held responsible for the performance of their assigned functions and the utilization of resources for that purpose; and that they not be held responsible for either more or less than the scope of their authority over activities and resources. The primary responsibility for the allocation and consumption of resources, whether they be in the form of funds or goods and services purchased and paid for elsewhere, is vested in the using organization.

A second principle is that authority and responsibility be delegated to the operating echelon where activities are performed and resources are utilized. Administration, and the responsibility therefore, should be "on the spot," not "absentee."

A third principle is that officials held responsible for performance should have a primary voice in the planning of how their activities will be performed and in estimating the resource requirements necessary to perform them. Such plans and estimates must be reviewed and adjusted by higher authority, and the planning official should be called upon to support and defend his plans. But basically the functions of planning and carrying out plans within approved missions should be vested at the same echelon.

A fourth principle is that the operating official should derive his authority and responsibility from one and only one higher unit. And this unit should be the source both of his program and his resources to perform that program. His plans and estimates should go to that unit; his directives and resources should come from it; and his accountability for performance should be to it.

A fifth principle is that fiscal responsibility and responsibility for other resources be merged with program responsibility at every echelon and not follow separate and unrelated or poorly related channels.

A sixth principle is that methods and criteria be established and utilized to hold operating officials accountable for results in relation to costs. This requires the measurement of work and of costs, the development of standards, and the comparison of work and costs with like activities outside and inside the agency and from year to year.

A seventh principle is that each official with responsibility be made in fact, responsible; that is, that he have a stake in and an incentive for exercising his responsibilities in an effective and efficient manner. Positively, this means that he should anticipate a reward for a job well done; negatively, a penalty for one poorly done. Ultimately, the system of responsibility must be tied in with the personnel system.

THE CONTEXT OF BUDGETING

The purposes and the principles enumerated above are, it is thought, useful generalizations for the evaluation of budget systems. And they are so used in this document. But it should be borne in mind that they are generalized; they are abstract; and they are impersonal. They are meaningful and useful only to the extent that they are applied to organizations and institutions which are themselves understood. Budgeting, like other social processes, is a human undertaking, carried on by people who are subject to a wide variety of influences and motivations. The process itself can be examined, evaluated, and improved only to a minor degree unless there is appreciation of the totality of the situations and the environment within which it is carried on. This contextual framework is of tremendous importance in national budgeting and perhaps particularly military budgeting, and its significance is commonly underestimated.

In an article published late in 1952, D. W. Brogan, eminent British political scientist, chided the American people for what he termed "The Illusion of American Omnipotence." [1] He referred to our recent disposition to attribute to ourselves, and more particularly to certain

---

[1] *Harper's Magazine*, December, 1952, pp. 21-8.

allegedly treacherous or incompetent leaders, full responsibility for the course of world events. He pointed out that if we assume American blame for the fall of Czechoslovakia or the revolution of China, we must also assume that the United States had within its power to determine the social and political developments in these countries and elsewhere in the world. He did not dispute that American policy may influence and perhaps modify events far from our shores. But the thought that we, or a few of our leaders, could halt or reverse the forces of change in China, developing out of a revolution that started with our blessings a quarter of a century ago, reflects, according to Brogan, a conceit that may be frustrating and demoralizing to ourselves and dangerous to our relations with others.

This same illusion, or at least a very parallel one, was illustrated during the course of the 1952 election campaign after Adlai Stevenson's remark that the extent of possible budget cuts would depend most heavily upon decisions made in Moscow. This suggestion of a restriction upon unlimited American discretion over a matter of domestic as well as international import attracted virulent attack. One suspects that the attack was effective. Yet the truth of the statement, however repugnant to national pride and however impolitic, could hardly be more obvious. The tendency in American attitudes and thought noted by Mr. Brogan in the field of foreign affairs is related to, and probably an outgrowth of, a widespread confidence in American mastery over our own internal affairs and destiny. The idea of omnipotence, identified with a relatively small number of political and administrative leaders, is a significant feature in our political culture. It is a source of strength and of challenge. "Nothing is impossible." Yet it also begets misunderstanding and frustration. Our national public life seems to be a machine-gun staccato of day-to-day climaxes, each linked with a few well-known names of public figures. It becomes difficult for the student, let alone the radio-listening public, to link the gun shots together, to find the strands of meaning which can make out of a series of actions a course, or a trend, or a direction of events. The imputation to the aimers and firers of the guns—the decision-makers—of omnipotence in aiming and timing the gunfire implies a freedom in their action which in many cases is quite unreal. This, of course, encourages us later on to hold them responsible for consequences, or alleged consequences, of events over which, in fact, they may have had little or no control.

There is no question that, with the expanding role of government in our national and international life, with the increasingly interlocking and interdependent structure of our society, and with the apparent centralization of political power in a relatively few officials, leadership in the governmental sphere has assumed a crucial and decisive role. What is left out of the focus upon these leaders, so dramatized by the press and the other media of mass communications, is that their decisions and pronouncements, including those affecting the budget, must grow out of a context that is full of unknowns, of prior commitments, and of influences that are relatively uncontrolled. The freedom of action of a President, or of a subcommittee of Congress, at any given moment in time is limited, and the degree to which the limitation is recognized is a measure of the sense of responsibility of the official or the group of officials involved.

Parts of the context are the large *areas of crucial importance to future plans which are unknown or relatively unresponsive to control.* These factors are particularly significant in military budgeting. The plans and capabilities of potential enemies, cited above in reference to Adlai Stevenson's statement, are perhaps the most significant. Future technical developments in the design of weapons are increasingly subject to planning and control but still constitute an area of high uncertainty. Industrial development and productivity, the potentialities of allies, and defensive ability to ward off bomb attacks on our industrial centers all introduce elements of uncertainty, varyingly responsive to public planning and control.

A second important element conditioning budgetary decision-making is that of *time.* It has become a popular recreation, unsuccessfully formalized in the legislative budget provision of the Legislative Reorganization Act of 1946, to settle in advance upon an expenditure figure for the coming fiscal year. There seems here to be an assumption that a President or a Congress has discretion for any given year to determine upon a figure of 90 or 80 or 70 or 50 billion dollars as a desirable budget. No President and no Congress can escape from the past, whether or not it is of his or its own making. A large part of the annual expenditure budget is in fact legally committed at least one year before the budget year. The Congress which went into office in January, 1953, for example, made appropriations for the fiscal year ending June 30, 1954, but a major proportion of the expenditures of that year already had been appropriated or otherwise committed by prior Congresses. The decisions which Congress made in the spring of 1953 will influence importantly the expenditures of fiscal year 1955, but the 83rd Congress will probably adjourn permanently soon after the beginning of that fiscal year, to be succeeded by the 84th Congress. Of course Presidents and Congresses can and do make important and crucial decisions affecting the next following budget year and even affecting the current one. But in public financial affairs, as in public policy matters, there is a continuity, an "on-going-ness," not easy to interrupt. The bulk of national programs and the national budgets which reflect their costs fall in this category.

The past is parent to the present and also, to a considerable degree, to the future. Current governmental authorities can interpret the past, can juggle the records of it, but they can not change it. The social, economic, and political forces that have grown out of the past and have given rise to public policies for the present do not, except under the pressure of total emergencies, cease or reverse themselves. A great many of these are legally or morally protected: service on the public debt, fulfillment of obligations for foreign aid, payment on social security, payment to contractors for goods and services, and retirement to civil servants. Others, amendable in legislation and appropriations, remain responsive to the forces and the needs which procreated them: build-up of the military establishment, support for farm prices, services to veterans, Federal aid in social welfare, highways, and many others. The degree of commitment, legal, political, and moral, of course varies widely among different programs. An important qualification for the statesman and the administrator is his awareness and understanding of these factors. It is indispensable to his determination of the points at which current actions will be both possible and desirable, the pace at which they should be accomplished, and the effects which may reasonably be expected.

Our political leaders seldom have the opportunity to "start from scratch." More often, their actions are of the order of accelerating or decelerating or changing the direction of programs and of movements. When they do initiate new undertakings, it is usually in response to forces and to needs that have been developed and articulated for a considerable period of time. Many, perhaps most, of their significant innovations require years, terms of office, and decades for full accomplishment. Roosevelt's TVA, a product of more than a decade of political gestations, did not complete even its physical program during his lifetime, even though he spent more than three terms in the White House. Truman's Point Four was just getting away from "home base" as he vacated office, a full four years to the day from the time of his original proposal. The military build-up, begun soon after the outbreak of hostilities in Korea, will not achieve its primary objective until 1955 or 1956, at which time it will be under the direction of a different President as well as a different Congress from those who initiated it.

The appreciation of the temporal context of budgeting is made more difficult because it is accomplished in periodic cycles. One of the distinguishing features, and one of the principal values, of the budget is that it recurs every year on a calendar basis, forcing a systematic re-examination of public policies and activities. The Constitution, the laws, and the necessities of official accountability have compelled a somewhat artificial division of time, for public purposes, into discrete fiscal years that end and begin at midnight of June 30. The fiscal year is indeed a very real and important matter in public administration and it has great program and operational significance, probably more than might be desirable. Practically all agency programs are geared to it, as is a large part of the procedure of Congress. In the fiscal realm, it has been frequently dramatized by the unseemly obligation of un-committed funds in late June; by the dying agencies which must go out of business by the end of the fiscal year; by the occasional failures of Congress to appropriate funds in time and the payless paydays of Federal employees.

The fiscal year is unquestionably a convenient and necessary device for administrative, accounting, and public control purposes. But to the extent that it encourages thinking of each year as an "autonomous" unit in time, independent of the year that preceded and the year that will follow, it is deceptive. Most public programs are growing or declining or maintaining an even keel through the months and years. Midnight of June 30 has no magic significance to the needs, the demands, and the reasons for public services. In fact, many fiscal and administrative inventions have been motivated at least partially by the desire to minimize the disruptive effects of fiscal-year autonomy—the distinction of obligations from expenditures, contract authorizations, corporation budgets, revolving funds, permanent appropriations, and "no-year" appropriations.

But the most important effect of "fiscal-year thinking" is its encouragement of the feeling that the administrative and legislative powers in a given year have complete authority and responsibility for the fiscal-year budget as such; that it must be considered and treated as an entity. Many of the most important decisions that go into the annual budget affect the expenditures for the fiscal year for which the budget is made and announced moderately, slightly, or not at all. The emphasis placed upon the totals for the fiscal year under consideration detracts from the interest in, and understanding of, the longer-run implications and impact of these decisions. And the anticipation of this over-stress upon fiscal-year totals by the decision-makers themselves must certainly affect the determinations that they make. If these officials are considered authoritative with respect to the oncoming fiscal-year budget and responsible for it, they will probably be at least tempted to make it as politically palatable as they can, even when it means transferring unpleasant surprises to the future. An indirect effect of the concept of executive-legislative omnipotence when it is coupled with that of annuality of the budget is to encourage short-run as against long-run thinking and planning.

A third important factor in the context of budget decisions is that of *the institutions and the organizations* involved in the process of budget-making and execution. It is no accident but an important governmental symbolism that the estimates which the President annually transmits to the Congress are widely known as "The President's Budget." The attachment of complete and final responsibility in the President is a fundamental and essential fact in our system of government and administration. But it would be a mistake to assume that the President personally produced the budget, or even that his office and his Bureau of the Budget produced it. The budget is a product of the entire administration. Decisions, small and large but cumulatively of real importance, are made by officials six to ten echelons away from the President. The legislative and the administrative heads can and do make crucial judgments on specific substantive questions raised by the budget process. But even in this activity they are very largely dependent upon the information which is presented to them and the manner and the form in which it is presented. They can influence the way decisions of others are made and the content of the decisions in many direct and many more indirect ways. But it is most important to appreciate that their means are the influencing of behaviors, attitudes, and motivations of other people, associated more or less distantly, rather than the making of all the decisions themselves.

The key requisites for the administrator and the legislator in budgeting are that they be adequately equipped with information to make the best possible decisions on the matters which they, from their particular vantage points, should make; and that they equip those below them with the perspectives and the objectives necessary to the making of the best decisions at their respective levels. The budget process is essentially a system of communications—perhaps the most highly developed and comprehensive formal system of communications in American government. The importance of the communications aspect increases with the size and complexity of the organization, for size implies distance between operating levels and administrative and legislative levels. If budget planning and control are relatively centralized, their wisdom and effectiveness depend heavily upon the operational information conveyed to central levels. If they are relatively decentralized, democratic control and responsibility depend upon the effectiveness with which objectives and perspectives may be conveyed from central to operating levels and assimilated by the latter. In either case, imperfections in communication detract from the true authority of the leaders and from the effective scope of their responsibility.

It is not enough that a President, a Congress, or a department head sincerely want to do the "right" thing, nor that they make wise decisions on the matters they should decide at their level, nor that procedures and organizational arrangements be perfected whereby such matters, and only such, reach them. It is equally important that they be able effectively to influence the decisions of subordinates in accordance with their understandings of problems and objectives. The degree of responsibility often associated with administrative heads by the press and the public is unreal and even impossible. For the leader must work with and through organization, a process which is usually difficult, subtle, and gradual. The pronouncement by spokesmen for the Hoover reports of 3 billion dollars of waste in the Federal establishment did not eliminate the waste. Similarly, the judgment of a President, a department head, or a bureau chief that there was waste in his establishment would not automatically eliminate it, even if the source of the waste were specifically identified. Some people in the organization first have to be stimulated to take action—and for many important areas of alleged waste, action would be required of thousands and even hundreds of thousands of personnel. The military chief of one of the service departments, concerned about the extravagant use of electricity because personnel failed to turn off the unused lights in their rooms and offices, suggested that an order be drafted for his signature directing all personnel to decrease their use of lights by 10 per cent. He dropped the idea when subordinates advised him that such an order would be unenforceable. If a four-star officer cannot direct such a simple change in behaviors of subordinates, who can? And what other recourse does he have to influence their motivations and behaviors in accordance with a need which he can observe and feel?

A going organization is a great package of systems, traditions, habits, values and beliefs, relationships, and behavioral patterns. In the main, these are inevitable elements of cooperative effort, and desirable ones. They form the basis for predictable behaviors, for group and individual reliability, for personal security and group morale. They also

constitute resistances and insurance against rapid change. An understanding of the institutional forces, their relative strengths and mean-
ings in the minds of the people linked by them, is essential to the
effective management and control of an agency's program and budget.
The institutions provide the framework within which and through
which—in some degree, by which and for which—budgets are formed
and executed. The budget process itself and the organizational arrangements for budgeting may now be regarded as highly institutionalized.
But the significance of the institutional context of budgeting is far
broader and deeper than this. The grades, ranks, compensation, and
specializations of personnel; the methods and procedures of working
together; the goals and aspirations of groups; the accustomed patterns
of formal and informal organization; the configurations of power within
the organization; and even the missions and established programs—all
of these affect and are affected by the budget and must be reckoned
with by the administrator or legislator seeking changes.

A fourth element of the context of public budgeting may be termed
the human or interpersonal factor. Though budgets and their supporting documents are almost deadly in their impersonality, and though
the official process is highly formalized, all budget decisions are made
by human beings as individuals or in association, working with and
sometimes against each other. The record and the literature in the
field unfortunately provide little in the way of description of the
actual processes by which most budgetary decisions are reached. We
see the official "position" that resulted and the formal reasons for it,
but we can only imagine the course of the path to the "position." The
very rigors and formalities of the process probably protect the budget
from many possible abuses on purely personal bases. Yet there is
reason to believe that the ambitions, professional interests, pride, and
even pet foibles and prejudices of individuals find their way into estimates, as well as into the use of appropriated funds. There are cases
of mutual "back-scratching" and "log-rolling" within the administrative structure as well as within Congress and between the two.

It is dangerous to generalize about the prevalence and impact of the
human factor in budgeting. But it may be worth noting certain interpersonal situations which appear to be both widespread and significant. For example, it is probable that most administrators tend to
identify their personal progress and welfare with that of their programs and organization. To some extent, the strength and security of
an organization is associated with its size, the rank of its personnel,
and the amount of funds available to it. The importance and indis-

pensability of an administrator's program and organization appears, and probably should appear, greater to him than to those in other organizations or to those at higher levels who must balance the demands of many different units. There is thus normally, though not universally, a fairly constant pressure for expansion from both organizational and personal sources.

A second factor working in the same direction has been termed the law of anticipated reactions. An administrator expecting higher echelons to cut his estimates will insure himself against serious damage by building them up to the maximum that he can reasonably defend—and sometimes beyond it. To the outsider this appears as "padding" and "empire-building," but the perpetrator can rationalize it as only common sense and self-protection. It is not unknown that budgets be padded as a favor to reviewing bodies; it gives them an opportunity to make and proclaim cuts without real damage. Indeed, the very expectation of budget review may encourage budget padding.

One view of budgeting is that it is a system of orderly competition in which the competition occurs not in the market place but in the councils of higher authority. Each administrator is competing with his associates for his share of the "pie," and the pie is usually not big enough to go around. But, as in private enterprise, combinations in restraint of competition are not uncommon, and they are about as difficult to deal with. Strong unitary agencies may develop a solid budgetary position in advance, stifling internal competition in order to present a united front before—and against—the next higher echelon, the Bureau of the Budget, and Congress. The same phenomenon sometimes occurs at the bureau level, the regional level, even the division level within agencies. The tendency is undoubtedly strengthened when the administrative personnel within the unit are strongly bound together by a common core of doctrine, professionalism, and career identification through the personnel system. Such restraints to free internal competition are a major problem in public budgeting, particularly in the military services, because they make intelligent review at higher levels more difficult and virtually force the top reviewing bodies to operate below their proper levels—or "give up the ghost."

Partly because of its competitive nature, the budget process tends to accentuate and dramatize conflicts and antagonisms between individuals and groups. In fact, it generates some of its own. Differences and conflicting objectives as between organizations, professional groups, echelons, field and headquarters, and staff and line, are probably a normal and, by and large, constructive part of the governmental environment. The budget process sometimes removes the protective clothing from the competitors and reduces these conflicts to a naked struggle for power or survival. Such struggles within agencies, or between them and the Bureau of the Budget or a Congressional sub-committee, may leave deep-seated hostilities in the minds of the participants, which are communicated to others in the organization. This potential hostility is endemic in many agencies, and has led at least one Federal budget officer privately to describe Federal budgeting as a process of mutual and endless suspicion of the other fellow. Budgeting is not merely an objective search for "truth"; it is a struggle between differing points of view and competing programs. And not least among the qualifications of an administrator and a budget officer are their abilities as tacticians and gladiators in the budget process.

Most of the human elements in the context of Federal budgeting are less theatrical than those mentioned above, but they are nonetheless important and probably more prevalent. Not a few budgeteers can probably call to mind without difficulty examples of professional or "line" officers who are typically resentful and resistant to real substantive questioning by nonprofessionals. They and their politically appointed superiors can probably recall their frustrations in trying to penetrate the plans and estimates of career-minded substantive officers. A fact attendant upon a good many budget review processes is the reluctance of a reviewer to analyze critically the estimates of an officer of higher rank or status, particularly when the future career of the former may be influenced by the latter.

Group relationships and friendships, particularly those that are reinforced by professional, working association, are often a significant influence even when unacknowledged. An example is the sometimes close professional tie between budget examiners at different echelons of the same organization. The efforts of some budget offices to clothe their activities with legitimacy by identifying themselves with the status and position if not the person of the top officers have effects on the way the process itself progresses, as do their sometimes parallel efforts to enshroud their determinations with secrecy. The impact of individual personalities upon the budget is frequently great: for example, the Patton-type administrator—dominant, aggressive, prone to "crash" decisions—who leaves to his harried staff the picking up of the pieces, the finding of funds for decisions already made, and the justification of the deeds. In contrast, there is the passive administrator, frustrated, bewildered, or, in some cases, fascinated by the red tape, to whom program becomes subordinate to process.

In the military services, these kinds of phenomena are complicated by the problems involved in civil-military relationships, the emphasis upon ranks and statuses, the officer-enlisted relationship, the regular-reserve relationship, and the officer rotation policy.

One other cluster of factors in the context of budgeting is the whole system of *political, economic, and social forces and pressures* working on the budget process from outside the organizations concerned, as well as from a combination of internal-external relations at various echelons. These are not discussed at length here, partly because they have been extensively explored in other studies.[2] Obviously, major budgetary policies reflect administrative and legislative responses to the total political situation, the current state of alarm, interest, or apathy of the public, the economic situation, the conditions and trend in prices, and other factors. The influences of producers and suppliers, of local groups seeking military construction, of private social and professional groups are equally well recognized.

The Budget and Rationality

The foregoing paragraphs have dwelt upon some of the principal kinds of factors that make up the environment in which national budgets are developed and administered. These included the unknown and uncontrollable or only partially controllable factors; time and its impact upon present budgetary behavior; organizational and institutional factors; personal and interpersonal factors; and political, social, and economic forces.

One intent of this presentation has been to indicate the boundaries of complete freedom of action and decision upon the budget at any one time. More positively, statesmen can be more effective if they recognize the totality of the conditions and forces affected in and by the budget. The discussion is thus to be considered less as a formulation of limitations than as an extension of the area of effective action. An un-

---

[2] Few subjects in the field of budgeting and appropriations have had more extensive treatment. See, for example, David B. Truman, *The Governmental Process* (New York: Alfred H. Knopf, 1951), especially his Chapter VIII on "The Ordeal of the Executive." In fact, a considerable part of the literature on politics and interest groups deals with this problem. The historical study by Lucius Wilmerding, *The Spending Power* (New Haven: Yale University Press, 1943), discusses this subject frequently. A large part of the work by Arthur Maass, *Muddy Waters: The Army Engineers and the Nation's Rivers* (Cambridge: Harvard University Press, 1951), deals with this problem in an area close to, though not covered by, this study. Finally, we should refer to two primary references in this field: Pendleton Herring, "The Politics of Fiscal Policy," *Yale Law Journal*, March, 1938, pp. 724-45; and Paul H. Appleby, "The Influence of the Political Order," *American Political Science Review*, April, 1948, pp. 272-83.

derstanding of the full context should help in focusing attention upon those points at which action decisions may truly be decisive.

Public administration has to do with social change, its direction, its speed, sometimes its prevention. The job of the politically responsible official is to bring about change in directions deemed desirable, or to stop it when undesirable. In determining what is or is not desirable, he is to some extent dependent upon public organizations themselves. Part of his responsibility is simply to assure that such organizations are responsive to changes in program needs. Another part is to utilize effectively the instruments that are available to bring about change in desired directions. And this requires understanding of all the factors entering into institutional behavior, the full context of governmental decision and action.

The complexities and the apparent contradictions of public budgeting should not be construed as arguments for an approach of either opportunism or determinism. The budget process remains one of the supreme examples of rationality in government. This is, in many ways, its principal feature. And it is proper to assume that those immediately concerned with it are, with few exceptions, capable and desirous of making their decisions in a rational manner. In budgetary terms, they will act favorably on proposals of which the social benefits, total or marginal, are expected to exceed the costs, and vice versa.

In public affairs, only a part of either costs or benefits can be measured precisely in dollar figures. It is often more than difficult, it is metaphysical, to weight short-term dollar costs against long-term social benefits or short-term benefits against long-term costs. It is hardly possible to give dollar values to benefits and costs that are largely social, institutional, or purely "human." Nonetheless valuations, or at least judgments, on such questions *are made* and almost *have to be made* in the budget process. It is at least to be hoped that such judgments will be better informed and wiser ones if they are reached with an understanding of how the budget proposals have been originated and processed and if the "actor," the judge himself, appreciates the context within which he himself is operating.

It is equally important that those of us in the audience see how the budget actions are taken "in depth," looking beyond and behind the dramatic and well-publicized episodes that dominate the stage from time to time. In perhaps no other organization in the national government is examination and analysis to this end more demanding in its challenge or potentially more rewarding than in the military establishment, to which the remaining chapters principally pertain.

chapter II

the setting of military budgeting

When I became Chief of Staff upon my return from Europe in 1945, I felt that all our war experience had rendered obsolete the defense organization then existing. I was convinced then as I am today that effective coordination of the services in war requires central planning in time of peace.

This is the essence of unity in the armed forces. But that unity must also extend to the procurement and administration of all the costly materiel and equipment of modern warfare. It was the hope of all of us who worked to achieve the passage of the National Defense Act of 1947 that this kind of unity was in the making.

This has not proved to be the case. Such unity as we have achieved is too much form and too little substance. . . .

DWIGHT D. EISENHOWER.[1]

The period from which this study springs is one for which we are little prepared by our past experience. After three years of undeclared war half-way around the world, we are now tensed in an uneasy truce. The beginning of the war occasioned, perhaps belatedly, the beginning of a tremendous build-up in our military preparedness, a build-up which is continuing with or without truce. In fact, only a fraction of our military strength, in material terms, has been used in Korea. Until 1953, not even that fraction was politically acknowledged in the annual military budgets. We have gradually diverted an increasing proportion of our productive resources to military purposes; and we have done it in a political and economic situation short of all-out war. Excepting the possible contingency of total war, the likelihood is that the present situation will persist—that of a democratic nation in "tiptoe" military posture.

---

[1] In an address in Baltimore, reported in the *New York Times*, September 26, 1952.

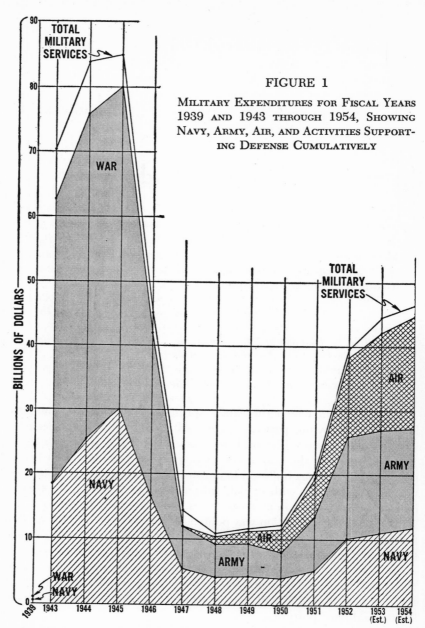

FIGURE 1

MILITARY EXPENDITURES FOR FISCAL YEARS
1939 AND 1943 THROUGH 1954, SHOWING
NAVY, ARMY, AIR, AND ACTIVITIES SUPPORT-
ING DEFENSE CUMULATIVELY

Based upon the *Budget of the United States Government for the Fiscal Year
Ending June 30, 1954,* Special Analysis I, and also the *Budgets* for prior years.

Our budgets, and particularly our military budgets, have assumed a new role and a new significance. The first, and more obvious, change is the increase in their dimension, both absolutely and relatively. The absolute picture is shown in Figure 1. Our military expenditures, those for the Defense and the three military departments, plus those assigned by the Bureau of the Budget for "Activities Supporting Defense," appear now to be leveling off between forty and fifty billions per year. This total is a little more than half of the expenditures for comparable activities at the peak of World War II and is something more than four times the peak expenditures for such purposes during World War I.[2] Peacetime military expenditures until 1939 had not exceeded one billion dollars, and between 1922 and 1940 never exceeded 20 per cent of total national expenditures.[3] In contrast, our national expenditures for military purposes are now running annually some 60 per cent of the total national expenditures and more than four times the total national expenditures in 1939.[4]

Historically, we may now divide the past twenty years of military budgeting into roughly four periods, with the fifth one in the offing. The first one, running roughly from 1933 through 1939, was the period of the depression and the New Deal during which military budgets were relatively small and received relatively little attention. For most of this period, the national budget amounted to considerably less than 10 billion dollars, and military expenditures ran 15 per cent or less of this total.

The second period, starting in fiscal year 1940 and ending with fiscal year 1945, was the war period. During the peak years, military expenditures rose to nearly 85 billion, almost 90 per cent of the national budget. This was followed by the postwar economy drive from about fiscal year 1946 through fiscal year 1950. It was characterized by the effort to minimize military expenditures, an effort that was partially

---

[2] For the comparison with World War I, see Otto D. Nelson, *National Security and the General Staff* (Washington: Infantry Journal Press, 1946), pp. 592-3.

[3] *Ibid.* See also the *Budgets of the United States Government* for these years.

[4] It should be borne in mind that the figures here charged to defense include only those attributed by the Bureau of the Budget to Military Services, most of which are expended directly by the Army, Navy, and Air Force Departments. A very substantial part of the remainder of the national budget is attributable to defense activities. For example, in 1952, when total national expenditures for nonmilitary items amounted to 27 billion, 5 billion of this total were charged to foreign military and economic assistance; 1.7 billion were charged to the development and control of atomic energy; 4.8 billion were charged to veterans' services

frustrated by the growing "cold war" psychology. Nonetheless, military expenditures dropped to around 12 billion dollars a year, a little under one-third of national expenditures.

The fourth period, the one in which we are still involved, was prompted very largely by the Communist aggression in Korea in June, 1950. It is the stage of post-Korea build-up, beginning with fiscal year 1951 and extending through 1954, and, in part, through 1955. Barring all-out war or an unexpected onset of all-out peace, it should blend into a fifth period in military budgets—the "plateau" stage of continued military readiness in a twilight world, half way between war and peace. The "build-up" period has been marked, in budgetary terms, by a quadrupling of our military expenditures and a doubling of their proportion to total national expenditures. The plateau period which is expected to follow will probably result in some reduction in total annual expenditures for military purposes, but the continuance of a relatively high level.[5]

The tabulation below, which juxtaposes data for selected years illustrative of each period, emphasizes these trends.

Period	Illustrative Years	Annual Military Expenditure (Fiscal Years) (billions)	Proportion of National Expenditure (Fiscal Years) (per cent)	Proportion of Gross National Product (Calendar Years) (per cent)
I New Deal (1933–39)	1939	1	12	1
II W. W. II (1940–45)	1944	84	88	41
III Postwar (1946–50)	1948	11	33	6
IV Build-up (1951–54)	1952	40	60	14 (est.)

and benefits, a cost of past wars; and 5.9 billion were the cost of interest on the public debt, most of which was a product of war. As a matter of fact, a considerable portion of the remaining 10 billion was directly or indirectly attributable to war and defense.

[5] Former President Truman in his last budget message estimated roughly that expenditures by the Department of Defense for military purposes would stay at a level "in the neighborhood of 35 to 40 billion dollars annually." "Budget Message of the President," in *The Budget of the United States Government for the Fiscal Year Ending June 30, 1954*, p. 13.

The contrasts among these four periods up to date are set forth in Figures 2 and 3, which show the proportions of military expenditures to the total national budget and to the gross national product respectively. It is apparent from these figures that we are still far below the

FIGURE 2

MILITARY EXPENDITURES AS A PROPORTION OF TOTAL BUDGET EXPENDITURES
For Fiscal Years 1939 and 1943 through 1953

Fiscal Year Ending June 30	Expenditures for Military Services (billions)	Total National Expenditures (billions)	Proportion of Military to Total Expenditures (per cent)
1939	1.1	9.0	12
1943	70.3	79.6	88
1944	83.8	95.3	88
1945	84.6	98.7	86
1946	45.1	60.7	74
1947	14.3	39.3	37
1948	11.0	33.8	33
1949	11.9	40.1	30
1950	12.3	40.2	31
1951	20.5	44.6	46
1952	39.7	66.1	60
1953 (est.)	44.4	74.6	60

Based upon the *Budget of the United States Government for the Fiscal Year Ending June 30, 1954,* Special Analysis I, and also the *Budgets* for prior years.

total war economy of the early and mid-forties, particularly in relation to the sharply rising gross national product. But it is equally apparent that we are well above any previous peacetime year in both the amount and the relative importance of military expenditures. And the extent to which the total economy is dependent upon military expenditures is only hinted by the figures.

Parallel and of at least equal importance to the great size of national military budgets is the new and different role they now play in the shaping of national policy. During the thirties, military expenditures were a minor segment of the national budget. They played only the slightest part in the drive toward fuller employment and were in fact subjected to much the same "penny-pinching" economy drives as they had been during the twenties. Military expenditures were authorized

FIGURE 3

GOVERNMENT PURCHASES OF GOODS AND SERVICES FOR NATIONAL SECURITY
AS A PROPORTION OF GROSS NATIONAL PRODUCT
Calendar Years 1939 and 1943 through 1952

Calendar Year	Government Purchases for National Security (billions)	Gross National Product (billions)	Proportion of Purchases for National Security to Gross National Product (per cent)
1939	1.2	91.3	1
1943	79.7	194.3	41
1944	87.5	213.7	41
1945	73.8	215.2	34
1946	18.5	211.1	9
1947	12.0	233.3	5
1948	15.5	259.0	6
1949	18.9	258.2	7
1950	18.3	284.2	6
1951	36.7	329.2	11
1952 (est.)	48.9	345.1	14

Derived from Table B-1, "Gross National Product or Expenditure, 1929–1952,"
Appendix B, "The Annual Review, January, 1953," The Council of Economic Advisors. Published with *The Economic Report of the President*, Transmitted to the Congress, January 14, 1953.

on a niggardly basis, pretty largely as a necessary rock bottom of national defense.[6]

The war reversed this trend but without changing the importance of the budget fundamentally. Budget dollars followed military requirements as they were estimated by the military officials. The short and critical items were supplies, transport, and manpower, not dollars. As Huzar later wrote "During the war years Congressmen were anxious that the Military Establishment should have all it needed. . . . By 1943 the authority delegated to administrative officers by law to transfer funds among appropriation titles minimized legislative questions about the sufficiency of individual items in military budgets, and the

[6] See particularly the accounts by Elias Huzar of the efforts of Army Chiefs of Staff MacArthur and Marshall to obtain more than minimal appropriations during this period, in *The Purse and the Sword* (Ithaca: Cornell University Press, 1950), pp. 133-156.

large carry-overs of unexpended funds made inquiries about the over-all sufficiency of the Army's estimates superfluous."[7] Or, to quote the words of one Congressman on the floor of the House: ". . . I am taking the word of the General Staff of the War Department, the people who are running this show. If they tell me this is what they need for the successful prosecution of this war and for ultimate victory, I am for it. Whether it staggers me according to its proportions or not, I am still for it."[8] At the war progressed, there was an increasing chorus of Congressional criticism of military extravagance and waste, notably by Senator Truman, but also by members of the appropriations committees. But at no time does the national expenditures budget appear to have dictated or limited military policy.[9]

As late as 1950 Huzar could write:

They [the committees on appropriations] have not considered it to be their responsibility to consider basic military policies. On these matters they have been strongly inclined to follow the leadership of the President, who is Commander in Chief of the armed forces, and of the Committees on Military Affairs [now Armed Services], which guide Congress in most of its legislation for the Army. In examining the military budgets, the subcommittees have concentrated their attention on administrative practices. Their chief challenges to the War Department's estimates have been directed not to the missions of the Military Establishment but to the means required to execute them.[10]

But in writing this and many succeeding passages, Huzar must have had his tongue in his cheek—or was indulging in a fiction which many Congressmen to this day like to expound. His following chapter, significantly titled "Military Appropriations and Military Policy," deals extensively with the postwar Congressional contests to change military policy, such as the Congressional struggles in 1948 and 1949 for a seventy-group air force. Simultaneous with the sharp decline in military appropriations following the close of the war was a sharp increase in their political volatility. Henceforward, it would be difficult if not

---

[7] *Ibid.*, pp. 158-9.

[8] Representative D. Lane Powers of the House Appropriations Committee, *Congressional Record*, p. 6156, June 19, 1943.

[9] This is not to say that considerations of an essentially budgetary character were not involved in military plans and programs. For an example of the application of economic-budgetary thinking to problems of military programming, see especially "The Feasibility Dispute: Determination of War Production Objectives for 1942 and 1943" (Washington, Committee on Public Administration Cases, 1950). But the dollar budget, as expressed in military appropriations and requests, does not appear to have represented such issues.

[10] Huzar, *op. cit.*, p. 104.

impossible to separate economic and political considerations from the military budget.

The Korean aggression and the military rebuilding operations which have followed its instigation have brought military budgeting forward in a way never before contemplated for governmental budgeting. On the budget have hinged not alone the military strategy and program but also the industrial and economic direction of the country, the acquisition and consumption of strategic materials, the political futures of participants—in short, the destinies of a democratic nation. Unlike most other national, and for that matter state and local, expenditures, military appropriations are not particularly limited by substantive legislation, processed through other committees.[11] And unlike in wartime, military appropriations today are not the mere sequel to substantive decisions made elsewhere. Within and upon the military budgeting process are brought to bear the strategic, economic, and political factors which themselves are determinative of our national future. Military budgeting is today more than an exercise in efficiency and economy. It is the stuff of our political governance.

The qualitative difference between our budgeting today and that in previous years was well expressed by former Secretary of Defense Robert A. Lovett in his opening statement in the House in behalf of the 1953 appropriations. He stated:

I would like to emphasize that the problem confronting this committee, the Congress, and the Department of Defense of accomplishing a program within the framework of the partial mobilization concept and which would permit the maintenance of a strong civilian economy [sic]. It has never before been attempted in this country. We have always operated military produc-

---

[11] Most military expenditures are authorized, in one way or another, by substantive legislation; and the appropriations committees are usually careful to make sure that there is substantive authority for appropriations. Substantive laws likewise are used to prescribe ceilings on military strength. They may, and have been, used to control the salaries of officers and men, the numbers of men who may be drafted, the manner in which troops may be transported, the amount allowed per man for subsistence, and even the bases and installations which the military establishment may develop. But, on the other hand, the big dollar amounts in military budgets are not controlled by substantive legislation. Appropriations are ultimately determinative of the amounts and types of matériel that may be procured, the number of civilians that may be employed, and, indirectly, the size of combat forces. For example, for fiscal year 1952 the military services could ask for about 105 billion and the President could ask a little over 60 billion on the basis of substantially similar substantive authority, aside from military public works. Furthermore, the substantive authority was not greatly changed from that for the year before, when the President asked originally for less than 14 billion of new obligating authority.

tion on the feast-or-famine basis of large production during actual war and little or no military production at other times. The building of a military organization capable of deterring aggression without destroying our economy is an extremely complicated problem.[12]

Earlier, Mr. Lovett had described how the military budgets were built up, based upon strategic force requirements, emanating originally from the Joint Chiefs of Staff. But he stressed four considerations of an essentially economic nature which the military departments took into account in determining their budget requirements:

First of all, the three military departments recognize and fully accept the fact that the essential foundation of our entire military structure is a sound, vital, and progressive economy. . . .

Secondly, we have tried to bear in mind that in preparation against the dangers of a hot war, we must not be trapped by our own efforts into losing the cold one. . . . All of our principal industries whether large or small have some break-even point in their operations below which it is impossible for them to continue in business. If it is humanly possible, therefore, we should earnestly seek to avoid causing these companies to drop below the break-even point which would cause unemployment and the loss of tax revenue. . . .

In the third place, and in the light of the factors mentioned above, the Military Departments have endeavored during the past year in particular to reschedule certain items of equipment in such a fashion as to avoid excessive peaks which might thereafter result in abrupt and permanent shutdowns. . . .

In the fourth place, we have tried to stretch out the procurement of certain types of items in those fields in which unusual technological advances give promise of substantially improved weapons within the next 2 or 3 years. . . .[13]

The impact of economic and other nonstrategic considerations such as these was felt most heavily by the military leaders, however, as a result of reviews and cuts imposed upon them from above. As Mr. Lovett explains elsewhere,[14] the original service requests were reduced by about 20 billion before they reached Congress and the majority of these reductions were imposed by the Secretary of Defense himself. But other civilian offices of the government participated. The result

---

[12] *Department of Defense and Related Independent Agencies, Appropriations for 1953,* Hearings before a House Subcommittee of the Committee on Appropriations, 82nd Cong., 1st sess., p. 90.

[13] *Ibid.,* pp. 87-8.

[14] *Ibid.,* p. 89.

was a budget which fell considerably short of what the military departments wanted.

In the words again of Mr. Lovett: [15]

It [the budget] does not give us, within the time that the military leaders feel desirable, the strengths which they feel necessary.

On the other hand, it is the best method of resolving that problem and taking a calculated risk that we have been able to find, and it represents the consensus of the military, the Office of Defense Mobilization, the National Security Council, the Bureau of the Budget, and the President in searching for a solution to an insoluble problem.

UNIFICATION AND THE BUDGET

The magnification of the importance of the budget and of military budgeting since the war has been accompanied and to some extent complicated by the issue of unification of the armed services. Not alone has the method of budgeting been severely affected by unification. To a considerable extent, the degree and the effectiveness of unification have depended upon the budgetary process within the Department of Defense. In spite of faltering beginnings after the passage of the unifying bill of 1947, the budget has rapidly developed as an important force, perhaps the most important force, toward real unification in the department.

The early impetus in World War II toward unification of the military agencies undoubtedly came from outside and above the forces themselves. Shortly after the ARCADIA conference of December 1941 and January 1942, the Joint Chiefs of Staff came into being "almost accidentally" and without benefit or restriction of a law or order.[16] This body was created in answer to the necessity that the American forces deal with the British on a unified basis as well as to meet the paramount need for unified strategic planning and direction. About six months later, on July 20, 1942, Admiral Leahy undertook his duties as the military chief of staff to the President and as a fourth member and presiding chairman of the Joint Chiefs. Meanwhile, also, unification at the top level in the field was achieved by the naming of theater commanders with jurisdiction over all forces in their areas. These commanders took their directions from the Joint Chiefs of Staff. Thus, there was a degree of unification at the top and in the field well before

---

[15] *Ibid.*, p. 97.

[16] See Ray S. Cline, *Washington Command Post: The Operations Division,* Office of the Chief of Military History, Department of the Army (Washington: Government Printing Office, 1951), pp. 98 ff.

unification became a critical issue among the military departments in the United States.[17]

A second major force toward unification came from the Army Air Forces when it was still a part of the War Department and the Army. Air Force pressure was a powerful force during and immediately after the war toward either a separate Department of Air or a unified department of defense in which Air would have equal status with Army and Navy. It was perhaps at least partly because of their respect for the growing popularity and political prestige of the Army Air Forces that the principal Army leaders—Secretary Patterson, General Marshall, General Eisenhower, and, later, General Collins—favored a unified department.

But the actual shape which unification was to assume seems to have been defined very largely by representatives of its earliest and staunchest opponent, the United States Navy. Discussion of the unification efforts to date must revolve largely around the name of James Forrestal, Under Secretary of the Navy from 1940 to 1944, Secretary of the Navy from 1944 till 1947, and then, until his resignation in March, 1949, the first Secretary of Defense. Second only to Forrestal as an influence in the unification movement was Ferdinand Eberstadt, a friend and adviser of Forrestal's from college days.[18] Before the war ended, Forrestal was prompted by a letter from Senator David I. Walsh, then Chairman of the Senate Committee on Naval Affairs, to undertake a study of, or preferably against, unification.[19] This became the basis of the "first" Eberstadt report, which was published subsequently under the auspices of the Senate Naval Affairs Committee on October 22, 1945.[20] In this report, Eberstadt came out against unifica-

---

[17] The idea of unification originated well before Pearl Harbor. The Senate Committee on Military Affairs reported in 1946 that no less than 60 unification bills had been introduced in Congress since 1921, and that the question had been studied by the House in 1932, the Baker Board in 1934, the Woodrum (House select) Committee in 1944, and the Joint Chiefs of Staff in 1944. See S. Rept. 1328 to accompany S. 2044, 79th Cong., 2nd sess., 1946.

[18] Walter Millis (ed.), *The Forrestal Diaries* (New York: Viking Press, 1951). On pages xviii and xix of his introduction, Millis describes the close relationship of Forrestal with Eberstadt starting in 1912, when Forrestal went to work for the *Daily Princetonian*, of which Eberstadt was then chairman. According to Millis, Eberstadt was to become "perhaps his closest friend and associate throughout Forrestal's later career" (p. xviii).

[19] The letter was dated May 15, 1945.

[20] Report to Hon. James Forrestal, *Unification of the War and Navy Departments and Postwar Organization for National Security*, Senate Committee Print, 79th Cong., 1st sess. According to *The Forrestal Diaries*, the report was completed September 25 (p. 64).

tion, but recommended three departments, War, Navy, and Air, each to be headed by a civilian secretary of cabinet level. He likewise recommended against a single military chief of staff, preferring the continuation of the Joint Chiefs of Staff structure. But he did recommend a number of coordinating agencies which were subsequently brought into being by the Act of 1947: the National Security Council, the National Security Resources Board, the Central Intelligence Agency, a statutory Joint Chiefs of Staff, a "Central Research and Development Agency," and a "Military Munitions Board." This report, though apparently never officially adopted by the Navy, became pretty much the Navy doctrine on unification for the next two years—a doctrine which opposed outright amalgamation under a hierarchical department and favored continuation and extension of coordinating devices among two or three departments.

In 1946, a unification bill, the so-called Thomas Bill, was introduced in the Congress but did not come to a vote. Representatives of the Navy opposed it.[21] In the latter part of that year, largely in response to President Truman's pressure, Secretary Forrestal of the Navy and Secretary Patterson of the Army worked out an agreement, involving some compromise on both sides, which was published January 17, 1947, and became the basis of Congressional discussions and action that year. Forrestal's main contentions in these discussions were that (1) a central secretary, if there must be one, have only coordinative powers; (2) there must not be a central single chief of staff; (3) the central secretary should not have general power or cognizance over administration within the departments.[22] Specifically, he argued that the Secretary's decision-making power should be limited to:

(1) Missions and means
(2) Cognizance of weapons
(3) Composition of forces

---

[21] The so-called Thomas Bill carried the Senate designation S. 2044. It was a product of a subcommittee on unification of the Senate Military Affairs Committee. This committee had, during the fall of 1945, held extensive hearings on the question of unification based upon the bills introduced by Senator Hill (S. 384) and by Senators Johnson and Kilgore (S. 1842) and upon the President's message of December 19, 1945, recommending unification. The Thomas Bill, which was reported to the Senate May 13, 1946, followed, in the main, Army specifications. It set up a single "Department of Common Defense" with a civilian secretary; provided an "autonomous" air force; provided subsecretaries for the three service departments; and gave broad central powers for unification and standardization of the armed forces. Although reported out of committee by a vote of 12 to 2, it never came to a vote in the Senate. See S. Rept. 1328.

[22] My summary of Forrestal's views as presented in The Forrestal Diaries, especially pp. 201-7.

(4) Finances
(5) Resolution of command disputes
(6) Personnel (training, education and recruiting) [23]

On other questions, the three departments would have authority to go directly to the President. On all internal matters, other than those specified, the departments should "run themselves."

The National Security Act of 1947 [24] followed the Forrestal specification in the main. It established most of the coordinating agencies originally proposed by Eberstadt—the National Security Council, the Central Intelligence Agency, the National Security Resources Board, the statutory Joint Chiefs of Staff, the Munitions Board, and the Research and Development Board. It set up the National Military Establishment, composed of the office of the newly established Secretary of Defense, the three service departments, and certain of the boards and their staffs. But the Secretary of Defense was cast in the role of the head of a loose federation of virtually autonomous units. His powers were limited to certain specified duties, comparable generally to Forrestal's original listing above and to a "general direction, authority, and control" over the departments.[25] Further, it reserved to the three "executive" departments "all powers and duties relating to such departments and not specifically conferred upon the Secretary of Defense." [26] It gave the departments explicit authority to submit any "report or recommendation" over the head of the Secretary of Defense to the Director of the Budget, to the President, and, implicitly, to the Congress.[27] The law established the Joint Chiefs of Staff to consist of the top military officials of the three service departments, the Joint Chiefs as a body to act as "principal military advisers to the President and the Secretary of Defense." [28] To these channels of responsibility may properly be added that of the Chiefs of Staff to the respective secretaries of their departments.

It is perhaps significant that up until the passage of the National Security Act of 1947, the budget received only passing attention as a factor involved in unification.[29] But after the bill passed, the budget

[23] *Ibid.,* p. 204.
[24] P. L. 253, 80th Cong., July 26, 1947.
[25] *Ibid.,* Sec. 202.
[26] *Ibid.*
[27] *Ibid.*
[28] *Ibid.,* Sec. 211.
[29] Although in *The Forrestal Diaries* the President is recorded as early as May 13, 1946 as having a primary interest in the budget problem: "what he wanted was a balanced system of national defense with particular reference to the integration of the budget" (p. 160).

became a matter of primary concern to the first Secretary of Defense. Forrestal's problems during late 1947 and more particularly during 1948 in preparing and presenting an integrated defense budget have had considerable significance in the development of unification as well as in recent budgeting in the Defense Department. The open appeals by the Air Force for more than the Defense Department had approved for it; the later requests by the Army for more than had been approved; the passing by Congress of appropriations above Presidential requests for the Air Force and the President's subsequent impounding of appropriated funds—all these attest to the significance of the budget and to the weakness of the position of the Secretary of Defense.[30] Forrestal tried, with doubtful success, to work through the Joint Chiefs of Staff. In the summer of 1948 and apparently at his instigation, the so-called McNarney Committee [31] was established as a Budget Advisory Committee to the Joint Chiefs of Staff. But that group, although it reduced military budgets to about 23½ billion, was unable to get them down nearly to the President's projected ceiling of 15 billion.[32] Although the Secretary of Defense could compel the Chiefs of Staff to re-examine their budgetary demands, he had no power to force them to arrive at real agreement within an approved ceiling.

At about the same time that Mr. Forrestal was undergoing these tribulations about the budget, the (Hoover) Commission on Organization of the Executive Branch of the Government, itself formed partly at his instigation,[33] had engaged a task force to study the operation of the National Security Organization under the provisions of the National Security Act of 1947. The report of this group, submitted on November 15, 1948, emphasized the relative weakness of the Secretary of Defense.[34] The task force was chaired by Ferdinand Eberstadt and its report has sometimes been labeled the "second" Eberstadt report. There is no doubt that Mr. Eberstadt, to some extent certainly influ-

---

[30] In his note on *The Forrestal Diaries,* entry of June 16, 1948, Millis writes: "But the core of the whole problem, as Forrestal clearly saw after the almost grotesque experiences of the spring, lay in the budget, in the manner of its construction, in the responsibility for its allocation and for its adjustment both to logical strategic plan and to the non-military limitations which could not be disregarded" (p. 449).

[31] Composed of General Joseph T. McNarney, Air Force; Vice Admiral Robert B. Carney, Navy; and Major General George J. Richards, Army. (*The Forrestal Diaries,* p. 450.)

[32] *Ibid.,* p. 503.

[33] *Ibid.,* p. 324.

[34] The Commission on Organization of the Executive Branch of the Government, Task Force Report on *National Security Organization,* Appendix G (Washington: Government Printing Office, 1949).

enced by Mr. Forrestal, had gone a long way in the three years following his first report. The new report emphasized the need to give the Secretary greater authority over the service departments with particular reference to their fund requests and their expenditures. This would require a considerable body of assistants for the Secretary, including an Under Secretary, a Controller, and other assistants. The task force recommended the requirement of controllers in each of the three departments and the making of similar arrangements for budgetary management in all the departments of defense. It made many other recommendations designed to improve the position and enlarge the authority of the Secretary, and to strengthen his relationships with all the various boards and committees set up by the act of 1947.

A few weeks later, the Hoover Commission itself submitted its recommendations on the National Security Organization.[35] It urged, in a much briefer report, most of the same things that its task force had recommended, excepting principally the proposals for controllers; and its report was phrased in stronger language. It advocated the vesting of much greater powers in the Secretary of Defense and in fact proposed that the three service secretaries be designated Under Secretaries of Defense. It urged specifically that "all administrative authority be centered in the Secretary of Defense, subject only to the authority of the President, including full and final authority over preparation of the military budget and over the expenditure of funds appropriated by the Congress." [36] The newly discovered importance of the budget is suggested by the fact that the Hoover Commission's recommendation number one was:

a. That full power over preparation of the budget and over expenditures as authorized by the Congress be vested in the Secretary of Defense, under the authority of the President.
b. That the Secretary of Defense direct and supervise a major overhaul of the entire budget system; . . .
c. That the armed services be required, at least in peacetime, to keep complete, accurate, and current inventories.[37]

On March 5, 1949, a few weeks after the two Hoover Commission reports were released for publication, President Truman submitted his message to Congress recommending substantial changes in the Na-

---

[35] The Commission on Organization of the Executive Branch of the Government, *The National Security Organization* (Washington: Government Printing Office, 1949).
[36] *Ibid.*, p. 17.
[37] *Ibid.* pp. 12-13.

tional Security Act of 1947. A bill, S. 1269, was drafted by the counsel
to the Senate Committee on Armed Services to reflect the President's
recommendations. This bill, renumbered and amended, ultimately became the National Security Act Amendments of 1949, Public Law 216,
which fundamentally modified the statutory framework for the Department of Defense and added provisions relating to fiscal management. The bill accorded basically with the Hoover Commission's recommendations. It greatly increased the authority of the Secretary of
Defense, added considerably to his staff, and provided a Chairman of
the Joint Chiefs of Staff who should be appointed by the President, responsible to the President and the Secretary of Defense, and ranking
first among the military officers in the United States. It reduced the
secretaries of the three departments by making them heads of "military
departments" and at the same time elevated the Secretary of Defense
to the rank of a full-scale head of an "executive department." It removed the heads of the military departments from the National Security Council. It made the chairmen of both the Munitions Board and
the Research and Development Board appointive by the Secretary of
Defense and advisory and assistant to him.

The theme and the objectives of the National Security Act Amendments were clearly the same as those proposed by the Hoover Commission. In three important respects they differed. The Commission had
recommended that the heads of the three service departments be made
Under Secretaries of Defense. The Commission had not recommended
explicitly that the National Military Establishment be eliminated as
such, although this was the plain effect of its proposals. Finally, the
Commission had not recommended that the Chairman of the Joint
Chiefs of Staff be the top military man in the services but had envisaged rather an official with neither vote nor power of decision who
would preside over its meetings and report to the Secretary of Defense.

During the spring of 1949, the Senate Committee on Armed Services
heard witnesses representing the top offices concerned in the new legislation, together with three outstanding private citizens, Mr. Hoover,
Mr. Eberstadt, and Robert P. Patterson, the former and last Secretary
of War. The most interesting and perhaps the most significant testimony was that of James Forrestal in one of his last official acts before
retiring.[38] Mr. Forrestal spoke vigorously and effectively for the proposed legislation. His year and a half incumbency as Secretary of Defense had led to a reversal in his position:

---

[38] He appeared before the Committee on Thursday, March 24, 1949. The following Monday, March 28, his successor, Louis Johnson, was sworn in.

I would like to address myself briefly to what I believe may be the chief objection raised to the proposed amendments; namely, that these amendments would vest in the Secretary of Defense too great a concentration of power. I have given long and serious thought to this objection because it is similar to an objection to which I lent my support 2 years ago.

After having viewed the problem at close range for the past 18 months, I must admit to you quite frankly that my position on the question has changed. I am now convinced that there are adequate checks and balances inherent in our governmental structure to prevent misuse of the broad authority which I feel must be vested in the Secretary of Defense. I am also convinced that a failure to endow this official with sufficient authority to control effectively the conduct of our military affairs will force upon us far greater security risks than will be the case if singleness of control and responsibility are achieved.[39]

It is interesting that the next witness on the bill, Mr. Eberstadt, testified on March 29 that the bill went substantially too far in giving blanket or "shot-gun" authority to the Secretary of Defense. He argued that the Secretary should be given certain specific new powers but that he should have no general administrative authority and that the National Military Establishment should be retained. In spite of his protestations that he and Mr. Forrestal were in agreement, it is evident from his testimony that Forrestal was ready to go a great deal further than Eberstadt.[40] But for our purposes, the most significant part of the Eberstadt testimony was his comment on the need for economy and efficiency in the Department of Defense. He said:

Our [task force] committee made certain recommendations relating to economy and I take the liberty of commending them to your attention. There will be no substantial advance in the field of economy until military budgetary procedures and fiscal policies have been overhauled from top to bottom.[41]

---

[39] *National Security Act Amendments of 1949,* Hearings before the Senate Committee on Armed Services on S. 1269 and S. 1843, 81st Cong., 1st sess. (1949), p. 9. The Committee also heard: Mr. Royall and Mr. Symington, Secretaries of the Army and the Air Force respectively, both of whom testified vigorously for the bill and for any measure that would strengthen unification; the three chiefs of staff, none of whom opposed the bill although they did present certain proposed modifications with respect to the Joint Chiefs provisions; Dan A. Kimball, then Assistant Secretary of the Navy for Air, who endorsed the principle of the bill; Frank Pace, then Director of the Budget, who endorsed the bill. Only General Clifton B. Cates, Commandant of the United States Marine Corps, opposed the bill outright.

[40] See particularly the Eberstadt testimony on p. 65 and following pages of the Hearings on the *National Security Act Amendments of 1949.*

[41] *Ibid.,* p. 57.

Promptly after this testimony, Senator Byrd asked Mr. Eberstadt to prepare, as part of the bill, legislation to provide efficiency and economy in the Department of Defense. The Chairman, Senator Tydings, endorsed the request, and thus was work on Title IV begun. This title, which became part of and was passed with the rest of the bill, is discussed in a later section.

At this point, it may be noted that the original bill, S. 1269, as revised by the Committee and renumbered as S. 1843, was reported to and debated by the Senate and passed by that body on a voice vote on May 26.[42] It had a rougher time in the House. The original amendments to the National Security Act were introduced in the House by Chairman Vinson of the Armed Services Committee on March 24, but were apparently not seriously considered by that Committee until after the Senate had passed its bill. Then the House Committee prepared its own version of the amendments, which was not markedly different from S. 1843. This version was ready to be reported to the House, when its opponents in the committee were able to muster a 13 to 12 vote (in which three Democrats voted with ten Republican members) to delay reporting out the unification features of the measure pending investigation of the B-36 controversy and the then current dispute over Secretary of Defense Louis Johnson. The House Committee then reported out unanimously Section 10 of the bill, which constituted only Title IV of the amendments.[43] This was introduced and passed the House without a roll call as H.R. 5632.[44] The Senate substituted its original bill for everything after the enacting clause of H.R. 5632.[45] The bill thus went to conference where it received certain amendments and was finally reported out and passed both houses.[46] The Senate passed it without debate and again without a roll call; the House passed it by a majority of 356 to 7.

The bill which finally emerged and became Public Law 216 when the President signed it on August 10, 1949, was substantially similar to the bill originally studied by the Senate Committee on the Armed Services. A number of language changes were made, some of which

---

[42] *Congressional Record*, May 26, 1949, p. 6879.

[43] The controversy in the Committee is described by its participants, mainly Chairman Vinson and Congressman Short, in the *Congressional Record*, July 18, 1949, pp. 9672-76.

[44] *Ibid.*, July 19, 1949, p. 9684.

[45] *Ibid.*, July 20, 1949, p. 9751.

[46] See Conference Rept. 1142 to accompany H. R. 5632, 81st Cong., 1st sess. The Senate passed the bill on July 28 (*Congressional Record*, p. 10345) and the House on August 1 (*Congressional Record*, p. 10592).

had important substantive effects. Thus the relationship of the Secretary of Defense to the Munitions and the Research and Development Boards was amended.[47] More important, the position of the Chairman of the Joint Chiefs was considerably modified by specifically depriving him of a vote on the Joint Chiefs, by prohibiting his exercise of command over the other service chiefs, and by specifying his duties in a rather narrow way.[48] The role and the responsibility of the Joint Chiefs, including its Chairman, remained equivocal. Public Law 216 obviously suffered from many compromises, as had its parent law in 1947. It was another step on a way toward unification that may yet be long. But not least of its "unifying" provisions were those in Title IV concerning financial management, which had been added as something of an afterthought. This section of the bill went through with hardly a dissenting Congressional voice and, as indicated above, provided the firm basis of agreement to which was ultimately attached the remainder of the bill.

TITLE IV

On May 5, 1949, Mr. Eberstadt returned to the Senate Armed Services Committee with a proposed new Title IV for the National Security Act to add to the Amendments that were still under consideration. In preparing this new title, he had been helped by members of the Committee's staff, by former members of the Hoover Commission's task forces on national security and budgeting and accounting, and by persons from the Office of the Secretary of Defense, most notably W. J. McNeil, then Special Assistant to the Secretary of Defense.[49] Since a large part of the balance of this study concerns departmental operations under Title IV, it may be well at this point to summarize its more important provisions.[50]

---

[47] P. L. 216, 81st Cong., Secs. 8 and 9, amending Secs. 213 and 214 respectively. The act as passed prescribed the duties of these boards. The original draft would have had them "assist the Secretary of Defense" in such duties as he might prescribe, including, at his discretion, those indicated in the bill.

[48] *Ibid.*, Sec. 7, amending Secs. 210-212.

[49] See the Hearings on the *National Security Act Amendments*, p. 202, for a complete list of those who worked on drafting the new title. It is apparent, however, that the leaders in this work were Messrs. Eberstadt and McNeil. It may be noted that Mr. McNeil had formerly been associated with Mr. Forrestal both in the Office of the Secretary of Defense and the Department of the Navy. So far as appears from the record at least, no representative from either the Army or the Air Force participated in preparing the bill, or, in fact, was called upon to testify about it.

[50] I have included in this summary only the provisions of Mr. Eberstadt's draft which were ultimately included in the law as it passed. The more important deletions and additions are referred to later. See the Hearings on the *National Security Act Amendments*, pp. 196-201, and P. L. 216, 81st Cong., Secs. 401 through 410.

Sec. 401 established the *Comptroller of the Department of Defense* to "advise and assist the Secretary of Defense" in his fiscal functions including, but not limited to:

> supervision and direction of preparation of budget estimates of the Department of Defense;

> supervision of principles, policies, and procedures in connection with: preparation and execution of budgets; fiscal, cost, operating, and capital property accounting; progress and statistical reporting;

> supervision of policies and procedures relating to expenditure and collection of funds;

> establishment of uniform terminologies, classifications, and procedures on such matters.

Sec. 402 required that in each department, budgeting, accounting, progress and statistical reporting, and administrative organization and managerial procedures "be organized and conducted in a *manner consistent with the operations of the Office of the Comptroller of the Department of Defense*"; set up a Comptroller in each of the three military departments "responsible for all budgeting, accounting, progress and statistical reporting, and for the administrative organization structure and managerial procedures relating thereto"; prescribed that the Comptroller in each military department be either military or civilian but that if military, he have a civilian deputy; and provided that he be immediately responsible either to the Secretary, Under Secretary, or an Assistant Secretary of his respective department.

Sec. 403 prescribed that *budget estimates* be prepared, presented, and justified and programs be administered "in such form and manner as the Secretary of Defense, subject to the authority and direction of the President, may determine" and on a performance basis; and that they be set forth in a readily comparable form.

Sec. 407 (passed as Sec. 405) provided for *working capital funds* for (1) financing of inventories of such stores, supplies, and equipment as the Secretary of Defense may designate, and for (2) providing working capital for such industrial-type activities and commercial-type activities as he may designate; and provided certain operating rules for such funds.

Sec. 408 (passed as Sec. 406) established *management funds* in each military department for the financing of material, personnel, and contractual services where two or more different appropriations are involved.

Sec. 412 (passed as Sec. 410) authorized the Secretary of Defense to require the maintenance of both *quantitative and monetary property records*, so far as practicable.

[Author's italics.]

Mr. Eberstadt's Title IV went through the Senate Committee and the Senate itself with very little debate. The hearings on Title IV in the Senate lasted through the morning committee sessions of May 5 and May 6. The only formal opposition to the amendments was that of the Bureau of the Budget, posed in a letter by F. J. Lawton, Acting Director, and voiced by Charles Stauffacher, Assistant Director in charge of Administrative Management.[51] The Budget Bureau's principal objection was to Sections 401 and 402 whereby the Comptroller was made mandatory upon the Secretary of Defense and the department secretaries and wherein his duties were prescribed. The Bureau contended that these contradicted the recommendations of the Hoover Commission that the Secretary of each department should have full control over his organization and specifically should be fully responsible for his budget. Unfortunately for the Bureau, however, Mr. Eberstadt had the day before assured the Committee that Mr. Hoover had fully endorsed the new title.[52]

Subsequently, the Senate Committee approved and recommended Title IV as a part of the National Security Act amendments.[53] A few relatively minor changes had been made in Mr. Eberstadt's wording, such as the inclusion of internal audit as a regular responsibility of the Defense Comptroller, and the elimination of references to the National Military Establishment. In the main, however, it was reported as recommended and passed the Senate without any proposed amendment.

The House Committee on Armed Services made four substantive changes in the proposed new title, all of which were retained in the conference committee versions and enacted. Three of these were amendments recommended to it by the House Committee on Appropriations.[54] These included the elimination of provisions: authorizing the Secretary of Defense to make transfers among appropriations up to 5 per cent of any appropriations (originally Section 404); prohibiting any military department or the Department of Defense from requesting any authorizing legislation from the Bureau of the Budget, the President, or the Congress without prior approval by the Secretary of Defense (originally Section 405); and inferentially authorizing the President to incur deficiencies in emergency situations (originally in Section 406).

The most important change made by the House Committee was the addition of a provision in Section 402(b):

---

[51] Lawton's letter appears on pp. 206-8 of the Senate Committee's Hearings on the subject, *National Security Act Amendments of 1949*. Stauffacher's testimony appears on pages 236-8.

[52] *Ibid.*, p. 208, and p. 216.

[53] S. Rept. 316 to accompany S. 1843, 81st Cong., 1st sess.

[54] The House Committee had referred it to the Committee on Appropriations for advice. *Congressional Record*, p. 9675.

Provided, That nothing herein shall preclude the comptroller from having concurrent responsibility to a Chief of Staff or a Chief of Naval Operations, a Vice Chief of Staff or a Vice Chief of Naval Operations, or a Deputy Chief of Staff or a Deputy Chief of Naval Operations, if the Secretary of the military department concerned should so prescribe.

This provision was apparently added on the insistence of a large number of military officers, mostly of the Army and Air Force, who had already requested of Chairman Vinson that they be permitted to testify on the bill. Mr. Vinson added the provision apparently as a concession to prevent the necessity of prolonged hearings and the possible defeat of the bill or a substantial part of it. The importance of this change is discussed in Chapter VI of this study.

No changes were subsequently offered on the floor of either house of Congress and in fact the support of this part of the act was virtually unanimous. Thus, with the exceptions stated above, the original recommendations of Mr. Eberstadt were enacted in much the same form as he had proposed. One major reason was of course that the title promised greater economy and efficiency in the military establishment; to oppose it was to favor sin. A second major reason was that this part of the bill was supported by virtually everyone, in the Administration and out, who had been consulted, excepting only the Bureau of the Budget.[55]

One other reason for the lack of opposition was probably that the title granted rather little in the way of new authority. On the Senate Floor, Senator Tydings, Chairman of the Committee on Armed Services, said:

I must admit that some of the provisions of this section might be accomplished without specific statutory direction, but the committee felt that it was necessary that some affirmative stand be taken by the Congress to direct that these necessary measures be undertaken without delay. The authority has existed for years but nothing constructive has happened in this field. The committee therefore feels that the Congress should direct that these necessary reforms be gotten underway by enacting this type of amendment.[56]

Senator Tydings' remarks with regard to the need for statutory direction were undoubtedly legally correct for most of the provisions of

---

[55] In his statement before the House, Congressman Short claimed that this part of the bill was supported by the Bureau of the Budget, the National Military Establishment, the Comptroller General, the Treasury Department, the Senate, the House Armed Services Committee, Mr. Hoover, and of course, Mr. Eberstadt. *Congressional Record,* July 18, 1949, pp. 9674-5.

[56] *Ibid.,* May 26, 1949, p. 6634.

Title IV, but there is some question as to the justice of his remark that "nothing constructive has happened in this field." The act required the establishment of comptrollers in all the military departments. Such offices were already in full operation in both the Air Force and the Army, a fact nowhere apparent in the published hearings on the subject.[57] The act made the "performance budget" mandatory for the entire department. But the Navy had already tried, and failed, to have the new type budget adopted by the Congress.[58] And the Air Force was that same spring presenting its budget on the "performance" basis. The act provided for working capital funds, and the Navy had operated the equivalent of a working capital stock fund for more than seventy years.[59]

But Title IV was a significant enactment of the Congress. It was the first Congressional expression in behalf of the "performance budget" idea.[60] Its authorizations of working capital funds of both the industrial and the stock type were legally as well as practically necessary, as was its provision of management funds. Its prescription of comptrollers at the departmental levels was a new departure, expressive particularly of the new emphasis upon accounting and fiscal management. Most of all, however, its emphasis upon economy and efficiency in military management remains its dominating feature. It is an interesting and not entirely irrelevant Congressional accident that its purpose came to be the dominant note of the preamble of the National Security Act Amendments of 1949: "An Act to reorganize fiscal management in the National Military Establishment, to promote economy and efficiency, and for other purposes." A study of the progress of Title IV through the Senate and House committees and through the two houses themselves supports the conclusion that the promise of greater economy

---

[57] See Chapter VI below.

[58] See Chapter IV below.

[59] The origination of the stock fund idea was provided in an act of June 19, 1878, that authorized payments for materials and services to be later adjusted against appropriations. Department of the Navy, Bureau of Supplies and Accounts, "The Navy Stock Fund and How it Works," *Monthly Newsletter*, May 15, 1952, pp. 11-14.

[60] More than a year later, the Congress passed the Budgeting and Accounting Procedures Act of 1950 (P. L. 784, 81st Cong.) which is generally construed as giving Congressional sanction to the performance budget. Its Sec. 102 (a), amending Sec. 201 of the Budget and Accounting Act of 1921, provided that the Budget set forth "functions and activities of the Government." However, explicit reference to the performance budget was eliminated from the bill on the grounds that it was unnecessary and might prove restrictive.

and efficiency was its principal "selling" factor.[61] It was designed, in the words of the House Committee on Armed Services, to "place the operation of the National Military Establishment on a sound budgetary and fiscal management basis." [62] The extent to which it has succeeded in this effort, or gives promise of succeeding, is properly one of the concerns of this study.

BUDGETS SINCE 1949

Public Law 216 had been in effect less than a year when war broke out in Korea, and the Navy Comptroller had been in operation less than one month. Obviously whatever effects the law might have had were barely underway before the entire military establishment was involved in a major crisis and before a new phase in our military budgeting, already described in this chapter, was begun. The "build-up" budgets started during fiscal year 1951 with a series of supplemental appropriations, totaling about three times more in new obligating authority than the original 1951 budget requests for the military departments. Fiscal year 1952 proved to be the most "expansive" in terms of obligating authority. The President, in January of 1951, submitted a one-line entry for military obligations of 60 billion dollars. During the fall and early winter of 1950–51, discussions among top military and civilian authorities of the government had reached this figure as an approximation of budgetary possibilities for the coming year. The three military departments themselves, working from the guidelines given them by the Secretary of Defense, arrived at a total approximately 45 billion dollars higher. But after this was pared down, the President in April presented to the Congress a "firm" budget just over 60 billion dollars.[63] The Congress actually voted, before the end of that fiscal year, more than 61 billion dollars.

Budget preparation in the military departments was again telescoped for fiscal year 1953 by the failure of Congress to adopt the 1952 appropriation until well after the new fiscal year had begun, and by the inability of the top civilian officials to agree in time on limiting figures. Most of the internal estimating activities were not conducted until late summer and fall of 1951. These were interrupted by the request of the Secretary of Defense that the services submit "point of departure"

---

[61] Observation based upon review of the Senate Committee hearings, the reports of both committees, and floor debates as recorded in the *Congressional Record*.

[62] *Reorganizing Fiscal Management in the National Military Establishment,* H. Rept. 1064 to accompany H. R. 5632, 81st Cong., 1st sess., p. 2.

[63] *Budget for the Military Functions of the Department of Defense for the Fiscal Year 1952,* April 30, 1951.

budgets within specified ceilings along with their regular estimates. The result was a Presidential recommendation of about 52 billion dollars which was subsequently reduced by Congress to about 48 billion.

The development of the Truman version of the 1954 budget followed a more orderly procedure. Estimating was begun in the spring of 1952 soon after receipt of guidelines from the Secretary of Defense. The military departments proceeded through established channels to the Bureau of the Budget and the President, receiving in his budget in January, 1953, approved requests totaling 41 billions of new obligating authority. The new Republican administration, however, brought about virtual abandonment of these figures and the beginning of a second and entirely new budget process for 1954 during the winter and spring of 1953. The first Eisenhower budget and the appropriations that followed it provided a considerable decrease in obligating authority, especially for the Air Force. The total finally requested for 1954 was about 36 billion.[64]

The past four years of defense build-up have witnessed, along with the tremendous increases in the amounts involved, some very significant changes of both a procedural and substantive nature. First may be mentioned the tremendous increase in importance of the time factor. While expenditures have been growing rapidly and will probably continue to grow through 1954, new obligational authority—the amounts appropriated by Congress—have actually been decreasing since fiscal year 1952. The factor of "lead-time"—the time between Congressional approval of an appropriation and the receipt of the goods or services authorized—has become increasingly, almost bewilderingly, important. No longer can the budget, or at least its military segment, be considered only as an annual proposition. As former President Truman wrote near the end of his last budget message:

This fact is that the financial program of the Government cannot be planned in terms of a single fiscal year. It must be planned in the light of security, economic, and budgetary goals—not just for the ensuing year but for three and even four years ahead.[65]

---

[64] The development of 1955 estimates, like that for each of the four preceding years, is "unusual." The designation of new chiefs of staff and the assignment to the new Joint Chiefs of responsibility for a fresh view and plan for the military establishment resulted in a delay in the initiation of work on the new budget. As of the middle of September, 1953, when departmental estimates are ordinarily submitted to the Bureau of the Budget, the Department of Defense had not yet issued budgetary guidelines to the service departments.

[65] *The Budget of the United States Government for the Fiscal Year Ending June 30, 1954,* p. M 54.

A second observation is that the constituent elements of the military budget have been changing in the direction of the Air Force. Prior to the onset of World War II, the Navy usually received the largest annual appropriation. During World War II, the Army, including its Army Air Forces, received the lion's share. Following the war, the Army continued to receive the greater part of the military budget until the Air Force was separated. For a few years, the three services received nearly the same amounts, whether or not by design. Following the approval of the 143-wing Air Force, that service moved into the lead, the Army running second, the Navy third. The Eisenhower administration has checked this trend, at least temporarily. But the gradual expansion of the Air Force in expenditure importance during the past few years is an unquestionable and significant fact. It reflects principally the costs of equipment and matériel.

This is related to a third observation: that during a period of build-up, the proportion of dollar resources required for matériel and production is greatly enlarged. During the pre-World War II period, personnel and current maintenance were by far the biggest factors in military expense. The same was true during the years immediately following the war. But after the Korean aggression, by far the largest part of the services' new obligations were for new and improved matériel. Its production, its requirements of materials, facilities, and manpower have also provided the limiting factors on the speed of the "build-up." And the maintenance of "warm" production facilities against the possibility of all-out war is the source of important problems in the planning of military programs.

A fourth important factor in recent budgets is Korea or, more accurately, the absence of Korea. The projected cost of combat in Korea was omitted from the annual budget estimates every year after fiscal year 1951 up to and including the Truman estimates for 1954. The military departments have been instructed each year to assume, in the compilation of their estimates, that there would be no further combat in Korea after the first of the fiscal year for which they were budgeting. This has meant, of course, that the actual cost of Korea must be taken up in supplemental estimates and in annual estimates for subsequent years.[66] This may have been because of the difficulty of estimat-

---

[66] Thus, the Army's 1953 estimates included about 2.8 billion to "recoup" expenditures for major equipment and ammunition expended in the Korea operation. In addition, the Army expected to request a supplemental appropriation of which nearly one billion would be for other Korea costs.

See *Department of the Army, Appropriations for 1953,* Hearings before a Subing so far in advance; or because, at the time the estimates were made, the Administration really predicted that the Korean hostilities would end before the budget period; or because of the political hazard of predicting continuation for another year and a half of an unpopular war. Its effects have been to complicate the estimating and reviewing processes and to put the services about a year behind in estimating and obtaining funds, particularly for procurement. The impact of this policy has been especially heavy upon the Army, which bears the brunt of most of the supply activities in Korea.[67]

The fifth observation about recent budgets is that they have largely been made without benefit, or restriction, of ceilings established prior to the budget process. During the postwar years, the military, like the other departments, had been compelled to budget under a ceiling, imposed by the President and the Bureau of the Budget. In fact, Forrestal himself had recorded that the President said that "about $6 billion a year of our national income would have to go to the service of the national debt and that, of the balance remaining, not more than one-third could be allocated to national defense and this would mean the most careful screening of requirements."[68] Truman's so-called "arithmetic" approach, whereby the military departments should get no more than one-third the national budget after fixed charges, was qualified in subsequent years and definitely abandoned with the Korean aggression. For fiscal years 1952 and 1953 especially, the military departments were virtually invited to build up their budgetary requirements to meet, in the safest possible manner, the force limits set by the Joint Chiefs of Staff. Then, when they had completed, or nearly completed, their budget requests on this basis, they were confronted with a ceiling or top limit imposed from above. This resulted in "crash" reductions in budgetary estimates, the reductions usually emanating from the civilian, or Secretary of Defense, side rather than from the military side.

This leads to the sixth observation: that military estimating has largely been performed, during recent years, on the basis of estimated requirements rather than that of available resources. In other words, the military departments have been encouraged to "build up a case" for what they think they may need rather than to work from what they

committee of the House Committee on Appropriations, 82nd Cong., 1st sess., Part I, p. 63.

[67] See particularly testimony of General Decker, Comptroller of the Army, in the House Hearings, *Department of the Army, Appropriations for 1953*, pp. 62-3.

[68] *The Forrestal Diaries*, p. 160.

reasonably expect they may be granted. The impact of this upon the budget is discussed in later pages. But it may be noted here that the "requirements" approach has implicit dangers, not alone that it may encourage inflated estimates but also in the "pass-the-buck" psychology it encourages among budgeteers. At the worst, it may make of the budget a mere "white paper" and a challenge to reviewers to cut and take responsibility for the consequences.

The "requirements" attitude has probably been accentuated by the separation of the Joint Chiefs of Staff from the budget process, a seventh observation about recent budgetary developments. Forrestal, it will be recalled, undertook to compel the Joint Chiefs as a body to arrive at acceptable budgetary figures. At least partially as a result of Title IV of Public Law 216, the Joint Chiefs has been effectively removed from the budget process, apart from the specifying of force figures at the beginning of the estimating. No longer does the Joint Chiefs have a Budget Advisory Committee, and no longer do the budgets of the service departments go through the Joint Staff. At the present time and for the last several years, the budget estimates have been prepared by the various services. The crucial cutting is done by the Secretary of Defense and his Comptroller or at their insistence. The effects of this transfer of authority are discussed in the next three chapters.

Finally should be mentioned the problem of civilian control. The question of civilian control has been a focal one in military reorganizations, even when it has not been openly referred to. One of the important arguments for strengthening the Secretary of Defense was to strengthen civilian control over military matters. And one of the important arguments against it was that it would weaken civilian control. Civilian control cannot, in fact, be separated from the problem of unification. The rise in power of the Comptroller of Defense *vis-a-vis* the Joint Chiefs of Staff may properly be considered from this standpoint, as may be the position of the Comptroller in relation to the three military departments. There can now be little question that one of the most effective tools of the Secretary of Defense, if not his most effective instrument of supervision over the three military departments, is his control of the military budget.

chapter III

plans, programs, and budgets

> *The American Army has also acquired a political maturity it sorely lacked at the outbreak of World War II. At times during that war we forgot that wars are fought for the resolution of political conflicts, and in the ground campaign for Europe we sometimes overlooked political considerations of vast importance. Today, after several years of cold war, we are intensely aware that a military effort cannot be separated from political objectives.*
>
> GENERAL OMAR N. BRADLEY.[1]

Had she been of a less poetic nature, Gertrude Stein might have proclaimed that "A budget is a plan is a plan is a plan." The sentiment would have been an accurate interpretation of the sense of the public budgeting movement—and to a lesser extent of the planning movement—for the past half century. Certainly a main reason for budgeting from the beginning was to facilitate and in fact compel planning. And it has frequently been pointed out that a plan is only a dream until it is budgeted.

But the statement that "the budget is a plan" may be more a declaration of principle than a description of actuality. Such has been the conclusion of many students of public budgeting, including the recent Hoover Commission. The budget may well be a plan in the sense that it prescribes conditioning and limiting factors upon future action. But the same budget may not be a plan in the sense that it reflects any planning. There is reason to suppose that much public budgeting is "historical," a mere transfer forward of the past into the future. There is also reason to believe that much planning occurs independently of budgeting

---

[1] *A Soldier's Story* (New York: Henry Holt and Company, 1951), p. xi.

47

and with very little relation to it. And one would betray no secrets in saying that some administrators view the budget more as a hindrance and impediment than as an instrument of planning.

The fact is that budgeting and planning are not exactly synonymous, even by definition. If we say a man *plans* a trip, we mean something a little different from the statement that he *budgets* a trip. The former expression signifies that he projects going somewhere at some future time by some means of transportation. The latter suggests that he is projecting how he is going to raise and allocate his available funds for the trip. Budgeting is the application of double-entry bookkeeping to planning. It compels the consideration of both sides of the ledger—what is to be done and what it is to cost. It is also of more than passing note that we usually think of the planning of the trip as coming before its budgeting. There is apparently some presumption that before we enter upon the process of budgeting we must have some kind of objective and program already in mind.

Another semantic distinction is suggested by the expression that a man carefully *budgets* his time, meaning that he allocates his scarce hours and minutes among the various things he wants to do so as to maximize the total value of all his minutes. The economist might say he endeavors to equalize the marginal return of the last minute expended on each different activity. Budgeting thus lays an emphasis upon the idea of *balancing:* of proposed activities with their probable costs; and of competing activities among each other, in relation to the costs of each. Further, its greater relative emphasis upon the resources side of the ledger lends to the connotation of *conservancy* associated with budgeting. It is no accident that the budget movement grew up with, and is today commonly identified with, the economy movement. In this sense, budgeting and planning are apposite if not opposite. In extreme form, the one means saving; the other, spending. The same people who urge better budgeting can condemn planning, and vice versa.

Perhaps a more useful way of looking at the distinction is to think of budgeting as one element or aspect of the total planning process. Planning involves first the conceiving of goals and the development of alternative courses of future action to achieve the goals. Second, it involves the reduction of these alternatives from a very large number to a small number and finally to one approved course of action, *the program.* Budgeting probably plays a slight part in the first phase but an increasingly important and decisive part in the second. It facilitates the choice-making process by providing a basis for systematic comparisons among alternatives which take into account their total impacts on both the debit and the credit sides. It thus encourages, and provides some of the tools for, an increasing degree of precision in the planning process. Budgeting is the ingredient of planning which disciplines the entire process.

Thus, despite the differing significances of the words, budgeting and planning are theoretically linked; in fact, one is part and parcel of the other. Yet, in large organizations, the distinctions between them may assume the proportions of barriers, far more than in the mind of the single individual who is presumed sovereign over his own activities. Partly this is because of the necessity of specialism. The managers and leaders of organization units are normally specialized in some function or some area in which their mission is to show work accomplishments. Insofar as they have a role in planning the future programs of their units, they have some incentive to project their specialist, functional aspirations. Budgeting has, of necessity and with support of law, produced its own specialism. It is a specialism of questioning plans, of balancing and counterbalancing demands for scarce resources. Some of its key words are "costs," "feasibility," "realistic," and "mark-up," meaning "mark-down." Many good budgeteers have the deserved reputations of being "no-men." This may have little to do with their personality profiles; the function itself almost forces them into the negative posture if they are to do their jobs effectively. The character of the budget process does not stimulate tendencies to risk-taking and innovation in relation to programs. Much the reverse, it is a vehicle for the questioning of invention and expansion, which are more characteristically associated with program planning and planners. The budget is properly associated with balance, and budgeting itself serves as a balance to the more positive elements of planning.

The separation of budgeting from program planning has been encouraged by many other factors. Not least of these is simply the dollar. Although budgeting need not be in terms of dollars, the dollar has provided the most common denominator for the objective measurement and comparison of values and costs. It has contributed to the association of budgeting with accounting and bookkeeping and to the development of techniques and processes which lay emphasis upon measurable units and precise analyses. These are not always associated with planners. The growing complexity of Federal accounting has placed a high premium upon mastery of the system and skill with the techniques. A good Federal budget man is readily transferable among agencies and programs. His knowledge of program is secondary to his knowledge of the process, and sometimes his sympathies are similarly related.

In subsequent pages we shall deal with other factors contributing to the divorce of the planning process from the budgeting process, with particular reference to the defense establishment. Organizational and procedural arrangements of the government as a whole as well as those of individual agencies encourage such separation. Many of these arrangements are consciously and purposefully projected, and with some reason. The budget plan and the program plan of a large agency may quite properly and necessarily *not* be the same thing. Their scope and coverage are almost certain to differ in some respects; their relation to time periods differs; the organization units and individuals primarily concerned for each may be different; the channels through which they proceed may well be parallel but not identical.

Nonetheless, budgeting and program planning must be intimately and frequently if not continuously related, even if they are not married. The need is obvious in all agencies; but it is most emphatic where it is most difficult—in the agency which is operating in uncertainty and in change. The problem of how, when, where to relate the two is one which has been given increasing attention within the defense establishment. In this chapter we shall discuss the background and the development of systematic plan and program systems in the Joint Chiefs of Staff, the Army, and the Air Force, with particular reference to their relationship with the budget process. In the following chapter, we shall deal with another aspect of the same problem, the performance budget.

BACKGROUND FOR MILITARY PLANNING AND BUDGETING

It is neither feasible nor necessary in this study to trace, even in the most summary form, the development of military planning up to the close of the Second World War. It is pertinent, however, to draw attention briefly to certain features and problems of this history, particularly as they relate to the development of budgeting. The present situation cannot be understood without appreciation of the shaping fingers of the past.

I. *Planning as a systematic organizational process is and has long been firmly embedded in military doctrine.* Evidences of the recognition of the need for planning and even of its specialization in particular officers and units have been traced to the earliest armies in recorded history. In fact, military histories to a considerable extent associate the development of military organization with the degree of advancement and institutionalization of the planning function.[2] The organizational sense of the word "staff" is, of course, commonly attributed to military organization, and planning is central among staff functions. Few civil agencies, private or public, plan with comparable consciousness, emphasis, or formalization of the function as such.

II. *Planning in the American military forces has emphasized the military aspects of command; that is to say, the operational, tactical, and logistical aspects.* Stated negatively, military planning has until quite recently given much less systematic attention to such factors as production, procurement, the economy in its relation to the military, and internal management other than tactical. To be sure, some of these areas have been deliberately kept beyond its scope for governmental and political reasons. But the planning of organization and of operations for tactical units, long recognized as a continuing function, has not been matched by comparable doctrine and technique for planning of departmental programs and organizations. In fact, planning by military agencies in the latter area is more comparable in its state of development to planning in other civil organizations of the government than it is to operational planning of the more military sort.

III. *The history of American military organization has been punctuated by periodic struggles to attain a centralized base of authority over both planning and operations.* These struggles have grown out of efforts to overcome the narrow and specialized points of view of semiautonomous bureaus, services, and departments; to broaden the scope of coordinated planning; and to establish a core of power to direct the implementation of plans. These struggles may be traced back to Revolutionary days. Characteristically, the need for a broader base of coordination is dramatized in war emergencies by scandalous or disastrous events; is alleviated temporarily by emergency measures; and culminates sometimes in permanent measures in the years following the war. In the past fifty years, we may trace to such a need and through such history the organization and development of: the Army General Staff; the reorganized Army Staff after World War I; the Army Air Forces and now the Air Force and its Air Staff;

---

[2] For example, see J. P. Hittle, *The Military Staff: Its History and Development* (Harrisburg, Pa.: The Military Service Publishing Co., 1949). Hittle writes: "From the standpoint of military history the development of the staff has paced the progress of military organization. The increased scope of battle necessitated, and was in turn made possible by, the use of staff officers. Great individual commanders attained great victories, but their success was largely dependent upon the thinking done by them before the battle—staff planning—which made it possible to achieve victory in the field" (pp. 11-12).

the Army Service Forces during the last war; the Joint Chiefs of Staff; the Combined Chiefs of Staff during the last war; the Secretary of Defense and all his subordinate units; the National Security Council; and many other agencies and coordinating arrangements. The struggle still goes on. It is a persistent problem and one for which there is probably no permanent solution. Forces of specialism and professionalism, of bureaucratism, and of politics apply continuing pressures toward unit autonomy and the "narrow view." It is doubtful that this country has entered any war before 1950 with either plans of adequately broad scope or the organizational mechanism to develop and execute such plans quickly. To a considerable extent the efforts to establish programming systems and indeed the performance budget described later in this and the following chapter, are in reality efforts to broaden the base for planning and control.

IV. *For many other reasons, the services have been relatively unsuccessful in the peacetime development of basic strategic and mobilization plans.* Of course, for a very large part of our history, the temper, aspirations, and foreign policy of the country effectively prevented such planning at all. Systematic planning for war which went beyond the protection of our shores and the support of the Monroe Doctrine was anathema—despite occasional lapses. As late as the fall of 1915, President Wilson is reported to have been "trembling and white with passion" on seeing a newspaper report that the General Staff was preparing a plan in the event of war with Germany.[3] In fact, until our entrance in World War II, war planning activity was tenderly guarded both for security and political reasons. War planning and warmongering could be identified in the popular mind, as witness the effort of a prominent midwest newspaper, some time before Pearl Harbor, to make political capital by its revelations of the Army's plan for war in Europe.

In the period between the great wars, however, significant strides were made in the organization for, and the development of, strategic and mobilization plans. Both Army and Navy set up War Plans Divisions soon after the First World War, and the Joint Army and Navy Board provided a coordinating mechanism in this and other fields of mutual interest. Much of this activity was more useful in its development of techniques and in the training of planners than in its substance. The Army during the twenties and thirties developed a variety of so-called "color" plans, different colors being used to designate different

---

[3] Reported in Otto D. Nelson, *National Security and the General Staff,* p. 218.

possible military contingencies. "As strategic planning in the broad sense, the early war plans, with the exception of ORANGE (war with Japan), were virtually meaningless because they bore so little relation to contemporary international and military alignments." [4] In 1939, work started on the RAINBOW plans, which were postulated on more realistic premises. Of the five plans developed in this series, RAINBOW 5, which contemplated the sending of American troops across the Atlantic to operate with England and France against one or both of the Axis powers, received increasingly concentrated attention as our entrance into war neared. It went formally into effect on December 7, 1941. "Though even RAINBOW 5 in many ways was inadequate for the crisis then at hand, it provided a sub-stratum of strategic agreement on which the subsequent development of British-American plans was based." [5]

Basic war planning during this period was weakened not only by political inhibitions and the difficulty of relating it to international realities. It was imperfectly related to the planning and control of current resources, operations, and deployments. Strategic planning provides the objective, but it is unrealistic unless it is supported by plans as to how we get from "here" to "there," i.e. mobilization plans. For much of this period, strategic planning was governed by the requirements approach—i.e. what the postulated contingency required; current plans and operations were governed by appropriations—i.e. what Congress would authorize from year to year; and mobilization planning was diffused among a variety of planning and operating agencies, military and civilian. To the confusion wrought by political uncertainties was added that of organizational uncertainty, lack of clear-cut responsibilities and relationships in the difficult process of converting a peaceful nation to a military nation. Underlying was the absence of an agreed definition of current, mobilization, and strategic plans, and a systematic method of relating them.

Illustrative of this kind of defect, in the words of Luther Gulick, was the failure of military leaders to ". . . envision even remotely the extent of prospective supply needs of a total war waged all over the world. This lack of imagination was duplicated by the industrial leaders, and we were told that steel and aluminum capacity, for example, were adequate and that conversion to war production of automobile and other plants was hardly necessary. . . . When war came,

---

[4] Ray S. Cline, *Washington Command Post: The Operations Division*, p. 36.
[5] *Ibid.*, p. 57

the picture was completely reversed; the military then knew no bounds in their demands." [6] Again: "The plans and designs made in the War and Navy Departments up to 1939 were not too valuable. The administrative plans drawn for M-Day were quite inappropriate. War was not what the planners thought, and did not come as they had imagined." [7]

Mr. Gulick's remarks are relatively temperate. The Bureau of the Budget report on *The United States at War* describes as "practically worthless" the initial estimates of the services as to their raw materials requirements, and it quotes other official documents of the period which depict military mobilization estimates in such terms as: "guess work"; "extremely diverse because of the many different assumptions"; "both imaginary and arbitrary"; requiring "almost unbelievable revision upward or downward"; "completely out of line with any realistic approximations." [8]

V. *There is little historical precedent for the correlation of the processes and organizations for military planning with those for budgeting.* In fact, many of the pressures up to the end of World War II were in the other direction. The divorce of the two activities has been furthered by its identification with other dichotomies of almost ancient origin: military—civil; central staff—bureau; operational—administrative; substantive—fiscal. In general, budgeting has been associated with each of the second words in this series—civil, bureau, administrative, and fiscal. The roles and relationships of the civil and military authorities vary among the service departments and are not clearly defined or definable in any of them. Nonetheless, the over-all trend in the emphasis of their functions is clear and unmistakable. The civilian secretaries and their staffs assume a substantial if not dominating role in the administrative activities of the departments, in the supervision of functions of civilian or business type, and in activities involving relationships with civil agencies within and outside the government. Specifically, the top civilian staffs exercise special influence in such areas as procurement, or, in naval terminology, producer-logistics, manpower control, civilian personnel management, and fiscal management. The military chiefs exercise recognized leadership in strategic and operational plans, in military intelligence, in consumer logistics,

---

[6] Luther Gulick, *Administrative Reflections from World War II* (University, Alabama: University of Alabama Press, 1948), p. 46.

[7] *Ibid.*, pp. 86-7.

[8] Subtitled, *Development and Administration of the War Program by the Federal Government* (Washington: Government Printing Office, 1946), p. 81.

and in military command. The split is not clean-cut and the gray areas where the two realms come together are sources of unending problems—such as military construction, mobilization plans, political intelligence, research and development, and, recently, the budget.[9]

Prior to 1921, appropriation estimates were annually prepared in the bureaus of the War and Navy Departments and transmitted to the respective secretaries. Here they were examined and transmitted to the Congress. The examination was seldom very thorough, for the secretaries lacked the time, knowledge, and staff to conduct a real review.[10] The defense of the estimates was principally by the bureaus themselves, and most of the appropriations were made to the bureau level and below. The establishment of a central planning agency in the War Department, the General Staff, apparently had only slight influence on this procedure, for the preparation and review of the budget estimates do not appear among its functions or accomplishments throughout its first two decades of development.[11]

The Budget and Accounting Act of 1921 required the departments to designate budget officers, and it resulted ultimately in the establishment of central budget units in both departments. In the Navy, the Chief of Naval Operations was the first budget officer. Subsequently, the office was filled by a line rear admiral who reported directly to the Secretary, an arrangement which in 1941 gave way to the Office of Budget and Reports. The chief of this office was a line officer directly responsible to the Secretary. This set-up remained until the Comptroller was established in 1950.[12] In the Army, the Office of Chief of Finance, an office of the Special Staff, became the budget office. During World War II, the budget function was transferred to the Services of Supply with the establishment of that command—a pretty clear indication of

---

[9] It is interesting to note that at one time in early Navy history, this situation was exactly reversed. Three senior naval officers, constituting a Board of Naval Commissioners, were responsible for supervising the administration of the department. The Secretary directed the forces afloat.

[10] See particularly the description of, and despair over, the process as reported by Henry L. Stimson, Secretary of War, first from 1911 to 1913, in *On Active Service in Peace and War*, with McGeorge Bundy (New York: Harper and Bros., 1947), especially pp. 72-4. Stimson discovered that "the authority of the Secretary of War in controlling expenditures in his own Department was negligible" (p. 72). His War Department experience was to give him valuable ammunition in fighting, later on, for the executive budget in the Constitutional Convention of the State of New York of 1915. See the *Revised Record* of that convention, p. 1611 ff.

[11] As these "functions and accomplishments" are reported in Nelson, *op. cit.*

[12] Department of the Navy, Office of the Comptroller, "The Naval Establishment: Its Growth and Necessity for Expansion, 1930–1950," NAVEXOS P-1038, July, 1951, pp. 92-3.

the "service" connotation of budgeting in the Army. After about a year it was returned to the Budget Division of the Special Staff where it remained until its incorporation in the Comptroller's Office in 1948. Until the Second World War, the essential role and procedure of budgeting was not fundamentally changed from that before 1921. The foci were the bureaus; the transmitting agents, the secretaries. The relation of budgeting to the core of military planning—the central military staff—was nebulous and occasional. This was an era of dollar famine for the services, and there is ample evidence that the availability of funds was the basic governing factor in military affairs. The budget's separation from the centrally integrating force of military planning contributed to the separatist power of the bureaus.

It should not be inferred from these remarks that military budgeting was outside of military control, or that budgeting activity was carried on principally by civilians. The reverse is the case. But budgeting was kept separate from the regular line channels of military directives and plans; it was considered primarily a tool of civilian-type management, responsive to civilian leadership; it was the business side of administration in contra-distinction to military command. World War II altered the situation basically in that the budgeting of dollars ceased to be a significant factor of control or planning. Dollars were not the critical scarce resource, and the significant plans and controls—though essentially budgetary in nature—applied to the fields of supply, equipment, manpower, and transport. For the most part, these were exercised through newly improvised organizations and procedures, outside the traditional budgetary channels.

VI. *The nexus between military plans and programs on the one hand and the budget, a political product, on the other is vital to each.* Past failures to relate the two in times of peace have resulted in the sterilization of military planning, a result not inconsistent with fairly negative American foreign policy objectives. But, as described in Chapter II above, the situation today is different. Military plans are ineffective unless they are supportable and supported by the budget; and budgets are meaningless unless they are based upon sound military planning, itself built upon approved objectives in foreign policy. To a very considerable extent, therefore, the key military problem of today is to relate the two so as to produce a force that is both militarily sound and politically understood and agreed upon. The effectiveness of military use of available resources depends in a very real sense upon our success in dealing with this problem. And so does the popular control of military goals and activities.

Present Framework for Planning and Programming

In spite of notable progress before and during the recent war, and of some brilliant achievements of planning during the war, the termination of hostilities left the services still in need of a firm doctrine and durable systems for integrating planning, programming, budgeting, and operating. The recognition of this need within the services has provided stimulus to a great deal of constructive thought, effort, and experiment in the last several years.

The period since World War II has witnessed a welter of activities, experiments, and improvisations as well as some very fundamental and firm changes. It is difficult to identify the main threads of this maze, particularly in the months since the Korean involvement, because the routines and schedules were largely upset by emergency needs. Nonetheless, certain underlying motifs seem to be discernible.

First, the drive toward greater and greater organizational unification has had tremendous effect upon both planning and budgeting. It is reflected in the growth in scope and power of central agencies at the Defense Department level and above. Procedural arrangements are becoming more and more linked to a single central focus. And unification at the very top has to some extent required a greater degree of unification of the services at the second level. Particularly in the Army, the staff in Washington is emerging into a more and more dominant position with respect to the programs and operations of subordinate units.

Second, there has been notable progress in the correlation and integration of planning and programming processes, not only among organizations concerned, but also among substantive elements of planning content and among the terms of time covered by different plans and programs. There is emerging an increasing body of doctrine covering these relationships. And the processes themselves are becoming increasingly formalized and routinized.

Third, the role and importance of the budget in the total military picture is being transformed. Its position is not yet clear, but certainly it is much different. It is now recognized in official doctrine as an instrument and in fact the expression of military plans; planning procedures are largely tailored to the requirements of the budget cycle; and, far from the step-child of the central military staffs, it is increasingly becoming one of their dominating concerns. A former Comptroller of the Army stated this emerging concept of the budget in emphatic, if optimistic, terms:

Within the Military establishment and with particular reference to the Department of the Army, the military budget is in reality a strategic and logistic plan expressed in program form, phased into an annual operating plan of correlated and integrated requirements, all assembled and collated through the use of common denominators, such as manpower, matériel, equipment, and, finally, dollars. Stated in other words, the budget, in its final analysis, at the time of preparation, is the expression in financial terms of the coordinated and balanced program and plan of operations of the Department of the Army which sets forth the requirements of the Army, within the period for which the plan is projected, to fulfill its responsibilities for National Defense under the then conceived international situation. Under this concept the budget is not merely a medium through which funds are obtained from Congress.[13]

A fourth trend is the magnification of the complexity of both the programming and budgeting processes. This development was probably an inevitable consequence of the size of the program, its impact upon virtually all spheres of activity, public and private, and the almost infinite variety of factors that must be considered. Organizational unification has added a whole new layer of units and agencies that contribute directly or indirectly to both plans and budgets—the Office of the Secretary of Defense and its various subunits, as well as the Joint Chiefs of Staff with its various committees and subunits. Another series of new agencies, likewise involved in military plans and budgets, has been established outside the Department of Defense, including the National Security Council, the Central Intelligence Agency, the Atomic Energy Commission, the Foreign Operations Administration, the Council of Economic Advisers, and others.

The problem of the complexity of procedures has been further aggravated by the emergency—the urgent need for new information and projections overlapping or overlaying established forms and reports. The need for simplifying and stabilizing is everywhere apparent, and efforts to this end are now being exerted at various echelons, including particularly the Joint Chiefs of Staff.

The general concepts as they appear in broad outline today are as follows:

1. The development and implementation of military plans and programs are primarily functions of central military command and staff. They are sub-

---

[13] Major General Edmond H. Leavey in a talk before the Washington Chapter of the Society for the Advancement of Management, February 14, 1949 (processed). The general's definition seems particularly sanguine in view of the fact that his statement was made two years before the Army budget structure was placed on the performance basis.

ject to civilian review and control at certain points, but the initiative and responsibility are essentially military. The aegis is the President in his capacity as Commander in Chief; next in line is the National Security Council; then the Joint Chiefs of Staff, an entirely military body; and finally the individual Chiefs of Staff and the Chief of Naval Operations and their staffs.

2. Budgeting is tied in with programming in a number of ways, but the processes are fundamentally distinct; the organizations and individuals concerned differ in part; and the procedure, the timing, the philosophy, and the classifications differ. The orientation of the budget process is toward the Congress and particularly its appropriations subcommittees, the President in his capacity as Chief Executive, the Bureau of the Budget, the Office of the Secretary of Defense and his Comptroller, and the civilian secretaries, the staff chiefs in their individual capacities, and the departmental comptrollers.

3. Planning and programming are considered properly to precede and provide the basis for budget estimates. The budget is a translation into dollar terms of program requirements. Operating programs are developed from the original programs by making such adjustments as may be required as a result of appropriations.

4 Planning, programming, and budgeting are all cyclical processes, and all are now geared to the fiscal year. That is, the fiscal year is the basic unit of time for the extension forward of all projections; and each fiscal year produces a new set of plans.

5. The basic procedures are substantially as follows:

a. The President, on the basis of advice of the National Security Council, determines in broad terms the policies and objectives of American foreign and military programs.

b. The Joint Chiefs of Staff determines the military forces required to achieve these objectives and phases them in time. The basic force requirements are normally reviewed and approved by the President and National Security Council. The Joint Chiefs also prepares comprehensive plans and guidances covering all the major areas of military activity and development, and transmits these to the three services and to other agencies at the Defense Department level.

c. The planning staffs of the three services prepare and supervise the preparation by lower echelons of plans and programs in detail, based upon the guidances received from JCS. Plans for mobilization are coordinated and tested for industrial feasibility in the Office, Secretary of Defense. This was done formerly by the Munitions Board. Similar coordinative and review activities are performed by the other offices at the defense level in their respective fields.

d. The plans and programs developed within the services are reviewed and approved by the individual chiefs of staff and thus became official for planning purposes.

e. The Secretary of Defense through his Assistant Secretary (Comptroller) develops budget guidelines and transmits them to the secretaries of the three service departments. These reflect the prior determinations of the National Security Council and the Joint Chiefs of Staff. They also take into consideration economic, financial, and political factors, and the views of the President, the Bureau of the Budget, and other agencies.

f. The three services prepare their budget estimates, basing them upon the plans and programs already developed and upon the policies set forth in the budget guidelines of the Secretary of Defense. These are reviewed, modified, and approved by the staff chief of each department and then by its secretary.

g. The Defense Comptroller and his staff, with the Bureau of the Budget, review the service estimates intensively, after which they are modified and sent forward as the Department of Defense budget.

h. After the President's budget is transmitted, and again after appropriations are passed, the services modify their plans and programs in accordance with the funds available. At this latter point, the programs become operating directives.

The above description and the accompanying diagram (Figure 4) are greatly oversimplified and are presented here primarily to provide a framework for subsequent discussions. For example, there is a reverse flow upward of recommendations and data from the services to the Joint Chiefs and the National Security Council prior to the formal directives and guidelines and, in fact, all through the process. It should be borne particularly in mind that several of the agencies involved are representative membership bodies, providing cross-filtration of points of view and influence. Thus, the Secretary of Defense and the Chairman of the Joint Chiefs of Staff participate in the National Security Council; the Joint Chiefs is a representative body, and its subordinate committees also consist of representatives of the services. Not shown on the chart are the budget advisory committees, described in Chapter V, and a variety of committees and councils at the service levels for the coordination of programs and plans.

PLANNING BY THE JOINT CHIEFS

From the standpoint of the development of the military plans that are precedent to military budgets, the Joint Chiefs of Staff and its constituent organizations are dominantly important. The Joint Chiefs, its committees, and the Joint Staff which services them are military

FIGURE 4

CHANNELS OF PLANS AND BUDGETS IN THE DEPARTMENT OF DEFENSE

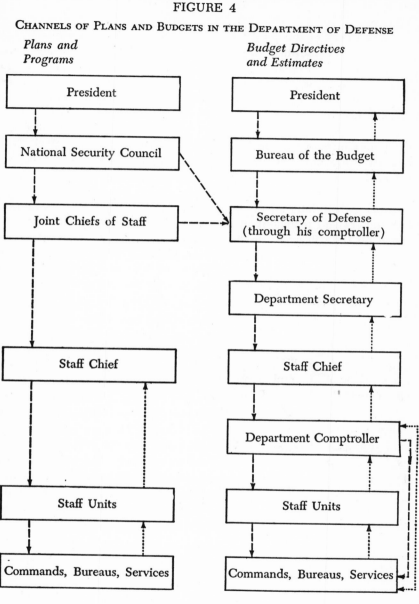

Plans and Programs

Budget Directives and Estimates

— — — — — — Guide Lines, Directives, Basic Plans.

·················· Proposed Plans, Estimates.

bodies consisting of officers serving ex officio or detailed or assigned to this duty for a limited number of years from the three services. The machinery of the Joint Chiefs thus provides continuing channels for the flow of information, plans, and points of view back and forth between the services and the coordinating center.

A major difficulty of military planning in the recent past has resulted from the tardiness or the sporadic arrival of the basic agreed plans from the hub of the wheel—the Joint Chiefs. It is therefore doubly significant that a new "plan for planning" was approved by the Joint Chiefs of Staff in 1952 and is now being put into effect. This is a carefully designed scheme for annual planning, geared to the calendar and comprehensive in its scope. When it is fully implemented, it should provide the services with a firm base from which to launch their internal planning activities. It will furnish assurance to planners and managers at lower echelons that the JCS plans will arrive on time in accordance with an understood schedule, thus reducing the necessity of anticipatory planning and "crash" adjustments.

Under the new scheme, the planning activities of the Joint Staff, as well as the plans themselves, are divided into three main types according to the time period covered. Long-range plans are projected annually a number of years in advance and are useful and necessary especially for the guidance of research and development activities. Short-range plans, likewise prepared annually, are designed to guide current operations and to provide immediate plans in the event of emergency. Unlike the long-range plans, which are essentially "requirements" documents, the short-range are premised on currently available resources and capabilities.

Standing midway between these two, both as to time covered and as to the type of planning approach, are plans of medium range. They are designed to translate national policy into strategy and objectives that are considered to be attainable. They are thus basically requirements statements, but they take into consideration current and foreseeable resource capabilities. These are the most important from the budget standpoint since they provide the premises for most of the programming of the services, for the preparation of the annual budgets, and for mobilization planning. For purposes of medium-range planning, a D-Day is assumed annually to occur on July 1 at the conclusion of a budget year. The plan itself covers the period following D-Day, but it forms the basis for the preparation of the

budget in the fiscal year preceding D-Day. Thus a plan applicable
to the fiscal years 1957 and 1958 would be based upon an assumed
D-Day of July 1, 1956 and would furnish the basis for the budget
for fiscal year 1956.

One of the difficulties of the projected scheme is the distance in
time between the development of the plan and the period to which
the plan applies. This problem is itself partly caused by the length
of time involved in the budget process. If one year, or a little less,
is allowed for the development of service programs based upon the
JCS plans, and another year, or a little more, is allowed for the development, review, and passage of the annual budget, it is apparent
that the JCS plans should be completed about two years before the
budget year is to begin, or three years before the assumed D-Day.
To this period must of course be added the several months that the
joint agencies themselves require for the development and consideration of the basic plan. It is apparent that this phase of the planning
process must proceed on assumptions that are vulnerable to frequent
and sometimes violent change in the intervening period.

Another difficulty, perhaps inevitable in a planning process of such
scope and dimension, is the tremendous complexity of the system.
Not only must the plans for different terms of time be meshed with
each other, but, at any given moment, plans of the same term but
applicable to different years will be in various stages of development
and application. These, too, must be related. And all must be related
to the planning and operations that are simultaneously proceeding
at both higher and lower echelons. A decision modifying one plan at
one time, as, for example, a cut imposed by the Bureau of the Budget
on the estimates for a given year, might directly or indirectly force
modifications on a whole series of JCS and service plans, not only
for that year but for many other years as well, and not only for
medium-range plans but for plans of both shorter and longer range.
In a fast-moving world, keeping plans up-to-date and in tune with the
times and with each other is no small problem.

The divorce between military planning and budgetary planning is
an additional difficulty. The Secretary of Defense and his staff aides
apparently have no official role in developing or reviewing the basic
plans of the joint agencies. When they undertake to analyze the
budgetary offspring of the joint plans, more than a year after their
preparation, they must either accept the premises as "givens" or
threaten to injure or warp the sense of the plans themselves, plans

which they had no official part in creating and for which they are not responsible. Conversely, the Joint Chiefs of Staff as a body has no further role or responsibility with respect to the annual budget although the budget is presumably predicated upon the basic objectives and plans JCS has initially approved.

THE ARMY PROGRAM SYSTEM

The services are dependent upon the planning of the Joint Chiefs, but in some respects their job is even broader and more difficult. They must contribute to and share in the JCS planning process; they must also develop their own plans and objectives within the framework laid down by JCS; and, most of all, they must convert plans into performance. This is the "cutting edge" of planning, and probably the point at which, more than any other, planning systems break down. Those processes which have to do with the reduction of planned objectives to specific directives and schedules for operations are encompassed in the word "programming." In the Army, the entire aspect of management concerned with the developing, executing, and following up of programs is encompassed in the formal expression "program management."

The expression is of recent origin, as is the system which it connotes. Although many of the elements of the imposing edifice which is Army programming are of long standing, their coordination in a single comprehensive scheme of doctrine, organization, and procedure is a significant current phenomenon. The system is still developing, still experimental in many respects, still incomplete. It is too early to evaluate it empirically, but it may be useful to examine and analyze its concepts and workings and perhaps identify some of its strengths and problems.

Like most organizational reform movements, the programming system grew out of an awareness of deficiencies, an awareness increasingly articulated following the end of the war. A series of studies of Army organization and management by groups within the Army—the Haislip Board,[14] the Management Division, and others—directed attention to the need for consciously formulated systems for program development and follow-up. One of the most far-reaching studies was that made by the private consulting firm of Cresap, McCormick, and

---

[14] The Haislip Board, known by the name of its chairman, was officially the War Department Policies and Review Board, established by order of the Chief of Staff, February 15, 1947. Its report was published August 11, 1947.

Paget in 1948 and 1949. Its findings and its proposals in the areas of programming, budgeting, and top staff organization added impetus to the development of a comprehensive program system. In general, it reported and deplored: the lack of correlation between planning and budgeting; the lack of general staff control over large portions of the budget; the absence of systematic machinery and responsibility for planning and for follow-up on the execution of plans; the failure to evaluate programs and policies in terms of cost; the lack of co-ordination among plans; and the lack of progress reporting.

The firm specifically proposed that there be established three deputy chiefs of staff, each charged with one of the three basic functions involved in programming:

> Deputy Chief of Staff, Plans—program development
> Deputy Chief of Staff, Operations—program execution
> Deputy Chief of Staff, Review—program review and analysis

The three-phase approach to programming which has somewhat inaccurately been likened to the legislative, executive, and judicial processes of government, has now become official doctrine of the Army. In April, 1950, a new top organization was announced establishing the programming structure along the general lines proposed by Cresap, McCormick, and Paget. There are now two Deputy Chiefs of Staff: one for Plans and Research, responsible, among other things, for program development; one for Operations and Administration, responsible for program execution. The Comptroller of the Army has the status, though not the title, of a third Deputy Chief of Staff and has the responsibility for program review and analysis.

Since 1949, work has been proceeding to develop and install a formalized programming system for both the Headquarters and the field. The work of the Army was divided into fourteen primary programs,[15] and each of these was classified into program segments. Appropriate Assistant Chiefs of Staff were named program directors of most of the various programs, and the heads of the various technical and administrative services became program segment directors. The primary programs and their directors are shown on the next page.

Within the Army, the direction and guidance of the development of all types of plans and programs are the responsibility of the Deputy Chief of Staff, Plans and Research, acting, of course, under the Chief

---

[15] The number of primary programs was subsequently increased to sixteen by the addition of two new programs for the civilian components—one for the National Guard and one for the Organized Reserve and R.O.T.C.

Primary Program	Program Director
1. Troop Program	G-1
2. Command and Management	G-1
3. Military Personnel	G-1
4. Civilian Personnel	Director, Civilian Personnel, Office of the Secretary of the Army
5. Intelligence	G-2
6. Training	G-3
7. Research and Development	G-4
8. Industrial Mobilization	G-4
9. Major Procurement	G-4
10. Supply	G-4
11. Services	G-4
12. Installations	G-4
13. Construction	G-4
14. Joint Projects	Various, as assigned

of Staff. But an important if not dominating role on substantive matters is played by the Program Advisory Committee (PAC), which is composed of top representatives of each major staff division. Its membership is virtually identical with that of the Budget Advisory Committee, described in Chapter V. It is aided in its work by a Junior Program Advisory Committee, consisting of middle-grade officers from the same staff divisions.

The process of program development is a recurring annual cycle. The timing of its sequence of steps is controlled ultimately by the deadline dates of the annual budget, and recent adjustments have been made to synchronize it with the planning schedule of the Joint Chiefs of Staff. The program process proceeds from the very broad and general to the detailed and specifically scheduled. In organization terms, it starts at or near the top, flows down the hierarchy, comes up for review and approval, and then goes down for execution. The Army's plan for programming, frequently revised in recent years, follows a general scheme roughly as follows.

Prior to the preparation by the Joint Chiefs of its medium-term plan, the Army prepares a preliminary report or estimate to be used in the development of the JCS plan. Immediately following the development of the JCS plan, and prior to its approval by the Joint Chiefs, the Army begins preparation of its *Estimate*, projecting the Army objectives in somewhat greater detail than the JCS plan. This *Estimate*, which should be completed in August, covers the same years as the comparable JCS plan, assumes a D-Day about three years hence, and provides the basis for programs and budgets applicable to the budget year that begins about two years hence.

The Army objectives stated in the *Estimate* provide the basis for the *Program Objectives,* a somewhat more explicit statement of objectives for each of the Primary Programs. These are prepared by or under the direction of the Program Advisory Committee and are reviewed and approved by the Chief of Staff and the Secretary of the Army. An entirely hypothetical illustration of the relationships among the Army mission, Army objective, and program objectives might be:

Army Mission: to provide ground forces for defense of strategic areas.

Army Objective (in the *Estimate*): two divisions to be ready to defend a tropical area.

Program Objectives:

1. Troop Program to provide for X divisions.
2. Training Program to provide for jungle training.
3. Major Procurement Program to provide jungle equipment.

On the basis of the approved *Program Objectives,* the Deputy Chief of Staff, Plans and Research, directs the preparation of a *Program Directive.* It is a finalized version of the *Objectives* and includes instructions, assumptions, and a prescribed schedule for the submission of approved programs. According to current doctrine, it should be issued by late fall of each year. On the basis of the *Directive,* the various program directors initiate work on the development of specific programs for which they are responsible. A large part of the work of program development is actually done below the level of the General Staff by the technical and administrative services. Each of these prepares programs applicable to its operations and consonant with the *Directive* and submits them to the program directors. Here they are reviewed, amended, correlated, and consolidated into *Program Documents.* These *Documents,* which constitute the programs themselves, are submitted back to the Deputy Chief of Staff, Plans and Research, and he, with the assistance of the Program Advisory Committee, reviews, correlates, and revises them as necessary. Upon approval, the *Documents* are published as the official programs of the Army.

Each organizational unit prepares a comprehensive organizational program, covering all the Primary Programs in which it has any responsibility. Since the structure of the Army does not follow program lines, most of the Primary Programs involve a large number of different agencies. All the technical services are responsible for parts of at least thirteen of the Primary Programs. This means that they operate under a system of multiple responsibility in respect to both program development and program execution. For example, the Chief of Engineers is responsible to G-1 for segments of three or more programs; to G-2, G-3, and the Director of Civilian Personnel, Office, Secretary of the Army, for parts of one program for each; and to G-4 for segments of seven programs.

Official doctrine stipulates that the various *Program Documents* provide the bases for the annual budget. In the recent past, however, the documents were not completed in time to be used in the budget directive, and development of the budget and the *Program Documents* proceeded concurrently. The official budget procedure begins after receipt by the Army of *Budget Guidelines* from the Secretary of Defense. Practice in recent years was to refer this document to the Program Advisory Committee, which revised the *Program Objectives* accordingly. These revised instructions were then used by the Budget Division of the Comptroller's Office and the Budget Advisory Committee in the preparation of the so-called *Army Program Guidance.* This document contained substantive program information to be used in budget preparation. It went out to the staff and operating agencies at the time of the procedural budget directive.

The *Program Documents* are intended to be completed and finalized more than a year prior to the fiscal year to which they primarily relate. Subsequent changes, necessitated by revisions in plans or by budgetary decisions, are to be accomplished by appropriate revisions in the programs. Then, the *Program Documents* become, in effect, operational directives, the basis for schedules and specific plans for execution.

Program planning in the Army is a complex and extended process. According to current doctrine, the time required for the preparation of the *Program Documents,* following the approval of an Army *Estimate,* is about six months. Of course, the Army planning which leads up to the JCS plan and then to the Army *Estimate* lasts more than six months. The planning process which culminates in the approval of the *Program Documents* must start more than two and one half years before the beginning of the fiscal year to which they primarily apply. And they must be finalized and approved more than one and one quarter years before that date.

Of course, the actual calendar in recent years has not been according to the "book." The first, or "Truman," budget for 1954 perhaps came closest to conformance with the prescribed procedure. The *Program Objectives* and the *Program Directive* for that year were issued in October and November, 1951, respectively. The *Objectives* were revised on the basis of the Defense *Guidelines* in April of 1952 and the *Army Program Guidance* was issued in April and May. Most of the *Program Documents* were completed sporadically from May to August of 1952.

In 1952, as in other years, a large part of the budget process was completed before some of the most important programs were finalized. This practice has largely been a product of necessity and is counter to the stated principle of the program—budget relationship. Nonetheless, it may have some merit. It has made possible some reduction in planning "lead-time"—the time between the drawing of plans and the period planned for. It has made possible the rapid development of Army budgetary instructions based upon broad program objectives rather than upon detailed program segments. In fact, the translation of the voluminous program documents into budget instructions might present an almost impossible job, for it would involve the correlation of two classification systems that are fundamentally different in many respects.[16] Finally, the present practice has perhaps discouraged in some degree the detailed specification and solidification of program requirements prior to realistic appraisal in terms of fiscal possibilities.

In certain respects, the Army programming system reflects a systematic effort to relate programming and budgeting into a coordinated procedure. Among these may be mentioned:

1. The Program Advisory Committee, the principal supervisory and coordinative body in programming, has virtually identical membership with that of the Budget Advisory Committee, which performs a similar function in budgeting. Programming and budgeting in some of the staff divisions are performed by the same individuals or by persons working in close association. Comparable coordinative arrangements are found in some of the commands and installations.
2. The *Army Program Guidance,* the major substantive budgetary instruction, is derived from the revised *Program Objectives,* which in turn reflect the OSD *Budget Guidelines.*

---

[16] See Chapter IV. It has been stated informally that the Comptroller of the Army would not use the program documents in his budget instructions even if they were available in time because of the excessive time and workload involved.

3. New programs and program changes are required to be costed and their costs taken into account before they are approved.
4. Programs are required to be amended in accordance with budgetary decisions.
5. Efforts are now being made to estimate the costs reflected in the *Estimate* so that they may be considered when this basic document is reviewed.

Nevertheless, one cannot escape the impression that the relation between budgets and programs is a product of annual re-improvisation and that at many key points it is conspicuously absent:

1. In fact, a very large part of the actual work in budgeting is performed by organizational units and people different from those engaged in programming.
2. Some of the most crucial determinations must be made on a hurried, emergency basis at various stages in the budget review process. Pressure of time prevents systematic consideration of program implications of these decisions by the program people. There is thus a continuing danger that programs will become out-of-date and even meaningless. Almost inevitably, programming takes a "back seat" to the compulsions of available funds in the actual direction of Army operations.
3. The costing of programs and the provision for program changes have not as yet been effective. Basic changes in some of the major programs are procedurally almost impossible; it would be more feasible to undertake a complete re-programming task than to modify the existing documents. As a consequence, approved programs may obsolesce rapidly because of operating decisions that cannot await the "red tape" of a program change.
4. The classification of programs and program segments differs from the budgetary classification structure, not only in class definitions but also in fundamental approach and philosophy. This problem, which is discussed at length in the next chapter, makes the correlation of the two increasingly difficult as each becomes more specific in its detail.
5. The program procedure and the various documents associated with it are extremely complex. This complexity, when added to that of the budget process, contributes to a lack of understanding of the system as a whole, and to the increased difficulty of coordinating its parts.
6. Neither the program system itself nor the need for it is wholly appreciated in the field or Headquarters.[17]

AIR FORCE PROGRAMMING

As is the case in the Army, the Air Force system for coordinated programming is of rather recent origin and is still in process of de-

---

[17] For example, one of the General Staff divisions in 1952 specifically proposed scrapping the program system and substituting a new, combined program-budget system.

velopment. The doctrine and the procedure for the program process and the calendar are in considerable part targets and objectives rather than descriptions of actualities. Nonetheless, the main factors of the program system and the major program documents are current elements in Air Force management. The Air Force has suffered like the Army, and to a greater extent, from the confusion attendant upon rapid and violent changes in over-all objectives, especially since the Korean hostilities began. It has been virtually impossible to firm up a complete and detailed program before a new one, radically different, is underway. This is illustrated by the sudden and successive changes of Air Force objectives from 269 wings (at the end of the war) to 55 to 48 to 95 to 143, and now, apparently, to the interim goal of 127 wings. These official targets do not reflect the unofficial one in 1948 and 1949 when the basic Air Force "objective" was the adoption of the 70-wing program.

The Air Force organizational structure is simpler and easier to adapt to a programming and budgeting system than that of the Army. It is fundamentally a functional organization both at Headquarters and in the field. The field commands of the Air Force in the United States are functional commands with nation-wide geographic jurisdiction. This has facilitated a relatively higher degree of decentralization from Headquarters in respect both to programming and budgeting. The contrast with the Army is most striking in the field of matériel and supply. The Air Force does not have to cope with technical services. Most of its procurement, supply, and maintenance activities are concentrated in a single command, the Air Matériel Command. The largest dollar portions of the Air Force program and of Air Force budget estimates are developed by this command, subject, of course, to guidance and review of major items by Headquarters.

Within Headquarters the primary organization is a series of five Deputy Chiefs of Staff (DCS), each with functional spheres of responsibility. These are the Deputy Chiefs of Staff for Personnel, Development, Operations, Matériel, and Comptroller.[18] Under each of the Deputy Chiefs of Staff are the various commands and activities within his functional field.

The Deputy Chief of Staff, Comptroller, as described elsewhere, is conceived primarily as a service organization for the other elements

---

[18] The Headquarters organization was modified in the fall of 1953 by an action to make the Deputy Chief of Staff, Development, responsible to the Deputy Chief of Staff, Matériel. The functions and title of the former office, however, remained unchanged

of the staff. His responsibility in the programming process is primarily the provision of statistical and financial information and analysis. Each of the other Deputy Chiefs of Staff and the Directors under him have responsibility for developing and synchronizing programs within their functional jurisdictions, subject, of course, to the general objectives and guidance approved by the Chief of Staff and from higher authorities. No single office below the Chief of Staff himself has centralized authority and responsibility for the Air Force program. Most of the Deputy Chiefs of Staff, including those for Development, Operations, and Matériel, have special programming officers attached directly to the Deputy Chief and above the level of the Directors. These are more in the nature of reviewing and coordinating offices than operating offices. The responsibility for leadership in the conduct of the programming system and for bringing together the various functional elements of the Air Force programs is vested in the Assistant for Programming to the Deputy Chief of Staff, Operations. It should be emphasized that the concept of this office is coordinative rather than substantive with respect to the programs. The substance of the programs is the total responsibility of the Air Staff.

The budget is conceived as a dollar translation of programs. The Budget Director and his office are thus intended to have little discretion with respect to the substantive content of programs and the budget estimates which represent them. In fact, there appears to be relatively little area for discretion in the budget estimating process either here or in the field until and unless it becomes necessary to distribute budget cuts.

The programming cycle is hinged quite directly to the budget calendar and the various deadlines which it imposes. Programming is fairly clearly defined in two sectors: the pre-budget sector, called planning—budgeting programs; and the post-budget sector, called operating programs. The former begins well before the issuance of the budget call and is intended to produce the basic as well as the detailed data necessary for budget planning. The operating program sector begins after, and is based upon, the President's budget. It is revised and firmed up after passage of appropriations by Congress and becomes an operational directive at that stage. These two segments of the programming process produce entirely different and distinct documents, but the documents deal with subject matter that is in large part identical.

Programming is conceived as an interpretative process proceeding from general statements of objectives to projections of specific requirements in terms of units, personnel, matériel, and work. The procedure for the development of planning—budgeting programs is roughly as follows.

On the basis of the planning guidances of the National Security Council and the Joint Chiefs of Staff, the Air Staff develops a statement of program objectives for the Air Force, setting forth in more specific terms the targets of the various functioning programs of the Air Force. This document, which is brought together by the Assistant for Programming, DCS-Operations, is a tentative proposal until reviewed and revised by the Air Council, a planning group of the top officers of the Air Force.

The Assistant for Programming develops and publishes the *Program Guidance* which provides the basic data for detailed program planning in all functional fields. This document, perhaps the most basic document in the whole programming system of the Air Force, is distributed to all the commands and all the Air Staff offices.

The various directorates of the Air Staff develop the program documents. These include a number of different volumes, several of which are formally approved and published, others of which are issued on a less formal basis. These documents include the basic programs in respect to troop strength, aircraft, installations, etc. Most of these programs are projected for a year and a half or more beyond the budget year.

The Budget Directorate prepares and issues the budget call for estimates. This is a lengthy document in two parts. The first part brings together the basic program information necessary for budgeting and is based entirely on the data produced by the above processes. The second part contains technical directions and instructions, largely of a fiscal and accounting nature.

The projected timing for this process is roughly comparable to that of the Army program system. The basic guidance from JCS should be received in the summer, about two years before the beginning of the fiscal year for which the program is developed. The *Program Guidance* should be produced by the late fall, and the budget directive should then be issued in the early spring.

The actual dates for the development of the 1954 program and budget were very much later. The *Program Guidance* was not published until April, 1952; the program documents were not issued until May, the same month in which the budget call went out.

The process for the operating programs follows a procedure similar to that for the planning—budgeting programs and includes an operating program guidance and operating program documents. The operating program documents should be issued in the spring, reflecting the President's budget and in anticipation of funds to be appropriated by Congress. These become a basis for initial financial planning for the new fiscal year and for the inital buying program of the Air Matériel Command. In the summer, the revision of these operating programs should be issued, based on actual appropriations. Other revisions are issued during the course of the fiscal year, and it is contemplated that operating programs will be issued on a quarterly basis.

The revision process attendant upon budget activity during the summer, fall, and winter preceding the beginning of the fiscal year results in changes and adjustments in both budget requirements and programs. The interpretation of the effect of budgetary reductions upon programs is a joint responsibility of the Assistant for Programming and the Budget Director. Major adjustments are referred to, and decided by, the Budget Advisory Committee. The lengthy and involved nature of the program process, however, is such that it is very difficult to keep the programs current and balanced as budget changes occur. One Air Force officer said that it takes six months to get a program revision through. This would be hard to verify, but the impression persists that once the budget process gets well underway, the programs are left behind and some of them become more or less academic exercises.

Like that of the Army, the Air Force classification for budget purposes differs considerably from that for program purposes. There appears to be less concern in the Air Force about reconciling the two, perhaps because the content of each is somewhat simpler. The program information that comes out in the budget call is in terms of the program structure rather than the budget structure, which means that such translation as is necessary is made by the estimating agencies themselves. The most difficult problem of conversion is in the matériel field where it is not always clear how program forecasts should be split among budget appropriations and projects (for example, as between the appropriations for procurement and for maintenance and operation).

Four most basic program documents are:

1. *Organization and Personnel* (the Troop Program), which contains a planned schedule of military and civilian spaces broken down by Table of Organization units, by command, by Table of Distribution units, and

by station totals.[19] From this program are derived detailed extensions showing personnel requirements by specialty, training programs, recruiting, personnel programs, etc.

2. *Aircraft and Flying Hours,* which covers all active aircraft and shows their allocation by type, model and series, and flying hours (the basic operational factor) by command.

3. *Projected Aircraft Inventory,* which covers and forecasts all aircraft, whether or not actively in use.

4. *Installations Program,* which is a schedule of installations including real estate and construction information as well as intended use of installation.

In addition to the above basic programs are others that treat with aircraft production and requirements, tactical availability of aircraft, conversion and equipping of aircraft, and base utilization.

In conclusion, it may be pertinent to point out certain of the features of the Air Force programming system and particularly those that contrast with that of the Army.

1. The clear differentiation between planning—budgeting and operating programs has distinct advantages over the Army system. The relationship between budget and appropriations on the one hand and programming on the other is much more clearly defined in the Air Force.

2. The budget organization appears to have a less discretionary role in the program process in the Air Force than in the Army, both in theory and in practice. The effort to make programming a staff-wide responsibility and to make it dominant in the planning and budgeting of Air Force operations appears to be successful. It may be noted that in the hearings in 1952 before the House Committee on Appropriations the Deputy Assistant for Programming for the first time made a presentation of Air Force programs as such. This presentation was made before, and as an introduction to, the presentation of the budget request by the Budget Director.

3. With exception of the aircraft program the programs are not costed prior to the budget process. It does not appear that cost considerations enter the planning system until they are forced on the organization during budgetary reviews.

4. Both programs and budgets are firmed up in a very detailed way far in advance of the period to which they apply. While it is clear that the Air Force with its heavy dependence upon long-lead items must plan and schedule years in advance, the present system clearly reduces flexibility and probably adds to total inaccuracy and lack of realism in planning.

CONCLUSIONS

One of Luther Gulick's *Administrative Reflections from World War II* was that: "Translation from purpose to program is the crucial step

---

[19] For definitions of those various types of tables and units, see Chapter V.

in administration." [20] Gulick was writing of an all-out war, not a semi-peace situation. Purpose is now neither as clear-cut, when alternatives are considered, nor as unanimous as it was then. We might today summarize the problem of effective military planning as having four major aspects:

1. The development and correlation of plans of long, medium, and short range.
2. The translation of these into programs of specific things to be done.
3. The translation of these programs into operations.
4. The continuous analysis and adjustment in all of these processes of requirements in terms of available or feasible resources and of political realities.

The recent developments in the Joint Chiefs of Staff, the Army, and the Air Force reflect sincere efforts to accomplish these objectives. In the Army particularly, they are significant manifestations of the drive toward providing a centrally coordinated basis for planning.

But certain reservations must be made. In the first place much of what has been discussed is a "paper" plan. The JCS proposal began to go into effect during 1953. The Army program system, while in operation in certain respects for some years, has yet to be tried on a full-scale basis. Some still scoff at it; and the budget, as passed, is still the ruling document whether or not the "program" has caught up with it. The Air Force, in spite of its programming system, is still regarded by many, including some of its own staff, as being an opportunistic and largely "unplanned" organization. The extent to which it has in the past departed from its own programs suggests doubts at least as to the future effectiveness of its system. It is apparent that the planning and programming systems described in the foregoing pages are still, in large part, plans and hopes.

In the second place, serious questions may be raised whether the systems, either as practiced or envisaged, provide satisfactory answers to the problems of relating plans and budgets. All of them require that plans and programs be completed more than a year before the budget year begins, which means more than two years before it ends. None of them has yet included a satisfactory way to take into account budgetary possibilities when plans and programs are first developed. All of them follow the sequential pattern whereby the plan and the program are developed before the budgetary process begins. All of them are highly centralized, either in Washington or at Wright Field.

[20] *Op. cit.* p. 78.

Finally, we may question the degree to which the planning and programming systems have been fitted into the pattern of budgetary administration. Do they tie in with the performance budget, which has been developed largely by a different body of personnel, under a different aegis, and with a somewhat different ideology? This question provides the general framework of the next chapter.

chapter IV

military performance budgets

The estimates do not raise for consideration questions which should be decided before appropriations are granted, nor does the form in which estimates are required by the Congress to be presented lay the foundation for the consideration of: Subjects of work to be done; the character of expenditures to be made; the best method of financing expenditures.

PRESIDENT WILLIAM HOWARD TAFT [1]

Do you have anything in the bill that would repeal a provision like this performance budget, which is costing the United States at least $5 billion a year at the present time.

REPRESENTATIVE JOHN TABER [2]

The story is told in Washington that former President Hoover himself invented the term "performance budget" to lend sales appeal to a different and improved method of Federal budgeting. Though some may question the adequacy of the expression as a description of all that Mr. Hoover had in mind, there can be little doubt that as a label it has effectively served its purpose. Probably no other single recommendation of the Hoover Commission has had more far-reaching effect nor resulted in more constructive efforts in the field of government management.[3]

---

[1] Message to the Senate and House of Representatives, June 12, 1912.

[2] *Department of Defense and Related Independent Agencies, Appropriations for 1953,* Hearings, Part 2, p. 140.

[3] The "performance budget" was a "theme song" of the Commission on Organization of the Executive Branch of the Government. Not only was it Recommendation Number 1 of the Commission's report on *Budgeting and Accounting,* but it was separately recommended in most of the reports for the various governmental

78

The central idea of the performance budget is deceptively simple. It is that the budget process be focused upon programs and functions —that is, accomplishments to be achieved, work to be done. Performance budgeting is essentially synonymous with what has long been referred to as program budgeting. It was the Commission's contention that the program approach in the Federal budget was subordinated and obscured in a welter of appropriation items, which followed no logic other than the accident of history. More particularly, it found that the primary emphasis in the Federal budget was upon organizational units, making it virtually impossible to correlate appropriations with programs and program costs; and upon objects or items of expenditure, swamping the purposes of expenditures under an ocean of meaningless detail.

It may be noted that some local governments and a number of Federal agencies, including particularly government corporations, were already operating budget systems that approximated "program" or "performance" budgeting.[4] At the time of the Hoover Commission studies, the Bureau of the Budget and other agencies were working toward revisions of budgetary operations in the same direction. A group in the Navy Department had undertaken to overhaul the Navy budget and appropriation structure soon after the war, and it was this group that brought the idea to the attention of Mr. Hoover. But the Commission reports were in considerable measure responsible for a government-wide attack on the problems of the budget system in the succeeding

departments, usually in the first part of each report. Likewise the Task Force Report on *Fiscal, Budgeting, and Accounting Activities,* Appendix F, recommended a "program or performance budget," carrying forward the more detailed proposals of A. E. Buck, the author of its Part Three on "Federal Budgeting," p. 10.

[4] A. E. Buck in his article on "Performance Budgeting for the Federal Government" (*Tax Review,* July, 1949), reports that the first experiment in program budgeting, then known as "cost-data" budgeting, was applied to the public works activities of the Borough of Richmond in New York City in 1912. The recent article by Catheryn Seckler-Hudson on "Performance Budgeting in the Government of the United States" (*Public Finance,* VII, 4, 1952, pp. 327-45), likewise stresses that program budgeting is not a new idea in the United States. She mentions among the predecessors of the performance budget proposal the report of Taft's Commission on Economy and Efficiency, and the practices of the Federal Departments of Interior and Agriculture, the State of California, and "progressive cities" (p. 329). Of the latter, perhaps the best known is Richmond, Virginia, about which John A. Donaho, then its budget director, was principally writing in his article on "The Performance Budget" (*Municipal Finance,* February, 1950, pp. 103-6). On the Federal level, the TVA has long been known for its program budget system, which was well described in the pamphlet by Donald C. Kull, *Budget Administration in the Tennessee Valley Authority,* published by the University of Tennessee Record, Extension Series XXIV, 3, Knoxville, May, 1948.

years. This work is still going on, but already significant results have been achieved in the substantial revisions of appropriation structures, the development of new classifications of expenditures, the emphasis in budget justifications and reviews upon functions, activities, work measurement, and programs.

As indicated above, a principal stimulator of this movement, as it may properly be called, was the military establishment and its sub-departments, particularly the Departments of Navy and Air Force. The Department of Defense as a whole still occupies a place among the leaders in the development of the new approach. The Navy in 1946 had presented its fiscal year 1948 budget in two alternate forms, one representing the traditional basis of Navy appropriations, the other on a program basis. After some argument with the Bureau of the Budget, both forms were submitted to Congress. However, the appropriation committees of the newly elected 80th Congress chose to ignore the new-style proposal. Subsequently, the idea of reorganizing appropriation structures along more rational lines was pushed from the level of the newly formed Department of Defense, notably by Secretary Forrestal and W. J. McNeil, his special assistant. This group, pressing its view on certain key Congressmen and Senators, and later upon Mr. Hoover himself, contributed to the emphatic views of the Hoover Commission on a revised budgeting system.

As described in Chapter II, the Congress in 1949 made the performance budget mandatory for the entire Department of Defense. Already, however, the newly created Department of the Air Force, under the necessity and with the opportunity of building a new budget system for itself, had set up a program or performance-type budget. The Navy followed in its budget for fiscal year 1951. At the beginning of fiscal year 1952, the Army revised its appropriations to complete the change-over in appropriations structure of the military departments.

In spite of the apparent simplicity of the concept and in spite of the modifications in budgetary classifications and appropriations, there is still much question as to whether these departments in fact have performance budgets. There is even some question whether what they have done is in the direction of performance budgets. As will be shown below, the present budget structures and systems of the Army, Navy, and Air Force differ markedly from each other. Obviously, the term means different things to different people. To a student of politics and of legislative bodies, it means perhaps a reduction of appropriation items, a rationalization of the appropriation structure in terms of programs, a presentation and review of budget requests in such a manner as to emphasize issues and make possible more effective choices. To a top administrator, it means these things and also greater flexibility and discretion in his operations, plus better control and accountability with regard to his subordinates. Down the line of an agency, it *may* mean a single source for funds, an enlargement of authority, flexibility, and responsibility in the use of funds, and a mechanism for relating program planning with financial planning. To the accountant, it means accrual accounting, cost accounting, segregation of capital from operating accounts, working capital funds, and many other techniques.

The simplicity of the performance budget is a delusion in another way. In fact, it is extremely difficult budgeting. One of the probable reasons that so much of our Federal budgeting has not reflected the program approach is that it is easier to budget and control funds simply on the basis of organization and object. For the performance budget does not replace these; it is in addition to them. Accounts still have to be kept, payments still have to be made, accountability still must be maintained in terms of organization and object. And the change-over to a performance system, as many hundreds of Federal employees would testify, is an enormous job.

The changes which we have come to associate with performance budgeting, such as simplification and reduction of appropriations, revision of classifications, and others, important as they are, are only a part of the concept. Underlying them is a notion which represents a quite radical departure from previous practice and previous ways of thinking. It is simply that when we budget and authorize funds we are providing for things to be *done* rather than for things to be *bought*. Moneys are furnished for activities and functions rather than for purchases and payments. Almost our entire experience and heritage in governmental financial control is the other way around. In a sense, this amounts to substituting ends for means as the focal points of financial planning and control. For example, performance budgeting might require that funds for basic training be estimated on the basis of the total numbers to be trained and the over-all cost of training each man, in contrast to previous practices of assuming the training goal, then adding up the salary, supply, and contractual costs to reach the goal. Congress would thus exert control on the number trained, the quality of training, and the total cost per man, rather than on the number and salaries of positions filled. The difference is not merely one of technique and method; it is a basic departure in way of thinking. It is not surprising that the performance budget has not been accomplished overnight. Not only must new estimating methods and control techniques be developed; the very minds of the citizen, the Congressman, and perhaps most of all, the administrator must be trained to think in different terms. For all of our history—and long before it—we have conceived of financial management in the accounting terms of items to be paid for rather than of programs to be accomplished. This has been true even of most "lump-sum" appropriations, estimates for which are usually based upon, and justified by, the addition of predicted items or elements of cost, the controls over which are exercised on the same bases.

This interpretation of the meaning of the performance budget is idealistic and perhaps unrealistic. Nonetheless, it is a logical extension of the significance of the more specific attributes associated with the expression.

In the following pages, the performance budget system of the Army, and, to a lesser extent, of the other military departments will be considered with particular emphasis upon the obstacles and problems in the application of this concept to military activities. This discussion will treat with: the problems of classification and how they have been handled; the problems involved in the segregation of capital from current expenditures; the problems involved in relating the budget to internal organization; the relations between the budget structure and the planning or program structure; and finally the problems injected by the factor of time. It may be noted in advance that some of these questions seem to be inherent in the theory itself; some are particularly applicable to the effort to adapt the concept to *military* activities, which are in some respects different from civilian functions; and some apply because of the way the concept has been adapted particularly in the Army. The analysis does not provide an evaluation of the performance concept generally, although some of the difficulties emphasized may well have pertinence in smaller and nonmilitary establishments.

The performance budget idea and its development in the military departments derive from a channel of influence different from that which gave rise to the recent developments in the fields of programming and planning. As was emphasized in Chapter II above, the former came very largely from pressures above and outside the military departments and their military personnel. Chapter III stressed that the planning and programming improvements have been generated largely by the central military corps itself. That they grew out of the same period in time is no accident. But they were developed by different people—which is no accident either. The Army's budget system, for example, is a response to a law in the drafting of which the Army had little part, and reflects the thinking of the Bureau of the Budget and of the Office, Secretary of Defense. These agencies know little of the Army programming system. And, in spite of the integration aspired for in the comptroller concept, the dichotomy existed in the past and still exists within the Army itself.

The Problem of Classification

. . . the process of classifying things really involves, or is a part of, the formation of hypotheses as to the nature of things. . . . Various classifications, however, may differ greatly in their logical or scientific utility, in the sense that the various traits selected as a basis of classification differ widely in their fruitfulness as principles of organizing our knowledge.[5]

The above quotation, drawn from the field of logic, has equal validity to organization and management. We might simply expand the last word to cover not only our knowledge but also our appropriations, budgets, accounts, programs, and functions. The way we classify things obviously reflects our view of the nature of things; it also conditions our subsequent perspectives, understandings, and decisions made within the framework of the established classification. Organization structure itself, to the extent that it is planned, is the product of the twin processes in logic of classification and division.

The first, and probably to date the most widespread, changes of the performance budget movement have been essentially classificatory in nature. A first step was the development by the Bureau of the Budget of a broad classification of the basic functions of the government as a whole.[6] Second was the overhauling of the appropriation structure for different agencies, along different lines, accompanied usually by a sharp reduction in the number of individual appropriations. Third was the development within agencies of classifications and divisions of activities, programs, functions, and projects. Accompanying all of these has been the modification of accounting systems, including the reclassification of accounts. The avowed theme of all these efforts has been to develop and substitute classifications and divisions based upon identifiable functions, programs, and kinds of work, rather than upon organization units and objects of payment. Another theme has been to

---

[5] Morris R. Cohen, and Ernest Nagel, *An Introduction to Logic and Scientific Method* (New York: Harcourt, Brace and Company, 1934), p. 223.

[6] The Bureau of the Budget anticipated the Hoover Commission by at least two years in its development of the functional classification for the *Budget* for fiscal year 1948. This classification, which has since been greatly improved, now provides the framework for the President's budget message and for some of the budget's basic tables. It is presented historically and in detail in "Special Analysis I."

segregate into separate classes activities and expenditures on the basis of their "character"—as between capital and current operating expenses and between activities which are exclusively governmental in nature and those of the so-called "business-type."

Classification and division by their very nature are processes that proceed from the broad and general to the increasingly specific; they go from the "top down." This fact has been a central element of performance budget theory. The primary consideration appears to be the usefulness of the classification in appraising and in decision-making at top executive and legislative levels. The subdivisions are then framed in such a way as to "feed into" the top classifications. This means that internal operating accounts and records, the internal division of work, and the structure for the allotment of funds should be accommodated to the structure at the top. The validity of this theory is discussed at a later point in this chapter. In some, perhaps most, agencies, the accommodation is not yet possible; the accounting and reporting systems and the organization structure are not capable, in their normal operations, of producing the necessary data or of controlling expenditures in accordance with what for top-level purposes may be the optimal classification of both funds and programs. A consequence has been the acceptance of compromises in the primary appropriation and program structures, some of them involving important deviations from the logic of program classification.[7]

An immediate effect of the performance system in the Navy and Army was the reform of obsolete appropriation structures by drastic reduction in the number of appropriations and by their redefinition in more logical and understandable terms. The Navy reduced from 52 to 21 titles; the Army from 21 to 8.[8] The new Air Force system provided a total of nine. The scope and dimensions of the new appropriation titles are illustrated by the fact that their average size, in terms of new obligational authority, has been running about one billion dollars per year.

But the conceptual bases for the primary classification of appropriation titles were quite different between the Navy on the one hand and the Air Force and Army on the other. The Navy molded its structure around the existing organizational structure of its bureau system.

---

[7] An example of this, discussed below, is the segregation in appropriations by all the military departments of the costs of military personnel.

[8] Not including four small appropriations of a rather special nature which were not included in the performance structure: two relating to the Alaska communications system; Promotion of Rifle Practice; and Civilian Relief in Korea, Army.

Each bureau was given one or more appropriations over which it has virtually exclusive jurisdiction and which, together, are roughly coextensive with its functions and responsibilities. The fundamental basis, therefore, is organizational rather than programmatic; the result is a classification that is functional in the same degree that the organization of Navy bureaus is functional. But the actual organization of the bureaus is more the product of history and tradition than of a logical analysis and division of functions. They could probably be described more accurately as units distinguished by subject matter and technical specialism than by function or program. The major organizational units of the Navy, together with the major appropriation titles over which each has responsibility, are shown in Figure 5.[9]

It is apparent that the classification of appropriations (which are in fact called programs in the Navy) was designed to accord with, and even strengthen, the basic organizational classification. In the words of one Navy authority on the subject:

The underlying philosophy of the performance budget is to parallel management responsibility with fiscal responsibility. Exceptions to this general rule are military personnel and service-wide operations. In general, technical bureaus are involved in the fiscal affairs of only those activities over which they have fiscal control.[10]

The appropriations, or "programs," reflect the intent to identify and group the major kinds of activities within the various bureaus on the basis of:

1. Segregation of capital from operating costs.
2. Single or closely related purposes or objectives.
3. Areas of primary significance or interest.

Compromises had to be made in certain cases, like Service-Wide Operations, for practical and operational reasons. But the aim was clearly to minimize such overlapping by confining complete control over the individual appropriations within individual bureaus.

The second level of Navy classification—the breakdown of appropriations into budget activities—represents more of a functional emphasis than does the first. As a result, many of the same "activities" appear

---

[9] Based on an analysis of the appropriations and their defense as reflected in the *Budget*, the Appropriation Bill, and the House and Senate Subcommittee Hearings on the Navy Department, for fiscal year 1953.

[10] Department of the Navy, Bureau of Supplies and Accounts, Commander Charles A. Blick, "Performance Budget for the Department of the Navy," *Monthly Newsletter*, February, 1950, p. 5.

FIGURE 5

MAJOR ORGANIZATION UNITS AND APPROPRIATION TITLES,
DEPARTMENT OF THE NAVY

Organization	*Appropriation Title*
Bureau of Personnel	Military Personnel, Navy
	Military Personnel, Naval Reserve
	Military Personnel, Officer Candidates
	Navy Personnel, General Expenses
Marine Corps	Military Personnel, Marine Corps
	Military Personnel, Marine Corps Reserve
	Marine Corps Troops and Facilities
Bureau of Aeronautics	Aircraft and Facilities
	Construction of Aircraft and Related Procurement
Bureau of Ships	Ships and Facilities
	Shipbuilding and Conversion
Bureau of Ordnance	Ordnance and Facilities
	Ordnance for Shipbuilding and Conversion
Bureau of Medicine and Surgery	Medical Care
Bureau of Yards and Docks	Civil Engineering
	Public Works
Office of Naval Research	Research
Bureau of Supplies and Accounts	Service-Wide Supply and Finance
Office of Chief of Naval Operations	Service-Wide Operations (Activities 1 through 7a)
Office of the Secretary of the Navy	Service-Wide Operations (Activities 7b through 12)
	Operation and Conservation of Naval Petroleum Reserves
	Naval Petroleum Reserve Numbered 4, Alaska

under different bureaus and applicable to different subject matter. Many of the appropriations include, for example, the activities of procurement, maintenance and operation, industrial mobilization, research and development, and others.

The appropriation structure of the Air Force is quite different, perhaps partly because it had no such bureau system of organization as the Navy. Its appropriations are in general broader in definition and fewer in number. They reflect pretty clearly the intent to (1) segregate capital from operating costs, and (2) group together broad categories or elements of cost. The air appropriations are:[11]

Aircraft and Related Procurement
Major Procurement Other than Aircraft
Acquisition and Construction of Real Property
Maintenance and Operations
Military Personnel Requirements
Research and Development
Reserve Personnel Requirements
Air National Guard
Contingencies

In 1950, the Department of Defense established a classification of "Budget Categories," applicable to the budgets of all three military departments. Its purpose is to provide a basis of summarizing and comparing the total costs of the three services. The framework of this classification is fundamentally similar to the appropriation structure of the Air Force, although there are important differences in definitions of the classes and in the activity breakdowns within each class. The primary categories of the Defense classification are: [12]

Military Personnel Costs
Maintenance and Operation
Major Procurement and Production Costs
Acquisition and Construction of Real Property
Civilian Components
Research and Development
Industrial Mobilization
Establishment-Wide Activities

The Department of Defense requires that each service submit its budget in two forms: according to its own appropriation and activity

---

[11] Based on the Air Force appropriations for fiscal year 1953, P. L. 488, 82nd Cong.
[12] Department of Defense, "Budget Category Definitions," May 17, 1950 (processed).

classification; and according to the Budget Category classification. This requirement has meant that each of the services must frame its own structure in such fashion as to facilitate rapid conversion of figures into the Budget Category groupings. For example, the program definitions and especially the activity definitions of the Navy system have been greatly influenced in the direction of matching the Defense Categories.

The Army appropriation structure, the last one to be developed, was clearly based upon the cost category concept of the Air Force and the Department of Defense. Here the effect in relation to organization structure was quite the reverse of that in the Navy. The technical and administrative services of the Army, in some respects the counterparts of the bureaus of the Navy, had formerly had their own clearly identified appropriations. Under the new system, these appropriations were lumped on the cost category basis. Each technical service now receives funds from several different appropriations in which it has only a partial interest. This effect is illustrated in the accompanying Figure 6. It may be noted further that the identity of the technical services is lost not only at the level of the appropriation classification; in the hierarchy of the subclassification of many of the appropriations, the technical services do not reappear until the third, fourth, and even fifth levels are reached.

One effect of the performance budget in the Army has thus been to lessen the independence and influence of the technical services, and, conversely, to strengthen greatly the position and the coordinating influence of the General Staff, *vis-a-vis* the budget. In fact, this would appear to be the most important effect of the new system to this date. The General Staff is now quite definitely *in* the line of command for budget purposes. No longer do the technical services appear before Congressional committees as independent pleaders for funds for their organizations. They still appear, it is true, but under the supervision and guidance of the Staff divisions and primarily for the purpose of providing technical supporting information. The appropriations are Army-wide in nature, and the primary responsibility for defending them rests in the General Staff divisions which likewise have Army-wide jurisdiction. It is still true, however, that the largest amounts of Army funds are actually estimated and administered by about half a dozen technical and administrative services, principally the Ordnance, Quartermaster, Finance, Engineer, Transportation, and Signal organizations.

The classification of appropriations is only the beginning of, and the framework for, a complex hierarchy of budget groupings which extends

FIGURE 6

Department of the Army Appropriation
Structure Before and After the Performance Budget

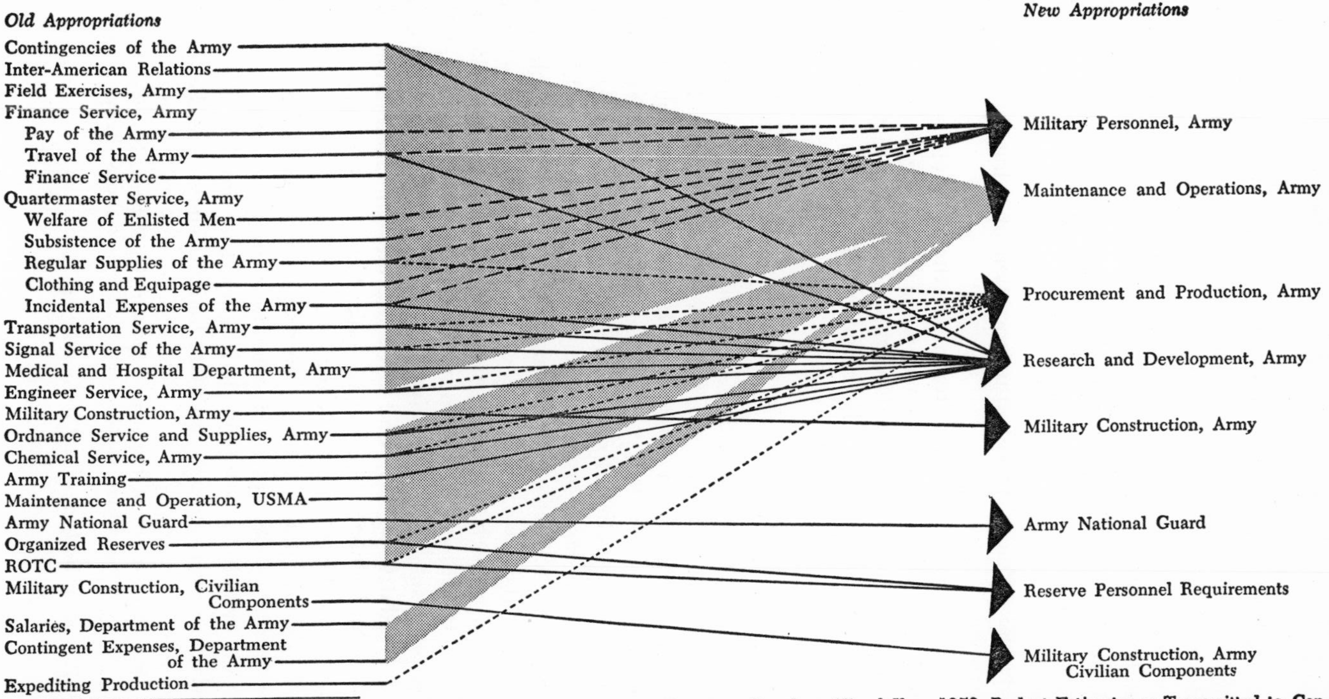

New Appropriations

Military Personnel, Army

Maintenance and Operations, Army

Procurement and Production, Army

Research and Development, Army

Military Construction, Army

Army National Guard

Reserve Personnel Requirements

Military Construction, Army Civilian Components

Old Appropriations

Contingencies of the Army
Inter-American Relations
Field Exercises, Army
Finance Service, Army
Pay of the Army
Travel of the Army
Finance Service
Quartermaster Service, Army
Welfare of Enlisted Men
Subsistence of the Army
Regular Supplies of the Army
Clothing and Equipage
Incidental Expenses of the Army
Transportation Service, Army
Signal Service of the Army
Medical and Hospital Department, Army
Engineer Service, Army
Military Construction, Army
Ordnance Service and Supplies, Army
Chemical Service, Army
Army Training
Maintenance and Operation, USMA
Army National Guard
Organized Reserves
ROTC
Military Construction, Civilian Components
Salaries, Department of the Army
Contingent Expenses, Department of the Army
Expediting Production

Based upon Department of the Army, "Pertinent Data on Revised Budget Structure Based on Fiscal Year 1952 Budget Estimates as Transmitted to Congress" (processed, undated).

to four or five levels. In the Army, the eight appropriations are divided among some 46 so-called "budget programs." These are in turn subdivided into about 140 "projects," and some of the projects are made up of "sub-projects," numbering more than 150. All of the above classifications are standardized and Army-wide.[13] In addition, the projects and sub-projects are divided at the installation level into so-called "station operating accounts" according to definitions usually prescribed at the technical service or command level. Finally, for budget purposes, all of these classifications are grouped on the basis of the government-wide objective classification which distinguishes payments for personal services, travel, transportation of things, and like objects of payment.

There is no clear-cut criterion for the subdivision of classes at various levels. Some are functional; some are on the basis of kinds of material or subject matter dealt with; some are objects of payment; and some are organizational. Examples of classifications are shown in Figure 7.

EVALUATION OF PERFORMANCE CLASSIFICATION

The Hoover Commission described a performance budget as one ". . . based upon functions, activities, and projects." It went on to explain that: "Under performance budgeting, attention is centered on the function or activity—on the accomplishment of the purpose—instead of on lists of employees or authorizations of purchases." [14] Obviously, in any large organization, there is a variety of different ways of defining "functions, activities, and projects," and the problem may soon be reduced to one of semantics and of differing perspectives. A more fruitful approach to the question is to appraise the classification in the degree to which it contributes to the over-all purposes of budgeting. The purposes fall into two basic classes: the improvement of executive and legislative review and decision, and the facilitation of effective internal administration. Let us look at the military performance structures from these points of view.

In the first place, there is no question that for the former purpose the present structures are tremendous improvements over the classifications which they superseded. They are simpler, clearer, more orderly, less overlapping, and more logical. They have the merit of utiliz-

---

[13] See Department of the Army, *Special Regulations*, No. 35-210-31, "Finance and Fiscal, Army Fiscal Code: General Appropriations—Fiscal Year 1953," June 4, 1952.
[14] Report on *Budgeting and Accounting*, p. 8.

FIGURE 7

EXAMPLES OF ARMY BUDGETARY CLASSIFICATION

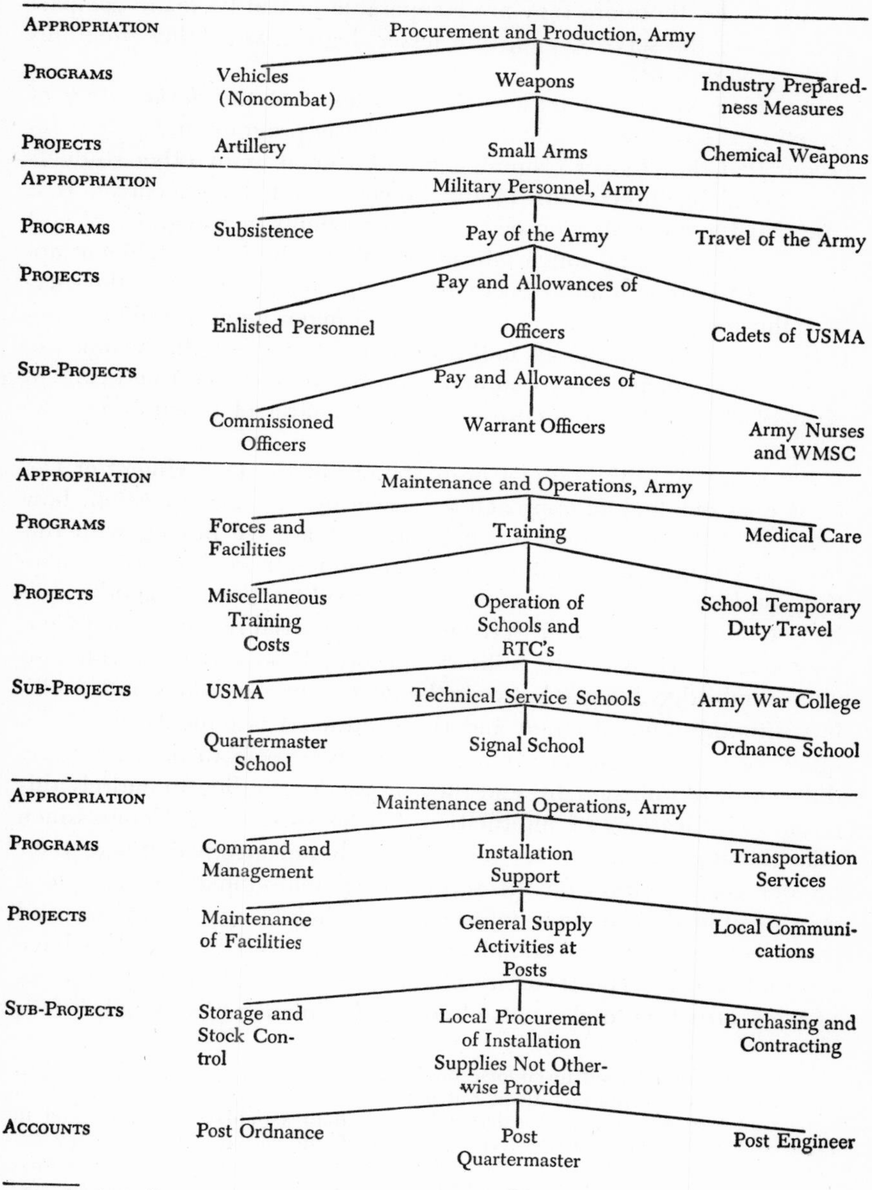

APPROPRIATION		Procurement and Production, Army	
PROGRAMS	Vehicles (Noncombat)	Weapons	Industry Prepared-ness Measures
PROJECTS	Artillery	Small Arms	Chemical Weapons
APPROPRIATION		Military Personnel, Army	
PROGRAMS	Subsistence	Pay of the Army	Travel of the Army
PROJECTS		Pay and Allowances of	
	Enlisted Personnel	Officers	Cadets of USMA
SUB-PROJECTS		Pay and Allowances of	
	Commissioned Officers	Warrant Officers	Army Nurses and WMSC
APPROPRIATION		Maintenance and Operations, Army	
PROGRAMS	Forces and Facilities	Training	Medical Care
PROJECTS	Miscellaneous Training Costs	Operation of Schools and RTC's	School Temporary Duty Travel
SUB-PROJECTS	USMA	Technical Service Schools	Army War College
	Quartermaster School	Signal School	Ordnance School
APPROPRIATION		Maintenance and Operations, Army	
PROGRAMS	Command and Management	Installation Support	Transportation Services
PROJECTS	Maintenance of Facilities	General Supply Activities at Posts	Local Communi-cations
SUB-PROJECTS	Storage and Stock Con-trol	Local Procurement of Installation Supplies Not Other-wise Provided	Purchasing and Contracting
ACCOUNTS	Post Ordnance	Post Quartermaster	Post Engineer

Based principally on Department of the Army, *Special Regulations* No. 35-210-31.

ing terms and categories that are commonly understood and that conform more or less to traditional accounting practice and military terminology. Furthermore they are comparable or can be made comparable among the services and, to a lesser degree, with other programs of the government.

But, for a variety of reasons they fall short of the *desideratum* of directing the reviewers' attention to the basic program and policy decisions that the Hoover Commission and a great many other students feel should be the concern of the Congress and the Executive. It is true that the concentration on major components or categories of cost reveals and points up much information that is basic to intelligent appraisal: the strength and direct costs of military personnel in the services; the amount or number and the cost of major items of military procurement, which are at least indicative of military strength; the amount, nature, location, and cost of military construction; the cost and content of medical activities; the cost and subject matter of research and development; and others.

But nowhere in the budget presentations of the Department of Defense does one find an approach to answering the basic question: how much protection (or how much insurance) are we buying with this budget? Or, in terms of alternatives, how much more (or less) protection would we obtain by the addition (or subtraction) of another billion or ten billion dollars? [15] Even a hasty perusal of the annual Congressional hearings on the military appropriations reveals a wide and almost unbridgeable gap between the general presentations of the military situation and program and the protracted arguments about detailed costs in the military budgets. The two seem to be on entirely different levels of thought; and they proceed according to entirely different classifications of information. To be sure, many Congressmen take the leap from one to the other with unconcerned grace; their greater concentration on the second level undoubtedly reflects to a considerable degree their interests, their habits and traditions, and their feeling of greater confidence and grasp. But in fact they have little alternative. The structure of the budget not alone slants the reviewers' attention to elements of cost and administrative detail; it fails

---

[15] I do not here intend to endorse or, in fact, dispute the suggestion that Congress should be given alternatives, but only to raise the question whether policymakers at the executive or legislative level or both should not be equipped to think in terms of such alternatives. The idea of alternative budgets is ably expounded by Verne B. Lewis in "Toward a Theory of Budgeting," *Public Administration Review*, Winter, 1952, pp. 42-54.

to provide the information in a form which permits an appraisal of the budget in terms of the fundamental purposes of military activity.

The budget classifications of all three services are basically groupings of the costs of *supporting* elements rather than of *operating* elements of the services. It is virtually impossible for a reviewer, or for the services themselves, to translate the one category into the other except by guesswork. The budget does not reveal the activities and costs of the fleet, of the strategic air force, or of the divisions of the Army. We do know from the budget some, but not all, of the costs attributed to military personnel, but we have only the roughest idea how much of those costs is attributable to Korea,[16] to defense of the United States, to the build-up in Europe, to productive activities, or to training. It would appear reasonable, even if idealistic, for a true performance budget to point up and to answer such questions as the following:

The program and the cost of combat operations; active defense of the United States; other operations and maintenance; and build-up for the future.

The program and cost of the basic components of air power—strategic, tactical, air defense, and air transport.

The programs and costs for divisions of the Army—the cost of building a division and of maintaining a division.

The program and cost of training of all major types.

The program and amounts of procurement for mobilization reserve.

The true costs of our various actual and proposed programs for supporting our allies around the globe.

The present budget structure contributes little to answering questions of this type. To a considerable degree, the performance classification gives the reviewing bodies no alternative to concentrating upon the very things the Hoover Commission said they should avoid: the administrative details. Conversely, it encourages and even compels the administrative and executive agencies to make and carry out policy decisions without effective political review.

With respect to the second purpose of facilitating internal adminis-

---

[16] In the House subcommittee hearings of early 1952, General Decker, Comptroller of the Army, ventured that Korea had cost the Army about 7 billion dollars in its first year and a half. But his figure was admittedly "rough," and it would be difficult to assess what it included. See *Department of the Army, Appropriations for 1953*, Hearings, p. 62.

tration, certain important difficulties and inconsistencies of the present classification structure should be noted:

1. *Military Personnel.* The separation of the direct costs of military personnel in distinct appropriations means that the costs attributed to all other appropriations and programs which involve utilization of military personnel are incomplete and inaccurate. These, of course, include all the important appropriations. Civilian salaries, on the other hand, are attributed to the appropriations, programs, and projects on which the civilians are working. Thus, most appropriations and programs include part but not all of their personnel costs. By the same token, the comparison of the utilization and the relative costs of military and civilian personnel on different programs and in different kinds of work is made more difficult.

2. *Matériel.* All the services provide separate appropriations for major procurement—that is, procurement of major items of equipment. Nonetheless, all of the other major appropriations also include funds for the purchase of supplies and matériel that are directly attributable to the "programs" which they cover. For example, a very large part of the appropriation, Maintenance and Operations, Army, is actually for the purchase of materials, supplies, organizational equipment, etc. And an important share of the appropriation for Military Personnel, Army, is for the purchase of food for the subsistence of the troops.

3. *Training.* In both the Army and the Air Force, training appears as a separate budget program under their respective appropriations for maintenance and operations. In the Navy, training makes up a substantial part of the appropriation for Naval Personnel, General Expenses. However, costs of training and education also are identified as parts of other appropriations, such as Marine Corps Troops and Facilities and Medical Care. Training is obviously a major activity of all the services. Yet its identification in separate budget programs is seriously misleading, for the actual coverage of the programs is only fractional. For example, the Army budget request for fiscal year 1953, which totaled over 14 billion dollars, included about 81 million dollars in its training budget program. As an indication of the actual cost of Army training, this figure is obviously absurd. Even after the overhead costs of operating installations are spread (see Installation Support below), the resultant figure of 214 million dollars remains ridiculously small. This situation arises because a great deal of actual training is carried out under other appropriations and programs; and also because the largest costs of the training presumably included here are attributed budget-wise to other appropriations, such as Military Personnel, and other budget programs, such as Forces and Facilities.

4. *Medical Care.* The Hoover Commission's almost classic example of per-

formance versus old-style budgeting was in the field of military medicine. It demonstrated the simplification of accounts at the Bethesda Medical Center resulting from the proposed consolidation of all costs in a new appropriation, Medical Care. This proposal, of course, rested on the somewhat questionable assumption that medical care should be considered a primary purpose or program of the Navy Department as a whole. The Commission's proposal has now become fact in the Navy system. But the identification of medical care in the Army or Air Force as a unity for appropriation purposes would appear to be inconsistent with their basic appropriation groupings. Nonetheless, the pressure in this direction has resulted in a seriously compromising situation in their budget structures. Thus the Army has established a budget program, Medical Care, within its appropriation for Maintenance and Operations. This is the only technical, supporting activity which is so distinguished; the other budget programs cut across the functional responsibilities of the various services and agencies. But the Medical Care program includes projects for medical training, medical procurement, medical supply distribution, and other functions which should logically appear as parts of other appropriations and budget programs. This inconsistency makes the other appropriations and programs incomplete and also has important organizational implications within the Army.

5. *Installation Support.* A particularly troublesome budgeting problem in the Army is the treatment of the costs of local services and overhead at Army installations. The typical large installation includes activities and organizations funded from different appropriations, budget programs, and budget projects. Thus an installation might have a training center, a hospital, a training division, and a laboratory. But a very large share of the total cost of the post is installation-wide, including such items as utilities, maintenance and repair of buildings, local transportation services, local communications, etc. In fact, at many installations these costs exceed the direct local costs of all other activities put together. If they are not distributed among the other "using" programs and projects, the costs of the latter are seriously understated. But in the absence of meters and other measuring devices and of a detailed system of local cost accounting, there is no sound basis for distributing them. Recent practice has been to distribute them statistically on whatever basis appears reasonable to the various commands, and the total figures so allocated are shown in the budget estimates. However, it is apparent that the resulting data are little more than "guesstimates," of little value in appraising true costs of budget programs.

CAPITAL AND CURRENT OPERATING EXPENSES

As has been shown earlier, all of the military appropriation classifications reflect an effort to distinguish funds to be used for capital investments and development from those for current operating expenses. Such a distinction, urged by the Hoover Commission, is in fact stipulated for the military budgets by the National Security Act Amendments of 1949.[17] The various appropriation titles for major procurement and production, for real estate and construction, and, in a special sense, for research and development, are pretty definite reflections of the effort to segregate capital items.

The usefulness either to reviewing bodies or administrators and, in fact, the validity of applying the customary business-type distinction between capital and current expenses in normal national government operations are debatable.[18] Some of the reasons for separate capital funding and accounting which apply in business and in local government—i.e. the spreading of costs over the years of return of nonrecurring expenses, the accumulation of reserves for paying off debts for major works and construction, the linking of long-range financial and works planning, the provision of justification for borrowing—are clearly irrelevant to the financing of most regular Federal activities. Except for those undertakings which are expected to be self-liquidating or self-supporting, government investments do not normally produce significant monetary return although they may and perhaps should result in social and economic "returns" to the country as a whole. Even such vague "returns" as increase in social welfare are hardly applicable to military expenditures. For these, whether construed as capital or operating, return a degree of protection or insurance, measurable only in the judgment of men or in the supreme test of war.

The capital versus current differentiation at the level of appropriations and major budget programs is in some respects at cross-purposes with the fundamental concept of budgeting and authorizing funds in terms of programs. Most major programs involve expenses of both types. If the longer-range or the nonrecurring types of expenses are segregated into a separate classification, the projected cost of the program is to that extent incomplete. Reviewing bodies must appraise the partial costs of a program or function at one time and then, later on, consider another part of the cost in an entirely different and perhaps

---

[17] P. L. 216, Sec. 403.

[18] On the applicability of the capital and current expense classification in Federal budgeting, see particularly Jesse Burkhead "The Outlook for Federal Budget-Making," *National Tax Journal*, December, 1949, pp. 294-6. See also Gerhard Colm, "Budget Planning, the Government Budget, the Financial Plan and the Nation's Economic Budget," February 15, 1950 (processed). An able discussion of this problem in relation to national governments generally is found in: United Nations, Department of Economic Affairs, *Budgetary Structure and Classification of Government Accounts* (New York: February, 1951), Ch. III.

not relatable context. Current practice of the House Appropriations Committee in reviewing military public works carries this dichotomy one step further. Military construction is now covered by a supplemental appropriation and is reviewed by a different subcommittee of the Appropriations Committee from those which consider the rest of the military budgets—and at a later time.

This is one important reason why it is impossible to glean from the present budget structure any but the haziest guess as to the actual or projected cost of the major operating programs of the military, such as the cost of the Korean action or the cost of training a division. For the cost of major items of equipment which are "consumed" is included under distinct appropriations, as are the costs of real estate and construction. Equally important, the structure of the capital-type appropriations directs the reviewers' attention again to an item-by-item and project-by-project analysis, only distantly relatable to program objectives. It may be noted that among present appropriations and primary budget programs, those for research and development and for medical care come nearest to being comprehensive and complete since both include the costs of major procurement and supplies incident to their operations. But both exclude the cost of real estate and construction.

The differentiation of capital from operating expenses inevitably raises knotty questions of definition. The Defense Department category of Major Procurement and Production Costs, presumed generally to be "capital" expenditures, is defined to cover: "Costs of acquisition of items of equipment of particular budget or planning significance and specifically designated for inclusion in this category." [19] It includes aircraft, ships, vehicles, artillery, weapons, guided missiles, electronics, special training equipment, railroad equipment, etc. It also includes that expendable item, ammunition. The Army's appropriation for Procurement and Production, Army, is comparable in the kinds of things covered. The definition of the appropriation provides for: ". . . procurement . . . , manufacture of armament and equipment, including concurrent spares, which generally have a long production lead time and an appreciable cost per unit." [20]

Obviously these definitions are not in strict accord with the customary economic or accounting interpretations of capital, which normally involve an anticipated turnover or return over a period of years beyond the current fiscal period. Ammunition, whether used against the Chinese or on a target range in the United States, "turns-over" rapidly.

---

[19] Department of Defense, "Budget Category Definitions," p. 7.
[20] Department of the Army, *Special Regulations* No. 35-210-31, p. 56.

And one may reasonably ask whether a major item of combat equipment, deployed with the expectation that it will be destroyed or replaced within a year, is not an operating rather than a capital expense. The investment character of the major procurement category appears to be only one of several criteria employed. Others include: "particular budget or planning significance"; "long production lead time"; large unit size or large unit cost; and administrative and accounting convenience. Most of the items are such that they are recorded, budgeted, and controlled on a unit-by-unit basis.

On the other hand, the various appropriations for maintenance and operations cover a very large amount of procurement, including equipment items of long life expectancy and usefulness. In the Army, for example, this appropriation includes all organizational equipment not budgeted under major procurement; mess equipment; office equipment; bakery equipment; etc. It also covers the procurement of large amounts of matériel for mobilization reserve—i.e., not expected to be consumed unless and until there is a total war.

Thus, as an expression of capital investment, the major procurement category is an overstatement, since it includes substantial amounts for goods for early consumption. And maintenance and operations as an expression of operating costs is an overstatement since it includes substantial amounts of investment for future use. The present budget structure does not reveal the basic fact about its "character"; how much of it is for the support of current operations and activities, and how much is for build-up for the future.

There would appear to be two quite different uses for character classifications of military expenditures, requiring two quite distinct sets of definitions to serve their respective purposes. The first would be to facilitate better internal management of property, inventories, and production. For example, materials of all kinds obtained for mobilization reserves must be distinguished, at least for bookkeeping purposes, from normal operating inventories of stocks for current use. The cost of mobilization reserves is properly considered an addition to capital assets. Likewise, it would appear desirable that depreciation accounting be applied to the capital investment involved in the various revolving fund activities in the fields of production and supply. These funds, once established, can be made truly self-sustaining only if the prices charged using units for their supplies and their products are inclusive of all their true costs, including the cost of their capital investment. In these fields, the normal accounting practices of private business would appear to be both pertinent and necessary.

The second kind of character classification would be one specifically designed for the reviewers and the policy-makers. It would show the amounts and the contents of the budgets and programs for the years under consideration that are needed for the support of operations and forces during each year, as against those which represent additions (or subtractions) in total assets during the year. In other words, it would tell the Congressman how much of the budget was for build-up, how much for operations and maintenance, and what the anticipated build-up would amount to at year-end. The word "assets" is used here, somewhat inadvisedly, in a sense much broader than that of tangible or redeemable properties. It would rather be an approach to the appraisal of the total worth of the establishment, and of its main components, toward the purposes it is intended to serve. Capital investment, under this definition, is the net increase in this total worth; conversely, in times of demobilization, the net decreases would constitute disinvestment. Capital would include not only the net increases of inventories of all kinds of matériel and the acquisition and construction of real estate; practically all research and most development are in this category. So is a large share of training, which likewise produces resources available for future use if needed. Even the cost of recruiting new personnel for new units is properly a "build-up" charge, distinct in its character from recruitment of replacements.

Information of this kind should be extremely valuable, even essential, to reviewers of the budget if they are to make intelligent decisions. And it would direct their attention to the types of policy questions which they are best able to judge and for which the American people should hold them responsible. This kind of data will not "grow out" of the present or even the future accounting systems of the military departments. The cost allocations would be approximations, perhaps quite rough. But even a general indication of the direction and speed of movement along these lines is more than we have now, and more than the present budget structure can produce.

BUDGET STRUCTURE AND ORGANIZATION STRUCTURE

In the foregoing paragraphs, I have undertaken to describe and illustrate certain basic deficiencies in the budget classification structure from the standpoints primarily of its value to internal administration and to reviewing officers at the top echelons of the departments, the executive, and the legislature. Some of these undoubtedly can be, and some are being, alleviated by adjustments in the classifications. But underlying many of them is a basic problem which goes to the very seat of performance budget theory and of existing legislation. It is the assumption that the information and the classifications most suitable for top-level and political appraisal and decision are, or can be made, the same as those that are most suitable for internal management and financial control. Bluntly, can the accounting and work classifications, reports, and controls of an organization be made to "add up" to the kinds of classification that the President and Congress need in order to make broad decisions on military policy?

The performance budget concept apparently includes a paradox. Much of the literature on the subject and even Public Law 216 carry an implicit assumption that the basic classification of an agency's programs is, or should be, identical to the organizational structure. It follows under this theory that if the organization structure does not accord with the "logical" program structure, the agency should be reorganized. This is an overstatement and an oversimplification of the case, but the implication nonetheless is present. Most of the writings have stressed the adoption of program classifications for purposes of improved review and of improved and more responsible administration, as though the needs of both were the same. For example, the Hoover Commission stressed the value of the performance structure primarily from the standpoints of effective executive and legislative review. But it went on to say: "The appropriation structure not only affects the presentation of the budget estimates, but runs to the root of management and fiscal responsibility. Departmental management is complicated and fiscal responsibility is diffused when single *bureaus* or *functions* are financed from diverse appropriations." [21] It assumed that bureaus and functions would be parallel, and its primary illustration, the Naval Medical Center at Bethesda, was premised on a single, comprehensive medical *program* exactly parallel with a single medical *organization*.

In 1949, Don S. Burrows, in an article describing the new Air Force program-type budget, set forth as three of the four basic principles of the program approach:

(1) To segregate fund requirements of distinct Air Force programs by appropriation and project.
(2) To eliminate multiple funding of single activities.
(3) To present budget estimates of program requirements.[22]

---

[21] Report on *Budgeting and Accounting*, p. 13. Author's italics.
[22] "A Program Approach to Federal Budgeting," *Harvard Business Review*, May, 1949, p. 283. The fourth principle was the segregation of capital and current expenses.

In Burrows' second principle, it is probable that by "activities" is meant organizational units. He expands on this principle as follows: "An Air Force Station Commander will receive funds from one appropriation to support his station. Formerly such activities were separately financed from some 20 sub-appropriations. If one of these sub-appropriations contained insufficient funds while another had excessive funds, he could not effect sensible adjustments. Hence, he might have funds in excess of requirements for medical attendants but be unable to provide adequate telephone service because funds for these purposes were in different appropriations." [23] From the example given, it would appear that the operation of the station as such must be considered an inclusive "program," and that, conversely, the rather widely diverse functions of medical service and communications are not programs for appropriation and budget purposes. In other words, the program base for the Air Force is pretty strictly an organizational one, under Burrows' thesis. This is actually the situation in the present Air Force budgeting for installations; virtually all funds for post operations are attributed to single budget projects. But an exception is the local medical program, most of which is charged to a distinct "functional" budget program.

The theoretical marriage of the programmatic and the organizational bases of the performance budget is perhaps best reflected, and for Defense Department purposes most importantly reflected, in the provisions of Public Law 216 of 1949 which prescribe the performance budget: "Sec. 403 (a) The budget estimates of the Department of Defense shall be prepared, presented, and justified, where practicable, and *authorized programs shall be administered,* in such form and manner as the Secretary of Defense, subject to the authority and direction of the President, may determine, so as to account for, and report, the cost of performance of readily identifiable functional programs and activities, with segregation of operating and capital programs. . . ." [24] The House Committee Report which recommended this bill makes the juxtaposition of program and organizational structure more emphatic. As one of the basic principles of the performance budget, it stated: "That there be a logical and, so far as practical, uniform grouping of projects or budget programs by the primary functions of the military departments, with this grouping paralleling, so far as possible, the

---

[23] *Ibid.*
[24] Author's italics.

organization and management structure." [25] The report supported this principle as follows: "The budget structure not only affects the presentation of budget estimates but runs to the root of management and fiscal responsibility. Management is handicapped when fiscal responsibility is diffused. The financing of an identifiable program from a single source of funds clearly fixes management responsibility, simplifies reporting, and permits departmental management and the Congress more easily to determine costs and to evaluate programs." [26] At other points in the report, the Committee criticizes the practices of multiple funding of single projects and programs and the "absentee administration" which arises when scattered organizational units have control of appropriations supporting such projects and programs.

Let us analyze these statements as they apply to the development and administration of the budget of a Federal agency. The process follows a sequence of steps roughly as follows:

Steps	*Organizations Involved*
1. initial formulation	operating units
2. Intra-agency review and consolidation	intermediate echelons
3. top-level review, decision	top echelon
4. Presidential (Bureau of Budget) review, decision	Bureau of Budget, President
5. Congressional review	appropriations committees and the two houses
6. appropriation	Congress
7. apportionment	Bureau of the Budget
8. allocation of funds and programs	top echelon
9. allotment of funds and subprograms	intermediate echelons
10. administration and obligation of funds	operating units

It may be noted that, according to this model, program and budget proposals come up (steps 1-3) through organizational channels. Likewise, apportioned funds and program directives go down through the same organizational channels (steps 8-10). To the extent that the "model" is followed, the natural, primary classification of estimates in budget formulation is certain to be organizational. And if the principle

---

[25] *Reorganizing Fiscal Management in the National Military Establishment,* H. Rept. 1064 to accompany H. R. 5632, 81st Cong., 1st sess., p. 5.
[26] *Ibid.*

of command is observed, it is absolutely essential that the primary classification of fund allocations and allotments be organizational. That is simply to say that persons authorized and responsible for organizations and the accomplishment of the missions of those organizations should also have control over the resources needed to accomplish the missions.

Steps 3, 4 and 5 are, in certain respects, similar. They all involve an over-all view of the agency, an evaluation of its various purposes and programs in relation to their costs. Obviously they bring to bear different points of view and differing breadths of perspective upon the subject agency, as they should. But the significant point here is that they require essentially the same types of information, presented in approximately similar forms. The Hoover Commission, and almost all students of budgeting, agree that the most desirable way of presenting such information for these purposes is in terms of agency programs and subprograms, and their costs.

This means that, unless organization structure and program classification are identical down to and including the operating level, there must be conversions in formulation from an organizational to a program classification between steps 2 and 3—and usually also between steps 1 and 2. It likewise means that step 8 and usually also 9 require a reconversion back to an organizational base. This does not mean that the program identification and classification need be lost in steps 1 and 2 of budget formulation nor in steps 9 and 10 of budget execution. It simply means that the prime classification at these stages is organizational, the secondary one, programmatic. The two can be identical only in organizations which (1) are considered for budget purposes to be unifunctional, or (2) are so structured that no unit below the top level participates in more than one function or program.

For illustration of the problem, let us refer again to the familiar medical care program of the Army. If we assume that medical care is an understood and accepted program for review, appropriation, *and* administrative purposes, the responsibility for planning, budgeting, and administering the program should presumably rest upon the shoulders of the head of the medical organization, the Surgeon General. So much of the medical funds as are used for the general hospitals and installations that are directly under his command raise no problem. But what of the station hospitals, infirmaries, and laboratories which are located at installations and are for the service of those installations? There is a station hospital at Fort Benning which is primarily a service agency to that post. Its head, like that of other unit heads on the post,

reports to the station commander who in turn reports to the commander of the Third Army, which is a regional organization for the South-
eastern section of the United States. The commander of the Third
Army reports to the Chief of Staff in Washington. If the Army followed the clear precept of financing each "identifiable program from a
single source of funds," the financial support for the Fort Benning
hospital should come directly from the Surgeon General to the head
of the hospital. This would apparently accomplish the House Committee's objectives; it "clearly fixes management responsibility, simplifies
reporting, and permits departmental management and the Congress
more easily to determine costs and to evaluate programs." It would
also accomplish certain other things that the House Committee specifically indicated the performance budget was designed to prevent: the
multiple funding of different projects and programs at Fort Benning,
and the absentee administration of medical funds from Washington.
If the same practice were extended to other of the basic budget programs, such as supply and training, each unit at Fort Benning would
presumably receive its funds directly from a budget program director
in Washington. The commander at Fort Benning would have no control over the financing and the funds of the units he was presumed to
command. His organization, insofar as it could remain an organization,
would be completely subject to multiple funding by absentee administrators. The same fate would befall the Third Army Commander.

Let us examine the alternative suggested by Mr. Burrows. Here we
consider the operation of installations a budget program *as such*. The
commander of Fort Benning under this system has complete control
over all funds to be expended at his station. They are, according to Mr.
Burrows' illustration, allotted in lump sum so that he may transfer
funds to and from his station hospital and his training center as the
needs appear to him. Likewise, he estimates his budget needs for the
station as a whole and forwards them through command channels to
Washington. Here they are presumably consolidated with the estimates of all other installations to produce a total estimate for a budget
program for operations of installations. Such a budget would accord
with the management and organizational purposes of the performance
budget; it would make fiscal and command responsibilities coextensive
at each echelon. But it would be quite unsuitable as a budget for the
review of the executive and the legislature. For now the Medical Care
budget program is seriously incomplete; it includes only the costs of
units under the direct command responsibility of the Surgeon General. And the Congressman, in the budget review process, would be

invited and almost compelled to explore in detail the problems of managing Fort Benning, Camp Drum, and Andrews Field.

The performance budget theorist may say that this problem is not the fault of the concept but a product of poor Army organization. On the other hand, it *must* occur in every organization which has regional and field offices having more than one major function. And the unifunctional field organization is the exception rather than the rule among major Federal agencies. Multifunctional field organizations are an almost inevitable accompaniment of complex programs, very often dictated by those same principles of economy and efficiency which support the performance budget concept.

In all the services, of course, compromises have been made on both sides of this dilemma. Organizational budget data are translated into programmatic terms and vice versa. But the program classifications have been materially modified in order that they may be readily derived from the going organizational and accounting practices. Likewise, organizational and management practices are being continually amended to facilitate funding and funds control in terms of the program classifications of the performance structure. It might be more fruitful in connection with each agency to examine the two separately and in their own terms. First, what kind of financial system and classification will best serve the needs of planning and managing the organization? Second, what system of classification will furnish the data in their most useful form for top management and political review and for appropriation purposes? Third, what techniques can be used to proceed from one type to the other and back again? It is probable that the answer to the third question would be for the agency to rely upon statistical rather than accounting devices and to develop indexes and short-cuts between program measurement and dollar costs.

BUDGET STRUCTURE AND PROGRAM STRUCTURE

It has already been noted in Chapter III that the military services operate program and planning systems, more or less related to their financial planning and administration. It is probably significant that the classifications developed for programming in both the Air Force and Army are distinctly different from those developed as a basis for the performance (or program) budgets. Some differences between the two are almost inevitable because of the different purposes they serve and their different applications to time periods; but the influence of considerations of accounting and financial administration upon the budget structures, particularly the "category of cost" concept, is perhaps the fundamental reason for discrepancies. In many respects, the program structure as it stands today would provide a more informative basis for budgetary review at the Presidential and Congressional levels than does the budget structure. To the lay student, at least, the class titles and their primary subdivisions seem more meaningful and suggestive of what the Army intends to *do* than are the appropriation and budget program titles.

In the Army particularly, the differences in classification have in themselves raised serious problems of management. Some of these were mentioned in a previous chapter: the difficulties and delays involved in translating the one to the other; the difficulty of keeping one up-to-date with the other because of the difficulty of making changes; and the length of time required for the entire process because of its sequential nature. The very coexistence of two different frameworks, each conceived as central for Army management, is a source of inevitable confusion, with the result that neither can fully perform its mission. The problem is magnified by the fact that there are actually three systems of responsibility, no two of which are exactly coterminous: the budgetary system, the program system, and the organizational framework of the Army.

The cross-relationships of the primary program and the budget structures are shown in Figure 8. It should be noted that this chart reflects the relationships at only the top levels of the two classifications. Within each of the budget appropriations and budget programs shown is a sub-hierarchy of budget projects, sub-projects, and accounts; and within each of the primary programs is a subject or functional classification and also a division of the program into its parts. It has already been pointed out that all the technical services participate as directors of parts of practically all the primary programs. They also participate in most of the budget programs as "operating agencies"; and the field armies have some responsibility with respect to most of the budget programs of the appropriation for Maintenance and Operations. Each of the primary programs is supervised by a General Staff office or division, known as program director, and each of the budget appropriations and programs is under a budget program director, likewise a General Staff office or division. But since the definitions of the classifications are not identical, the scope of direction and responsibility of the staff offices and divisions are not substantively coequal for budget and program purposes, and neither conforms exactly with the organizational responsibilities prescribed by the Army organizational directive.

FIGURE 8

RELATIONSHIP OF PRIMARY PROGRAMS AND PERFORMANCE BUDGET
PROGRAMS

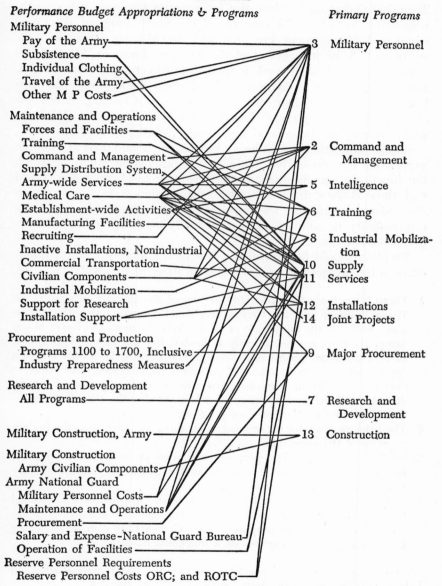

Performance Budget Appropriations & Programs

Military Personnel
  Pay of the Army
  Subsistence
  Individual Clothing
  Travel of the Army
  Other M P Costs

Maintenance and Operations
  Forces and Facilities
  Training
  Command and Management
  Supply Distribution System
  Army-wide Services
  Medical Care
  Establishment-wide Activities
  Manufacturing Facilities
  Recruiting
  Inactive Installations, Nonindustrial
  Commercial Transportation
  Civilian Components
  Industrial Mobilization
  Support for Research
  Installation Support

Procurement and Production
  Programs 1100 to 1700, Inclusive
  Industry Preparedness Measures

Research and Development
  All Programs

Military Construction, Army

Military Construction
  Army Civilian Components
Army National Guard
  Military Personnel Costs
  Maintenance and Operations
  Procurement
  Salary and Expense-National Guard Bureau
  Operation of Facilities
Reserve Personnel Requirements
  Reserve Personnel Costs ORC; and ROTC

Primary Programs

3 Military Personnel

2 Command and
  Management

5 Intelligence

6 Training

8 Industrial Mobiliza-
  tion

10 Supply

11 Services

12 Installations

14 Joint Projects

9 Major Procurement

7 Research and
  Development

13 Construction

(Copied from the Army chart of March 20, 1952, on the subject. Note that two
primary programs, #1, the Troop Program, and #4, the Civilian Personnel Program, are not included since they have no direct relation to budgeted appropriations and programs.)

For example, the Army's organizational directive provides that: "The Assistant Chief of Staff, G-4, . . . directs and controls the Technical Staffs and Services." [27] The Quartermaster Corps is one of these Technical Staffs and Services. But for program purposes, it is directly responsible to G-1 for its segments of the Troop Program, the Command and Management Program, and the Military Personnel Program; to G-3 for its segment of the Training Program. Most of the Quartermaster's budget work is under the direct supervision of G-4. But it has primary estimating and executing responsibility for two budget programs, Subsistence and Individual Clothing, which for appropriation purposes are classed under Military Personnel, an appropriation under the general supervisory jurisdiction of G-1.

Similar illustrations might be multiplied. Such situations of multiple supervision are almost inevitable in complex organizations in which the functional classifications at the operating level are not identical with those at the staff level. But here the problem is, in a sense, three-dimensional because of the imposition of two types of supervisory responsibility in addition to that normally exerted by heads of organizational units.

Attention should be drawn to a few of the more important differences in the budget and program classifications of the Army:

1. There is no budget counterpart for two of the primary programs, the Troop Program and the Civilian Personnel Program. The Troop Program, probably the most basic of all, projects the units and forces of the Army. Its costs are not directly estimated but are reflected in almost all of the budget programs indirectly. The Civilian Personnel Program applies primarily to functions of personnel management rather than to numbers and pay of personnel. The costs of civilian personnel are reflected in all the budget programs which involve the use of civilians— as well as in the other primary programs.
2. The primary program for training is far more inclusive than the budget program of the same title.
3. Medical Care for budget purposes is treated as an inclusive program; in the program system, it appears as a segment of practically every primary program.
4. Parts of the costs and activities of the civilian components, the National Guard and the Organized Reserve, are segregated in three distinct appropriations for budget purposes. These elements are distributed among the various primary programs on a functional basis.

---

[27] Department of the Army, *Special Regulations* No. 10-5-1, "Organization and Functions: Department of the Army," April 11, 1950, as amended.

An examination of the subclassifications of the two systems reveals perhaps more basic problems of reconciliation because of their indication of differing conceptual approaches to the subject matter. The comparative sub-breakdowns of the appropriation and the primary program for military personnel are as follows: [28]

Budget Program and Project	Primary Program Subject Classification
Pay of the Army	Personnel Procurement
Pay and Allowances of Officers	
Pay and Allowances of Enlisted Personnel	Personnel Management
	Personnel Classification and Job Analysis
Pay and Allowances of Cadets, USMA	
Subsistence	
Procurement of Subsistence Supplies	Officer Career Management and Enlisted Personnel Management
Commutation of Rations	
Individual Clothing	Promotions
Purchase of Individual Clothing	Pay and Awards
Monetary Allowances in Lieu of Clothing	Discipline
Travel of the Army	Travel of Dependents
Permanent Change of Station—Individual	
Permanent Change of Station—Organizational Units	Distribution
Other Military Personnel Costs	
Welfare and Morale Activities	Separation
Troop Information and Education Activities	
Apprehension of Deserters	
Courts, Commissions, and Boards	
Chaplains' Supplies and Equipment	
Education of Dependents	
Interest on Soldiers' Deposits	
Death Gratuity	
Awards and Medals	

[28] Derived from the budgetary classification in Department of the Army, *Special Regulations,* No. 35-210-31; and the program classification shown in Department of the Army, *Special Regulations,* No. 11-10-30, "Army Programs: Execution and Review and Analysis of the Military Personnel Program (Army Program No. 3)," December 28, 1951, paragraph 4.

The performance budget classification appears to be a grouping of major *objects* of cost that are associated directly with troops, considered primarily as individuals rather than units. The primary program classification is a grouping of the major *functions* involved in the management of military personnel. The program heading of "Pay and Awards" refers to the administration of the pay and awards system, rather than to the actual manpower requirements and allotments for pay, which are specifically excluded from the program.[29] However, a presentation of fund requirements is included in the program document, but the "fund requirements for pay and allowances do not have . . . direct association with any of the Program activities." [30]

Another illustration of conflicts among comparative subclassifications in the budget and the primary programs is in the area of training: [31]

Budget Projects and Illustrative Sub-Projects	Primary Program Subject Classification
Operation of Schools and Replacement Training Centers	Basic and Branch Material Individual Training at RTC's, Oversea Commands, etc.
U.S. Military Academy	
Command and General Staff Colleges	Individual Training by the Army School System, at Civilian Institutions, etc.
Language Schools	
Technical Service Schools	Unit Training
Replacement Training Centers	Army-wide and Joint Training Exercises
Miscellaneous Training Costs	
Training at Civilian Institutions	Civilian Components Training, Including ORC, ROTC, and National Guard
Production and Distribution of Training Films	
Training Aids	Training Through Army Extension Courses
Training Publications	
School Temporary Duty (Travel)	Provision of Specified Facilities Such as Training Aid Centers and Instructional Material, Publications, Films, etc.
Army Service TDY	
Other School TDY	
	Specialized Post-Cycle Training

Again there appears to be a distinction in both scope and kind between the two classifications, though it is less marked than in the

---

[29] Department of the Army, *Special Regulations,* No. 11-10-30, paragraph 4.
[30] *Ibid.*

[31] Based upon Department of the Army, *Special Regulations,* No. 35-210-52, and *Special Regulations,* No. 11-10-60. "Army Programs: Execution and Review and Analysis of the Training Program (Army Program No. 6)," October 22, 1951, paragraph 4.

case of military personnel. The budgetary classification segregates by type the organizations that exclusively perform training and certain categories or objects of cost directly attributable to training work. The program classification distinguishes the different kinds of training activity, such as basic, individual, and unit training. Unit training is not specifically treated anywhere in the budget classification, its cost being spread among a variety of programs.

The structures of some of the primary programs are basically similar to their budgetary counterparts. Thus the Construction Program and the Research and Development Program are parallel to their opposite number appropriations. The Major Procurement program has a classification of the major items of procurement identical to that of the Major Procurement and Production appropriation. Both are primarily on an object basis. However, the program is more comprehensive in that it covers not only procurement and the letting of contracts but the scheduling of deliveries.

The Army Staff is vigorously undertaking to improve the program-budget relationship in two broad directions. The first is to bring the basic classifications into alignment by adjustments and redefinitions of both. Its proposal, which went forward to the Defense Department in the fall of 1952, is illustrated in diagrammatic form on Figure 9. Among its principal features are: elimination of two of the appropriations for civilian components; elimination of the budget program for Forces and Facilities; broadening of the budget program, Training; establishment of a comprehensive budget program for Services; establishment of a primary program for the Army National Guard; elimination of the budget program, Medical Care, and substituting therefor a Medical project as part of the Services program; and transfer of the budget programs for Subsistence and Individual Clothing to the budget program covering supplies.[32]

The second promising field of current Army effort is a project aiming to identify and standardize, at the operating level, the basic activities of all organizations of the Army. From these would be developed a standard Army-wide classification of Army functions from the bottom up rather than from the top down. These would provide a uniform system of phonetics for the whole language of Army management. The ultimate objective of this effort would be a common standard for work

---

[32] Department of the Army, Office of the Chief of Staff, Memorandum for Chairman, the Steering Group, Program and Budget Management Project, "Working Group Report and Recommendations," March 24, 1952, and subsequent amendments (processed).

FIGURE 9

RELATION OF ARMY BUDGET AND PROGRAM STRUCTURES AS PROPOSED BY
THE DEPARTMENT OF THE ARMY, 1952 [a]

Proposed Performance Budget Structure	Proposed Primary Program Structure
——————	Troop Program (Not Budgeted)
——————	Civilian Personnel Program (Not Budgeted)
——————	Installations (Not Budgeted)
Military Personnel, Army (Appropriation)———	Military Personnel Program
Maintenance and Operations, Army (Appropriation)	
Command and Management (Program)———	Command and Management Program
Evaluation System (Program)———	Intelligence Program
Training (Program)———	Training Program
Supply Distribution and Maintenance (Program)———	Supply Distribution and Maintenance Program
Services (Program)	Services Program
Finance and Audit (Project)———	Finance and Audit Services
Administrative (Project)———	Administrative Services
Protective Services (Project)———	Protective Services
Welfare, Morale and Related Activities (Project)———	Welfare, Morale and Related Activities
Medical (Project)———	
Communications (Project)———	
Transportation (Project)———	
Other Specialized QM Services (Project)———	Logistical Services
Maintenance of Facilities (Project)———	
Real Estate Management (Project)———	
Supplies and Procurement Activities (Program)———	
Industrial Mobilization (Program)———	Industrial Mobilization Program
Matériel, Army (Appropriation)———	Matériel Program
Research and Development, Army (Appropriation)———	Research and Development Program
Military Construction, Army (Appropriation)———	Construction Program
Army National Guard (Appropriation)———	Army National Guard Program
Joint Projects (Appropriation)———	Joint Projects Program

[a] Copied from the Army chart of July 2, 1952, on the subject.

measurement, procedural planning, cost accounts, fiscal accounts, organization structure, programming and reporting, and, finally, budgeting.

Both of these undertakings should, if completed and approved, effect material improvements in the reconciliation of programming and budgeting and thus in Army management as a whole. But there still remains, in all the services, a fundamental and to some extent inherent reason why programs and budgets must be distinguished and why the "ideal" performance budget cannot become a complete actuality. One aspect of this underlying problem is organizational; the other, temporal. The organizational aspect, in its simplest terms, derives from the fact that there is an organizational distinction, more or less clearly recognized, between producing and supplying elements on the one hand and using units on the other. The end product of military activity, of both programs and budgets, is in the main represented by the performance of the using units. But most of the resources which the using units require are furnished them gratis. They have little role and little responsibility for estimating the financial support they need, for defending it, and for expending it except in the finalized form of supplies, equipment, and services. To many of these units, dollar budgeting is fractional or completely irrelevant. Thus a very substantial proportion of the most fundamental elements of military performance is in fact only remotely related to funds in terms of organizational responsibility. Yet the identification of funds with performance would seem to be a definition of performance budgeting.

On the other hand, the biggest part of military budgets and of military budgeting is of, by, for, and to the logistical organizations, logistical being used here in its broader sense of support for military operations. These units usually have command as well as financial responsibility for obtaining and producing goods and services, and for distributing them. They have varying degrees of control over the way they are consumed and maintained or operated. But the main responsibility for utilization and for generating requirements rests not with the suppliers, but with the users. Thus, with few exceptions, the responsibility for performance and that for budgets are not identified in the military organizations.

Military plans generally start with strategic objectives and the operational requirements to accomplish them. Military programs encompass both the operations to support the objectives and the logistics to support the operations. Their classification is therefore designed to show in logical relationship the programs and functions involved in operations and logistics, whether or not these involve large costs, direct or indirect. The budget, however, is structured around elements of direct cost. As a total picture of the military program and of military performance, it is heavily biased in the direction of the supplying and service activities, and within them, to the elements of those activities that are most important in terms of dollar significance. Under the present organizational and administrative system of the military services, a revamping of budget classifications to make them conform exactly to the logical structuring of programs and plans would probably be neither feasible nor desirable for purposes of internal management.

Insofar as the performance budget is defined to signify the identification of command and functional responsibility with financial responsibility, it is probably impossible of attainment. It would clearly be unrealistic to fund a commander on the hills of Korea with dollars and direct him to buy his guns and ammunition. Within the continental United States and particularly among the more or less stationary activities, there is much promise that responsibility for budget and responsibility for operation and utilization can be brought closer together. The stock funds and the industrial funds, discussed later, are steps in this direction. So are the various efforts to establish comprehensive costing systems, the pricing both of supplies and military personnel, and notably the recently inaugurated appropriation and expense accounting system of the Air Force.[33] The logical extension of the performance budget idea is a budget in which the primary responsibility for estimating fiscal needs as well as for expending appropriated funds would rest upon the consuming units rather than upon suppliers. Only under such a system could the operating programs and the budget structure come into perfect harmony.

THE DIMENSION OF TIME

The second aspect of the inherent problem of correlating the program and the performance budget is the time factor. It is a source of misunderstanding and confusion in the minds of the lay public, the Congress, and to a considerable degree the military planners themselves. This confusion is reflected in statements that the budget is a simple translation into dollars of a program or that the appropriate

---

[33] The new and somewhat experimental Air Force appropriation and expense accounting system contemplates that local users charge themselves actual costs of goods and services whether or not they pay for them. The resulting reports are to be used for comparative and management purposes, and, it is hoped ultimately, to support budget estimates. *Air Force Letter*, No. 177-4, June 12, 1952.

time segment of the defense program serves as basis for preparation of each annual budget. The fact of the matter is that the budget for a fiscal year is an expression of only a part of a program for that fiscal year *and* of parts of programs for several years after that fiscal year.

Part of this problem is the familiar distinction between obligations and expenditures. Budgets by and large are requests for appropriations which in turn are authority to obligate funds. Some of the funds will be spent during the budget fiscal year. Others will not be expended until one, two, three, and in a few cases more years after the fiscal year. The funds which are not spent until subsequent years are for the most part for long-lead items such as construction and major procurement.

Programs on the other hand are guides and directives for action during the period for which they apply. They project proposed accomplishments during that period in such terms as units or ships to be activated and maintained, stocks to be delivered and utilized, personnel to be trained. Some military programs, it is true, are immediately related to fiscal obligations. That is, for practical purposes, the programs, the obligation schedules, and the expenditure schedules are virtually identical. Pay and allowances of personnel, purchase of perishable supplies, and some utility charges are in this category. Some, such as depot supply, relate closely to expenditures and accrued expenditures rather than obligations. Others such as operation and maintenance of units and stations, if translated into fiscal terms, would have to be expressed on a cost basis. That is, the resources applied to the operation and maintenance of military forces would be accounted for when delivered and made available for use and consumption by using units. Many military operating programs fall into the latter category. Much of the matériel the services use in carrying out their programs for a given year is paid for many months before it is used, and much of it must be obligated for a long time before that.

A direct translation of many military programs into dollars would produce substantially a statement of accrued costs at the user level. It might well have little relation to the budget of the same year for the same items. It is probable that less than half of the funds appropriated to the Army for fiscal year 1953 are for the support of operations in that year, and the proportion is even smaller for the Air Force. This means that more than half of the 1953 appropriations are for the support of programs after fiscal 1953. To that extent the Army, the Department of Defense, the President, and the Congress have made decisions with respect to the 1953 budget which commit the country to fiscal requirements and to military programs for 1954 and 1955.

The Army budget for fiscal year 1954 will not be a translation of the Army program for fiscal year 1954. Rather will it be a partial translation of programs for each of the fiscal years 1954, 1955, and 1956, developed after taking consideration of program resources growing out of budget appropriations for 1951, 1952, and 1953, still available for obligation, expenditure, or use.

The problem is neither new nor unique, but it has recently attained tremendous proportions in military planning and budgeting. The increasing mechanization of the military forces results both in increasing lead times of items of equipment and increasing importance of long-lead items in the total military scheme. It also results in longer time requirements for training and therefore a high operating lead time for personnel planning. The extension of our military interests beyond the shores of North America involves lengthening of supply lines and added time between procurement and use of matériel.

Furthermore, the problem is particularly acute because of rapid changes in the over-all force program. If we were operating on an even keel—that is, with a stable force and stable deployment—our matériel requirements would presumably stay about equal year in and year out, regardless of lead times. Of course, new scientific developments, tactics, and strategy would continue to bring about innovations and disturbances of such an equilibrium.

From the standpoint of current military programming and budgeting, there is some short-range advantage in this situation. When the services develop their operating programs for the next ensuing fiscal year, they are assured by virtue of prior appropriations that a very substantial portion of such programs is fiscally firm. Much of the uncertainty attendant upon the budget review process has been removed. Furthermore, much of the remainder of the programs for any given year is quite immune to budgetary reductions in that year. This includes some items for which obligations and expenditures within the fiscal period are identical or nearly so—military pay and allowances, subsistence, and similar items. Most of these are related directly to basic program factors already approved and fixed, explicitly or implicitly, by prior year actions on long-lead items. For example, the troop program is the principal basis for estimating long-lead procurement. Once procurement proposals have been approved and funded, it would be contradictory to cut back on the troop program so as to save relatively small sums for personnel pay and allowances.

This very advantage to the planners in the services is a direct reflection of the limitations of the reviewing and authorizing agencies of the Executive Office and Congress. In the annual military budgets they are confronted by a *fait accompli*—a "fate" largely "accomplished" by their own action in prior years. When they tackle the 1954 budget requests, they find that most of the program and the expenditures for 1954 are fixed by prior action. In their struggle to balance the budget or to lower expenditures and taxes in the current year, they must chip away for relatively small savings in those areas in which obligations have not already been authorized. This perhaps explains the Congressional emphasis and restrictions upon such items as travel, civilian salaries, printing and binding, promotions, and papers and pencils. They are the kinds of expenditures that are most "accessible" for the current year. Much of the budget is beyond recall.

By the same token, the most important choices made by the military establishment, the Executive, and the Congress in the budget process of a given fiscal year are those which pertain to programs of subsequent fiscal years. They are important not only in terms of their own intrinsic size and cost but also because, as elements of an integrated over-all program, they very largely determine the dimensions of the other elements for which appropriations will be sought in later years. Subsequent failure to make such appropriations must result in imbalances in the over-all program if the program was initially balanced.

A longer fiscal period—a biennial or a quadrennial budget, as suggested by some—might alleviate the problem but it would not eliminate it. No matter how long the fiscal period, there is certain to be a carry-over from one period's budget to the next one's program. And the problem does not argue for dissociating budget from program. The reverse is true unless we are to depart from the premise that program is the basis for budget. But each must be framed in its own temporal terms and in terms of the purpose which it serves. The fiscal 1954 budget does not equal the fiscal 1954 program but it is based upon, and derives from, program objectives of 1954, 1955, 1956 and even later years. And it can be formulated, reviewed, and evaluated intelligently only in relation to ongoing program objectives that extend beyond the current year's time limits—as shown diagrammatically on the next page.

A complete program system would comprehend, for a given programming period, all the activities planned to be performed and accomplished. In a period of stability when the goal is merely to maintain an existing force at its current strength and degree of readiness, a simple picture of anticipated *activity* might be adequate, provided it

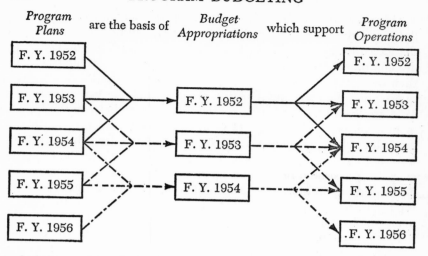

included provision for maintenance, replacement, replacement training, and similar features. However, during a period of build-up or of demobilization, the status of available resources at the beginning and at the end of the program period must be taken into account. The former depends upon programs of prior years; the latter, upon anticipated programs for later years. Thus, just as a budget for any year relates in part to programs of future years, the program for any year depends upon program objectives of later years. The short-range budget is linked to a medium-range program which is linked to a long-range estimate.

Translated into terms of resource requirements, the program for a given year would take a generalized form of the following order:

Resources (in personnel, units, facilities, matériel) consumed, used, or lost during program year

PLUS

Resources to be available at end of program year to turn over to subsequent year

MINUS

Resources available at beginning of year, received from prior years

EQUALS

Resources required to become available during program year.

The emphasis in this formula should be placed upon the word "available." The essential distinction between the fiscal budget and the program grows out of the time-distance between the decision to make something available and actual availability. This time-distance obviously varies widely among different elements of the program. For some, it is so small as to be irrelevant; for others, it is so long as to be irrelevant to operations (though not for development) during the program period; and for the rest, it requires careful differential phasing in the period between the time of planning and the end of the program year. The important point is that the program year be looked at as a whole; the subsequent processes of scheduling and budgeting work backward from it.

Figure 10 is a highly oversimplified and completely hypothetical illustration of the time relation discussed above. The example is in the field of supply and procurement but essentially the same conclusions would apply in the case of construction, or of personnel recruitment, training, and organization of units. Section A shows expected user requirements, and its fourth column is presumably derived from the application of consumption experience rates to projected unit (or perhaps individual) strengths, 1953 through 1956. "Returns to Depots," likewise based on experience rates, includes unused and re-issuable items as well as others for salvage or discard. For purposes of this section, it has been assumed that user supply levels will be maintained at approximately six-month consumption requirements.

Section B projects the program accounts for central supply. Columns 5 and 4 are identical with Columns 2 and 3 respectively of Section A. Here it is assumed that: 50 per cent of the items returned to the depots (Column 4) are lost (Column 6); that the depots will maintain a twelve-month supply level; and that a mobilization reserve of 1,000 items (a three-month supply) will be built up by the end of fiscal year 1954 and maintained at that level thereafter. Column 3, "Procurement," is derived by adding the net increases in supply level (Column 2) and mobilization reserve (Column 1) to the losses in the period from issue and other losses, and then deducting returns from users.

Column 3 in Section B becomes Column 1, "Deliveries," in Section C, the Procurement Program. Here we have assumed administrative and production lead times totaling ten to fifteen months. It may be noted that, for example, the major part of deliveries planned for 1954, 2,075, are ordered and funded in 1953, and the second largest part, 1,100, are ordered and funded in 1952. Columns 3 and 4 of Section C show the total funding requirements—that is, the budget requirements

—for fiscal years 1953 and 1954, respectively. They each amount to a great deal more than the actual projected consumption for the corresponding years, shown in Column 4 of Section A. But if it be assumed that unit strengths level off after 1955 at about 4,000 and that rates of consumption and loss stay the same, annual funding would also level off to equal annual consumption plus net losses—i.e. about 4,200 items.

In this hypothetical illustration, it would obviously be impossible to determine the fiscal year 1954 budget requirement without projecting the user program as well as the central supply program at least through fiscal year 1956. Even if procurement lead time were zero, it would be necessary to project these programs at least through fiscal year 1955.

It may be noted also that the principal variable in this table is user consumption, Column 4 in Section A. With the exception of mobilization reserve, which presumably depends upon other considerations, and the procurement schedule, every calculation on the figure can be projected by applying to anticipated consumption, factors presumably drawn from experience and policy decision. For most types of supply, the anticipated consumption depends upon the strength and deployment of troops or units of different types, or both.

A final observation about Figure 10 is that the projection of the programs and budgets for given fiscal years depends heavily upon the validity of the information about resources on hand and on order at the beginning of the period in question. That is to say that the projected "On Hand" data at the beginning of the period shown in Column 1, Section A, and Columns 1 and 2, Section B, must be firm and that the funding for fiscal years prior to the budget year must be known or anticipated with reasonable assurance. These are the "jumping-off" points. It may be postulated that the further in advance of the period planned or budgeted for, the greater the uncertainty and probability of error in these base figures. If, for example, our table had been developed during fiscal year 1952 as a basis for the 1954 budget request, errors might occur with respect to actual consumption, actual losses, and actual delivery schedules during both fiscal years 1952 and 1953. Furthermore, at the time these 1954 budget requirements were estimated, actual appropriations would not have been known for fiscal year 1953, with the result that Column 3 in Section C might be erroneous.

The type of analysis developed in these pages is not new to the Army or to the other military forces. In fact, as described in the next chapter, a large part of military estimates are initially developed in much this way. But it does not appear that this type of problem has been

FIGURE 10

HYPOTHETICAL PROGRAMS FOR ITEM X

SECTION A

Item X—User Requirements (Projected)

	On Hand Beginning of Period	Receipts in Period (*from Depot Supply*)	Returns to Depots	Consumption and Other
	IN-PUT	IN-PUT	OUT-PUT — Losses in Period	OUT-PUT — Losses in Period
	(1)	(2)	(3)	(4)
F. Y. 1953	1,000	2,450	200	2,000
F. Y. 1954	1,250	3,000	250	2,500
F. Y. 1955	1,500	3,800	300	3,000
F. Y. 1956	2,000	4,400	400	4,000
F. Y. 1957	2,000			

SECTION B

Item X—Program for Central Depot Supply

	On Hand Beginning of Period — Mobilization Reserve	On Hand Beginning of Period — Current Disposable	Receipts in Period — Procurement	Receipts in Period — Returns from Users	Losses in Period — Issue	Losses in Period — Other Losses
	(1)	(2)	(3)	(4)	(5)	(6)
F. Y. 1953	200	2,000	3,150	200	2,450	100
F. Y. 1954	500	2,500	3,875	250	3,000	125
F. Y. 1955	1,000	3,000	4,650	300	3,800	150
F. Y. 1956	1,000	4,000	4,200	400	4,400	200
F. Y. 1957	1,000	4,000				

SECTION C

Item X—Procurement Program

Procurement Schedule (Funding)

	Deliveries	F.Y.1952 and Prior Years	F.Y.1953	F.Y.1954	F.Y.1955	F.Y.1956
	(1)	(2)	(3)	(4)	(5)	(6)
F. Y. 1953	3,150	2,750	400			
F. Y. 1954	3,875	1,100	2,075	700		
F. Y. 1955	4,650		1,400	2,650	600	
F. Y. 1956	4,200			1,300	2,600	300
		3,850	3,875	4,650		

thoroughly treated in the discussions on the performance budget nor in the review of military budget estimates, particularly at the Congressional level. Basically, the problem is one of relating the performance budget for a given fiscal year to plans and programs for future fiscal years. It seems reasonable to hypothesize from the foregoing discussion that, in a performance budgeting system:

1. Program planning for future fiscal years must be directly related to long-range objectives and estimates of forces.
2. Budget plans for a given fiscal year must be built upon program plans not only for that year but for a period into the future, along the following lines:
    a. a comprehensive program, covering all phases of operations and resources, at least one full fiscal year beyond the budget year;
    b. programs for long-lead elements (one year or more lead time) extending two or more years beyond the budget year, depending on the lead time. (This would mean projection of force requirements upon which long-lead elements are based at least two full years beyond the budget year.)
    c. long-range programs for such elements as construction and research and development several years beyond the budget year. (This would require long-range planning guidance on anticipated strengths of forces, strategic and tactical factors, and general patterns of deployment.)
3. Program plans should be developed as late as possible in relation to the beginning of the budget year.
4. Program projections on which the budget is based should be submitted with the annual budget, and review of the annual budget by higher authorities should be made on the basis of budget year *plus* future year programs rather than upon budget year expenditures and obligations.

CONCLUSIONS

In this chapter, some of the obstacles to the concept of the performance budget in the military services have been emphasized. These are primarily classificatory, organizational, programmatic, and temporal in character. It may be proper to close by referring to the more positive side, the achievements in the direction of the concept in the past few years. Certainly there is now greater appreciation of the relations of programs and appropriations; there are efforts underway, described in this and the preceding chapter, to provide mechanisms for better relating them; there is growing appreciation of the classification problem and of the time problem. In the Army, perhaps the greatest achievement of the performance budget has been organizational; it has helped to provide an integrated base for planning and control in the General Staff.

The question as to whether the Army and the other services have performance budgets seems neither answerable nor pertinent. The basic idea, as originally stated by the Hoover Commission, that the performance budget is one based upon "functions, activities, and projects" depends on many problems of definition and application in individual agencies. The proper question is less whether an agency has or does not have it, than whether or not it is working in the direction of the concept in all of its ramifications. The performance budget is more a statement of direction and of intent than a description of a current condition. There can be little doubt that the Army, the Navy, and the Air Force have been working *toward* it. But the road has been difficult. Its effects on the budget process, as distinguished from the budget structure, are one of the concerns of the next chapter.

chapter V

the budget process

It is essential to know actual as well as theoretical method of dipping ice cream, as they differ considerably.

DEPARTMENT OF THE ARMY.[1]

The observer aspiring to understand and describe budgeting in the military establishment today can hardly avoid the risks of oversimplifying, overgeneralizing, and downright inaccuracy. The process is so huge in over-all dimensions, so intricate in detail, and so complex as to defy comprehension by a single mind. And it is changing rapidly from year to year and month to month. The formalized directives and doctrines on the subject are more in the nature of objectives and targets than of actualities. The fact of the matter is that the process has not "settled down" to the point where it can be described as a firm system. This is partly because the organizations and procedures for budgeting are themselves quite new and experimental. It is partly because, since June of 1950, the budget operations have been carried on in an environment of endemic emergency. Quick shifts in direction and emphasis have been normal, uncertainty has been high, and indecision or tardy decision at top policy levels has been common. It may well be that this condition will be permanent, and that the budget process, if it can be properly called a process, must be oriented to such a framework, if it can be properly called a framework.

In spite of these hazards, I shall undertake in the succeeding pages to sketch out the salient features of the internal budgeting operation, giving emphasis to what appear to be the principal problem areas. Most of the specific references will be to Army practices.

[1] *Pamphlet 20-325*, paragraph 4, as quoted in *The New Yorker*, December 13, 1952, p. 77.

ORGANIZATION FOR BUDGETING

Under Public Law 216 and the directives of the Secretaries of Defense and the Army, the central responsibility for budgeting is vested in comptrollers at the levels of Office of Secretary of Defense and the staffs of the services. In the Army and Air Force, counterpart comptrollers supervise the budgeting for the commands, technical services, and armies in the field, and for the major installations. Responsibility for budgeting at Army installations not having comptrollers usually rests upon a post fiscal officer or budget and fiscal officer.

Within the Army, the responsibility of the various comptrollers extends to the technical direction, coordination, and supervision of the procedures; the consolidation and review of estimates; and the planning and supervision of the presentation of estimates before higher reviewing bodies. In theory, and for the most part in practice as well, the comptroller's jurisdiction does not extend to amending the programs or policies which provide the substance of the budget. He reviews the estimates from the standpoints of accuracy, technical and procedural correctness, and conformance with policies and instructions. He may, of course, question interpretations of policy and program and may raise questions about the programs themselves, especially when they result in unusual or apparently excessive increases in cost. But most decisions on such questions are made by line or program officers.

The Comptroller of the Army, like his counterparts in the other military departments, is the top budget officer of the department. In practice, most of his operating responsibilities are delegated to, and carried out by, the Chief, Budget Division, who is officially designated as Assistant Budget Officer of the Department of the Army.

The Budget Division, Office of the Comptroller of the Army, includes a small staff unit, the Plans Branch, for liaison, coordination, and the development and supervision of policies, presentations, and other papers. The larger Estimates and Funding Branch handles the spadework—the preparation of budget directives, the detailed review of estimates, negotiations and conferences with other staff units in Headquarters and with the field, and the issuance of fund allocations. It is organized into sections on the basis of major appropriations. This permits a degree of specialization and continuity within the staff with respect to the substance of the budget and acquaintance with counterpart budget specialists in other staff and operating units. The following observations, most of which would probably apply to many other Federal budget offices, may be made about this branch of the Budget Division:

1. Its staff is primarily concerned with the technical and procedural aspects of budgeting.
2. Its operations are customarily carried on under high-pressure, emergency conditions; it is a "fire-fighting" outfit under almost continuous stress to meet deadlines and implement policy decisions and policy changes; it has little time for planning or reflection.
3. Its personnel seldom get out into the field to see the budget "in action" and to add meat and meaning to the papers and figures that are their stock-in-trade; this puts them at a disadvantage in dealing not only with the field representatives but also with budget reviewers of higher echelons, particularly the analysts of the Bureau of the Budget who make a practice of regular field visits.
4. The Army officer rotation policy means that some of the key staff are "green" in their jobs and, in effect, in a training status; this defect may be partially compensated by the fact that incoming officers bring a field point of view to their work, but it is doubtful that many have had previous experience that is relevant to their Headquarters assignment.

The Budget Advisory Committees

Each of the three services has a Budget Advisory Committee (BAC) and, on paper, the functions and responsibilities of each are comparable. The BAC is an example of the familiar standing committee device designed to bring to bear the viewpoints and representations of various functional units of the staff upon substantive budget questions. Its membership therefore includes ranking officers at the top, or near the top, of each staff division—or, in the case of the Navy, each of the operating bureaus. In all three departments, its capacity is officially only advisory, and its corporate responsibility in the case of Army and Air Force is to the Chief of Staff. All the BAC's are part-time bodies so that their members, as individuals, retain their affiliations and primary allegiances in the offices which they represent. In practice, a BAC can, through its recommendations, exercise considerable decision-making authority. Though appeal can be taken from its judgments to the Chief of Staff, in most cases its verdict is virtually final as far as the service position is concerned.

There is, however, a wide variation among the departments as to the actual operations of the BAC. In the Army, it convenes, holds hearings, and renders decisions at most of the key points in the entire budget process—from the issuance of the budget directive to the allocation of appropriated funds. Its hearings on budget estimates are extended over several weeks and are quite comprehensive. The Air Force BAC has similar functions but holds less extensive hearings. Its hearings on the

1954 estimates were held daily over a two-week period. The Navy BAC customarily convenes for one day to hear and discuss the major features of the departmental budget. Most of the budgetary decisions are already reached and approved by the Chief of Naval Operations before this meeting. The Navy BAC thus does not appear to play an important part in the making of budgetary decisions.

The membership of the Army and Air Force BAC's reflects an effort to unify budgeting and programming. In the Air Force, the Committee consists primarily of the principal programming officers from each of the deputy chiefs of staff. In the Army, the BAC is virtually identical in membership with the Program Advisory Committee, which plays a similar role in connection with the Army program system. The actual memberships of these two committees are as follows:

Air Force [2]

Director of the Budget, Deputy Chief of Staff/Comptroller, Chairman
Assistant for Programming, Deputy Chief of Staff/Operations
Director of Operations, Deputy Chief of Staff/Operations
Assistant for Matériel Program Control, Deputy Chief of Staff/Matériel
Director of Personnel Planning, Deputy Chief of Staff/Personnel
Assistant for Development Programming, Deputy Chief of Staff/Development
The Assistant Secretary of the Air Force (Management), without vote
The Under Secretary and the Assistant Secretary of the Air Force or their
    representatives—"to be invited as observers when matters under their
    cognizance are to be considered"

Army [3]

Chief, Budget Division, Office of the Comptroller of the Army, Chairman
Deputy Assistant Chief of Staff, G-1, Personnel
Deputy Assistant Chief of Staff, G-2, Intelligence
Deputy Assistant Chief of Staff, G-3, Operations
Deputy Assistant Chief of Staff, G-4, Logistics
Assistant for Planning Coordination, Office of the Deputy Chief of Staff for
    Plans and Research, without vote
Representative of Office of the Chief, Army Field Forces, without vote
Special Assistant to the Chief of Staff for Civilian Component Affairs
    (when civilian component affairs are under consideration)

---

[2] Headquarters, United States Air Force, *Headquarters Office Instruction,* No. 14-15, "Boards and Committees: Air Force Budget Advisory Committee," April 16, 1952.

[3] Department of the Army, *Army Regulation,* No. 15-35, "Boards, Commissions, and Committees: Budget Advisory Committee," October 2, 1951.

In both Army and Air Force, representatives of the Comptroller budget offices provide the secretariat for the committee, develop procedures and agenda, record minutes and see to the implementation of BAC determinations.

Budget Program Directors and Operating Agencies

Under the Army and Air Force performance budget scheme, each of the appropriations is classified into a number of budget programs (called "Activities" in the Navy). The headquarters staff office having primary concern with the subject matter of the budget program is given certain supervisory and review responsibilities with respect to it. In the Army the heads of these responsible staff offices are designated as budget "program directors." In general, they correspond to the offices represented on the BAC. The budget program directors are not exactly parallel to the "program directors" prescribed by the Program Management system, principally because the classifications differ.[4]

Under the budget program directors are the "Operating Agencies." These are the primary operating organizations to which funds are allocated. In the Air Force, they are the commands and overseas air forces. In the Army, they include offices of the Special Staff, the various technical and administrative services, the continental armies, the overseas armies, and certain special offices or agencies empowered to spend funds, such as the U. S. Military Academy, the National Guard Bureau, and the Office, Secretary of the Army.

The actual preparation of estimates is done by, or under immediate direction of, the "Operating Agencies." Likewise they allot and supervise the expenditure of funds allocated to them by the Secretary (actually the Comptroller).

The role of the Army's budget program directors at the various stages of the budget process is not entirely clear and is, in fact, a source of considerable discussion. The channel of official communications such as the budget directive and budget estimates is direct between the Office of the Comptroller of the Army and the operating agencies. Directives going downward are normally cleared with the appropriate program directors in advance, and many of them are actually prepared by the program directors or jointly. Through their representation on the BAC, the program directors, of course, have a formal opportunity to participate in the basic decisions. Estimates and requests from the operating agencies to Headquarters go directly to the

---

[4] See Chapters III and IV above.

Comptroller of the Army, but copies are normally sent simultaneously to the program directors.

The program directors exercise a varying amount of supervision, direction, and review of the budgetary work of the operating agencies. By far the most important of the program directors is the Assistant Chief of Staff, G-4, Logistics, who is program director for all or most of four of the largest appropriations—Procurement and Production, Maintenance and Operations, Military Construction, and Research and Development. G-4 has cognizance of most of the budgetary activities of the technical services as well as of the overseas and continental armies. Its guidance and review with respect to the technical services are direct and continuous. But the armies deal directly with the Office of the Comptroller as well as with G-4.

The second most important of the budget program directors in the Army is the Assistant Chief of Staff, G-1, Personnel, who has cognizance of the largest portion of the Military Personnel appropriation and a review responsibility with respect to civilian personnel estimates which are scattered among all the appropriations. G-1 provides detailed military personnel data to the Office, Chief of Finance, which is the operating agency for the budget programs, Pay of the Army, Travel of the Army, and others. G-1 supervises the dollar estimating of these programs.

All of the major operating agencies have specialized budget units, usually as part of a comptroller office. Their budgetary functions are roughly comparable to those of the Headquarters Budget Division, including liaison with higher echelons, issuance of instructions, supervision of the preparation of estimates, review and consolidation of estimates, allotting of funds, and monitoring of expenditures within allotments. The comptrollers in the Air commands, the Army technical services, and the field armies normally coordinate the substantive review of estimates by appropriate staff offices and by commanders at their level. In some cases in both the Air Force and the Army, budget advisory committees have been established at the operating agency level, following the general organizational pattern of the Headquarters. It does not appear that these have been widely effective as yet, due largely to lack of interest and knowledge on the part of staff officers, lack of confidence that action taken at this level is effective or important, and lack of sufficient time for a real hearing and review. Perhaps the most effective budgetary work at these levels is that performed by the offices of the technical and administrative specialists, such as the engineers, the quartermasters, the signal officers, and others.

The Working Level

In the various supply services of the Army and the Matériel Command of the Air Force, the development of basic estimating data is performed in large part by requirements sections of subject matter or commodity divisions. Much of this work in the larger agencies is mechanically computed by the application of standard cost or price figures to projected unit requirements. As will be discussed later, most of the supply and procurement estimates are centrally developed on a world-wide basis. With the exception of locally procured items, the budgeting of matériel is not decentralized to the installation level.

The organization for budgeting at the installation level in both the Army and the Air Force is roughly comparable to that at higher echelons. The larger installations have set up post comptrollers, whose functions include the supervision and coordination of budget estimating and execution. Comptrollers of the larger posts have separate budget units. At the installations of the Army where a comptroller has not been established, the central budget work is performed normally by a fiscal officer or a budget and fiscal officer. In other words, budgeting is almost universally affiliated with accounting and other financial functions under an officer directly responsible to the commander or chief of staff.

The functions of local comptrollers and budget officers are likewise similar to those of their counterparts at higher echelons. They receive directives and instructions, interpret them as they apply to post budgeting, and issue instructions to operating units on the post; they supervise and guide in the development of estimates; they review estimates from the technical standpoint and for conformance with general and installation policy; they consolidate the estimates into an installation budget, and after obtaining the signature of the post commander, forward it to the next higher echelon; they receive the allotments of funds and distribute them among the operating units; and they supervise and review expenditures during the course of the budget year.

The actual development of budget estimates is, by and large, the responsibility of operating units on the post—not the comptroller. Large units may themselves have specialized budget officers or administrative officers to do this work. Some of the larger posts have established the equivalent of budget advisory committees, consisting of the principal staff officers at the post. The effectiveness of these groups has probably not been very great, due largely to the same factors as at the command level—lack of adequate interest, knowledge, and time. However, the post comptroller or budget officer normally seeks substantive review by functional staff officers of estimates within their cognizance.

Conclusions Relative to Budgetary Organization

The following general observations may be made about organization for budgeting in the Army and Air Force Departments:

1. The comptroller system is designed to provide a series of counterpart budget organizations at each level of command from the Department of Defense to the individual installations. This is illustrated in the accompanying simplified diagram of organization for budgeting (Figure 11).
2. The role of the comptrollers at each level with respect to the budget is conceived as a *staff aid* to the commander at that level. This has two connotations. First, the comptroller's direct line of responsibility is to his commander and not to the counterpart comptroller at the next higher echelon. However, a "dotted-line" relationship does exist between comptrollers at different levels involving technical and functional instruction and communication. Second, in his staff role, the comptroller is not empowered with substantive authority as to the content of the budget. His functions with respect to policy and program are essentially interpreting, coordinating, reviewing for conformance, and executing. But some comptrollers are in fact involved in program decisions.
3. At every echelon, the substantive staff officers are drawn into the budget process, as the initial estimators, or by structural arrangements, such as the budget advisory committees, or by participating in negotiations, supervision, and review.
4. The association of budgeting work with statistics and other activities, brought about by the establishment of comptrollers, has not materially affected the budget operation, since the functions themselves have not been integrated.
5. With few exceptions below the Department of Defense level, budgeting is directed by military personnel; most of the comptrollers and important budget officers are military. A large number of the journeymen staff are civilians having backgrounds and qualifications comparable to budget staffs in other Federal agencies. In general, these qualifications emphasize competence in technique and detail and accounting; some are predominantly experienced in the general management work characterized in the government by the expression, "O and M." Relatively few are experienced in military operations and programming.
6. With few exceptions, the comptroller functions do not extend to the development of budget estimates nor to the actual allocation of funds. By and large, the determination of budget requirements is made by substantive operating and staff units.

FIGURE 11

MODEL OF ORGANIZATION FOR BUDGETING IN ARMY AND AIR FORCE

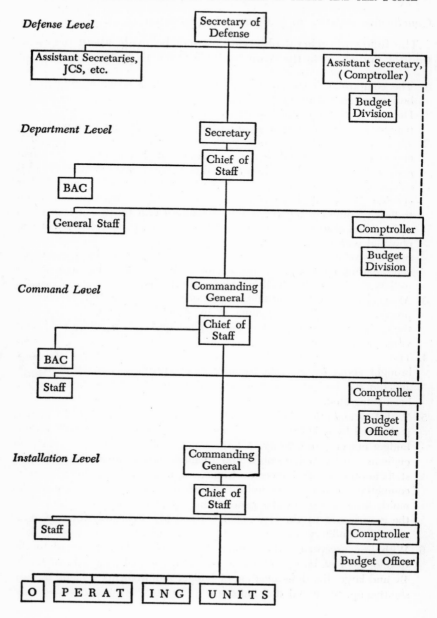

The budget process in large public organizations may perhaps best be analyzed from the standpoint of an "ideal" pattern or model depicting a series of communications within and between organizations. More particularly it is a *system* of communications, regularized and cyclical. These communications flow up and down the hierarchy between the operating levels at the bottom and the policy levels at the top, through various intermediate levels. Coordination of cross-functional and cross-area elements is achieved through the bringing together of comparable data from the various operating units at the same organization levels *and* at the same time.

A primary purpose of communications is of course to facilitate informed decision-making. The "ideal" budget process should therefore be designed to facilitate or even necessitate that decisions be made at the right points in the organization and at the proper times. As information moves upward in the organization, it becomes more various and comprehensive in scope and less specific in manageable detail. The possible types of decisions at top levels become "strategic" or generalized since they must apply to a wide variety of areas and functions. As information moves downward, the reverse is true. The pertinent information must be increasingly specific and "operational."

Another aspect of the process is that it is sequential; one step follows another in more or less orderly fashion. The generalized pattern of basic steps may be described as:

Objectives $\longrightarrow$ Plans $\longrightarrow$ Authorization of Means $\longrightarrow$ Operations

Each of these steps requires prediction and foresight, based upon intelligence about the things planned for, and upon experience. The budget process must therefore bring to bear, at the appropriate points of decision, experience and intelligence data.

The model budget process thus becomes a series of sequential movements up and down an organization. The upward flow is characterized by coordination, consolidation, and generalization; the downward one, by interpretation and specification.

One further feature is that of legitimization. The end result of the process—operations—cannot proceed until authority has been formally established through appropriations. Where any significant modifications are made in the course of the process, these must be translated back into operating plans. This in effect requires secondary and corrective processes.

An oversimplified graphic presentation of the "model" budget process is shown on the accompanying diagram (Figure 12). The vertical dimension here is organizational hierarchy, from operating unit at the bottom to superior agencies (Congress, National Security Council, Bureau of the Budget) at the top; the horizontal dimension is time. In this model the planning and programming processes are assumed to have been completed with the first step, the authorization of budgeting programs, and the budget process begins with the second step.

In the welter of budgetary activity that is normal the year round in the military departments, this idealized schema is hardly visible to the naked eye. In the first place, the process as shown covers a period of more than two years for any given fiscal year, not counting the time involved in prebudgetary programming. At any given time, a department is concerned with either two or three different annual budgets. Thus in April, 1952, the Department of the Army was involved in steps 11, 12, 13, and 14 for the fiscal year 1952 budget; in steps 5 and 6 for fiscal year 1953; and in steps 2 and 3 for fiscal year 1954. And the budget processes for different fiscal years are not isolable; they interact upon each other. A decision made by Congress with respect to the 1953 appropriation might well cause a major modification of funding and operations in fiscal year 1952 and in estimates for fiscal year 1954.

A second difficulty is that there is a considerable degree of overlapping and of backtracking in the process for a given fiscal year. The funding process, steps 6 through 10, normally must proceed before appropriations, step 5, are legislated. Thus specific operating plans must be made before there is firm information as to funds available.

Likewise, tardiness and incompleteness of policy and program decisions (steps 1 and 2) have forced step 3, the development of estimates, to proceed in advance and on the basis of hazy assumptions. Step 4, the review of estimates, has to some extent displaced step 1 in the determination of basic policies and objectives.

Another very important variation from the *schema*, which is described at greater length in subsequent pages, is the fact that a very large proportion of military dollar requirements are in fact estimated centrally. Step 3 is carried on not at the "operating" level but at a command or technical service headquarters on a world-wide or nation-wide basis.

Other variations from the pattern, some perhaps inevitable, will appear from the description of the actual process in succeeding pages. This discussion will be presented in five sections corresponding to certain of the steps shown on the chart, as follows:

FIGURE 12

CONCEPTUAL PATTERN OF THE BUDGET PROCESS IN RELATION
TO ORGANIZATIONAL HIERARCHY

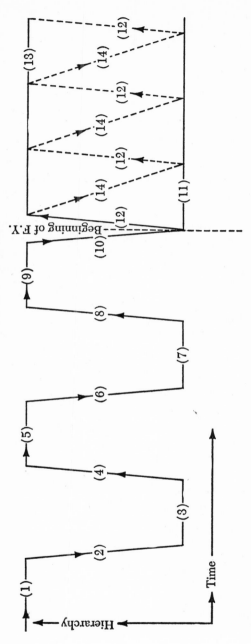

Steps

(1) Determination of program and budget policy
(2) Interpretation and specification
(3) Development of estimates
(4) Review, coordination, and consolidation of estimates
(5) Appropriation
(6) Interpretation and instructions for funding estimates
(7) Development of funding plan
(8) Review, coordination, and consolidation

Steps

(9) Apportionment of funds; adjustment of program
(10) Allocation and allotment of funds; operating program schedules
(11) Operations and obligation of funds
(12) Reports on program and budget
(13) Review and analysis of program and budget and revisions as necessary
(14) Directives revising program and funding

Budget Directives	(Step 2)
Budget Estimating: Central	(Step 3)
Budget Estimating: Field	(Step 3)
Budget Review	(Step 4)
Funding	(Steps 6 through 10)

The steps involving Congressional appropriations (step 5) and budget administration (steps 11 through 14) are not treated directly since they are beyond the scope of this study.

BUDGET DIRECTIVES

Budget directives normally contain two fairly distinct types of information and instructions: procedural and technical guidance as to the forms to be used, the techniques for computation, and the supporting data to be supplied; and substantive information as to programs, policies, and assumptions to be used in making estimates. These may be combined in the same document or issued separately.

The basic procedural guidance for all Federal budgeting is contained in the Bureau of the Budget *Circular* No. A-11, "Instructions for the Preparation and Submission of Annual Budget Estimates." Annually, usually in the late spring, the Bureau transmits a revised edition of the *Circular*, or revised pages, along with a Transmittal Memorandum from its director.[5] This is the *official* beginning of the annual Federal budget cycle.

Normally, the Bureau transmits at about the same time individual memoranda to the heads of agencies setting forth basic program assumptions, policies, and dollar ceilings. Ceilings are not now applicable to military appropriations, and the substantive premises for military estimates are contained in a budget guidance letter from the Secretary of Defense. This letter, usually referred to as the *Budget Guidelines*, is the "trigger" which sets off the formal budget processes in the three military departments. It was issued late in 1951 (in September) for the 1953 estimates because of delay in top policy decisions that year. In 1952, the *Guidelines* for the 1954 budget were issued on April 7, three weeks before the Bureau of the Budget transmittal.

The OSD *Guidelines* are drafted by the Office of the Assistant Secretary of Defense (Comptroller). They are based upon the national military and defense policies approved by the National Security Council and the President, the force requirements approved by the Joint

---

[5] The Transmittal Memorandum for the fiscal year 1954 estimates was dated April 28, 1952.

Chiefs of Staff, and considerations and limitations introduced by other Defense Department agencies. The Bureau of the Budget may assist in the preparation of the *Guidelines,* and in the past, it has had the opportunity to review and advise on them before they were issued.

The *Guidelines* are quite general in content. They do not prescribe dollar ceilings but rather set forth general statements of policy and objectives. In the absence of specific definitions of such expressions as "Minimum Industrial Sustaining Rate," they have left a great deal of latitude for interpretation and judgment by the services. This has probably been an intentional policy. Operating in an uncharted field for the last four years, the Secretary of Defense has preferred to firm up policy and program on a case-by-case or "common law" basis in the review process rather than commit himself in advance to precise policy statements.

It should be recalled from the earlier discussion of programming that the services have already developed program statements in some detail prior to the receipt of the OSD *Guidelines.* These must be reconciled, to the extent possible, with the OSD instructions in the preparation of service budget directives. This task falls upon the budget agencies under the departmental comptrollers, usually working in close collaboration with the program agencies. The programming staffs immediately revise the basic, over-all program objectives as required by the OSD *Guidelines.* The budget divisions then draft program guidances or incorporate the revised program objectives into their budget directives.

The departmental budget calls are then issued in two parts—the procedural and technical instructions in considerable detail, and the substantive program guidance. They may be issued as a single document, as in the Air Force, or in two separate documents, as in the Army. This is usually done as soon as possible after receipt of the OSD *Guidelines.* The departmental budget calls for fiscal year 1954 were issued in April and early May of 1952.

The Army Program Guidance, which is the substantive part of the budget call, is prepared by the Plans and Policy Branch of the Budget Division, Office of the Comptroller of the Army. It is a fairly brief and general document, like the OSD *Guidelines,* but is supported by annexes in some detail. Its principal parts are:

1. A general section setting forth the basic program objectives and particularly the fundamental decisions relative to troop units and strengths— major units in the active Army, manning and degree of readiness of the active Army, Army Reserve Forces, etc.

2. Guidance with respect to each of the major appropriations and each budget program of the Maintenance and Operations appropriation.
3. Annexes containing more detailed information relative to military personnel, as follows:

> Annex A—world-wide deployment, strength, gains and losses by month; army command strength by month; man-years by grade; officer accessions; strength by deployment and by assignment.
>
> Annex B—deployment and strength schedules for the active army by major combat units, major command strengths and deployment.
>
> Annex C—schedules of the Field Exercise Program and student and trainee loads at service schools and training centers.

4. Two additional sections concerned with Procurement and Production and with Military Construction; these are sent only to the General Staff and the technical and administrative services, not to the army commands.

The Army Budget Directive, the procedural instruction for budgeting, is prepared by technicians of the Estimates and Funding Branch of the Budget Division, Office of the Comptroller of the Army. It is issued in two "editions," one addressed primarily to the continental and overseas armies, and the other to the offices of the staff and the technical and administrative services. These documents included for fiscal year 1954 general statements about the purposes, procedures, and policies governing the budget process. They also included specific information and instructions on: the budget time table; the Fiscal Code and changes in budgetary classification; the form and content of estimates and supporting justifications, including workload data; and prescription of certain supplementary tables. The directive sent to the armies laid emphasis upon the appropriations and budget programs for which they have a primary responsibility for estimating, such as certain programs of the appropriations for Military Personnel and Maintenance and Operations. The later edition to the technical services and other offices emphasized instructions relative to Procurement and Production, Military Construction, Research and Development, and certain programs that are centrally estimated under Maintenance and Operations.

In spite of a generally approved policy of decentralization, practice varies widely among the operating agencies as to their disposition of budget directives. The usual procedure among the field armies is to reproduce them in whole or in part, add certain amplifications applicable to some or all of their subordinate organizations, and forward them to the installations. A few, such as the Third Army, have developed their own budget manuals to which the annual directive is geared. Some, particularly the technical services, have endeavored to relate their budgeting process to accounts, cost accounts, and work measurement and reporting systems.

A large portion of the budget job itself, however, is done by the headquarters of the operating agencies themselves, and, for the most part, directives from the Army staff have permitted such centralization. This is particularly true of the technical and supply services which develop most of their estimates centrally, sometimes without even calling upon subordinate installations for budget estimates, even for purely local costs. Likewise, at least one of the continental armies, the First, does virtually the entire estimating job in its own headquarters, calling upon the field installations only for certain supporting workload information. In spite of the considerable efforts to develop firm programs as a basis for budget estimates, there is a dearth of usable program information at the army and at the installation levels. The program information contained in the budget calls is largely on a world or nation-wide basis. It does not tell the station commander what workloads he may expect, what specific units he must train or service during the budget year, or for what work output he will be responsible. His budget directive may therefore include only a general instruction to assume a strength and workload comparable to the current year. It may be noted parenthetically that the average installation commander has relatively little foreknowledge of his workload from other sources and virtually no control over it; and the armies and commands are in little better position. The vast majority of program decisions are made centrally, and unless they are projected *in detail* over two years in advance, they cannot be used as guidance in the installation budgeting process.

The portions of the budget calls having the most pertinence to the budget work performed by the armies and the installations under them are, therefore, the technical and procedural instructions. The substantive program data have in recent years been of relatively limited value.[6] On the other hand, the program information in the budget directive is of dominant and indispensable importance to those organizations responsible for budgeting for matériel, construction, military personnel, and other elements which are estimated on a world-wide or nation-wide basis.

---

[6] One officer, a budget official in an Army headquarters, told the author that the Army Program Guidance was of *no* value in the field.

Budget Estimating: General

The military departments pursue the general principle that the organizational unit to which funds are allocated for specified purposes should have coequal responsibility for the estimating of dollar requirements for those same purposes. Thus, a procuring agency, such as the Quartermaster Corps, estimates the dollar needs for those items which it is responsible for supplying and for which it receives funds. The Chief of Finance estimates the dollars needed for Pay of the Army and likewise receives the funds for that purpose. And the First Army develops the estimates for those types of obligations which will actually be incurred under its command. Generally speaking, the estimates of funds flow *upward* through a channel identical to that followed by *allocated* funds downward.

Although there have been significant efforts under the performance budget system to decentralize estimating responsibility to the operational level, the general principle does not apply uniformly. For example, the Office of the Quartermaster General centrally estimates the dollar requirements for subsistence without calling upon individual installations or even commands for estimates of their requirements. However, many of the dollars ultimately received by that office for subsistence are allotted and suballotted out to lower levels which have authority to purchase food to meet their current needs. We have already noted that the headquarters of a continental army may do the entire estimating job without calling upon the installations for estimates. Virtually all the funds, when they are received, are nonetheless allotted to the installations which actually obligate and expend the funds. Likewise, the cost of Pay of the Army, estimated by and allocated to the Chief of Finance, is actually expended at the installation level by drawing upon an open, or unspecified, allotment.

It may be said that the Army is now striving to decentralize, to the extent possible, the responsibility for estimating fund requirements down to the installation level. Most installations must prepare and submit budget estimates for the requirements for which they can spend dollars. In general, however, their budget responsibility does not extend to the estimation of their user needs for goods and services which are furnished them from funds under the control of other organizations.

This situation results in the coexistence of two methods of budget estimating which are quite different both conceptually and technically. The first, which we may call the "field" system, follows the traditional scheme of budget development. The commander of each organizational unit estimates his dollar needs, item by item or class by class. His estimates are then reviewed, compared with those of other unit commanders, and consolidated with them by the addition of like items or classes. This becomes the installation budget, which in turn goes through a similar process at the field army level to produce a field army budget. Although other mathematical processes are involved and factorial methods are being used increasingly, the fundamental one is that of *addition:* the addition of estimated costs of like items and classes of different organizational units.

The second type of process is "central," not so much in the usual organizational connotation of the term as in the sense that it is carried on at one central place for the establishment as a whole. This process involves the translation of the over-all program into requirements for the item budgeted, usually by the application of experience and other factors; and then the application to these requirements of an average unit cost or costs. It is essentially *factorial* estimating in which the basic mathematical process is not addition but *multiplication.* It may be noted that it matters little in this kind of budgeting who or what unit will require or will use what amounts; nor does it matter where the goods and services are needed, except to the extent that different areas may call for the use of different factors.

Before undertaking a more intensive examination of these two processes, it may be useful to indicate their relative importance in the totality of military estimates. From the standpoint of budgetary activity—or work directly attributable to the budget estimating process—it would appear that what we have termed "field budgeting" plays a very substantial role. But in terms of the proportion of total dollars budgeted, the central, factorial system is dominant. This is apparently true in all three services. Although an accurate breakdown of military dollars on the basis of budgetary method is not available, Figure 13 offers evidence. This table, which is based upon the cost category (not the appropriation) classification of the Secretary of Defense, shows, for each of the services, the differing proportions of different cost elements for 1950, the last "normal" pre-Korea year, and for 1952.

In "normal" times, costs associated with military personnel have been the largest single category. The major elements, pay and allowances, individual clothing, and subsistence, are estimated by central agencies in all three services.

During the "build-up" period, and perhaps henceforth, procurement and production, which covers major procurement for items such as

FIGURE 13

MAJOR COST CATEGORIES AS PERCENTAGES OF TOTAL NEW OBLIGATING
AUTHORITY IN THE THREE MILITARY DEPARTMENTS,
FISCAL YEARS 1950 AND 1952 [a]

	Army		Navy		Air Force	
	1950	1952	1950	1952	1950	1952
	Per Cent	Per Cent	Per Cent	Per Cent	Per Cent	Per Cent
Military Personnel Costs	42	21	37	19	28	14
Operation and Maintenance	35	25	31	22	23	15
Procurement and Production	6	42	17	49	35	58
Acquisition and Construction of Real Property	2	5	2	5	4	10
Research and Development	3	2	6	3	5	2
All Other	12	5	7	2	5	1
Total Per Cent	100	100	100	100	100	100
Total Dollars (in billions)	$ 4.3	$20.8	$ 4.0	$16.0	$ 4.6	$22.0

[a] Based on data provided by the Assistant Secretary of Defense (Comptroller) in *Department of Defense, Appropriations for 1953,* Hearings, pp. 164-5.

weapons, aircraft, vehicles, and ships, is the largest cost category. It is estimated almost entirely by central agencies, though part of this work is delegated within the procuring organizations.

Most of the dollars which are estimated by field agencies and installations fall within the category of operation and maintenance. It includes maintenance and overhead at installations, local fixed charges and contracts, local purchases, some of the costs of training, and others. But very substantial parts of this category, too, are estimated by central procuring agencies. These include organizational equipment for troops, maintenance equipment and spare parts, operations of depot supply, medical supplies and equipment, and many others.

The construction program is largely estimated by, and funded to, central agencies, notably the Corps of Engineers, but the planning process is considerably decentralized within that organization, and using organizations participate in programming. The plans and budget estimates for research and development follow somewhat special channels, different in all three departments. The "All Other" includes civilian component expenditures, establishment-wide activities, contingencies, and similar items, which, too, are handled in a variety of ways, some decentralized to operating units.

It is apparent that the majority of military dollars are budgeted by central agencies, responsible for procurement and disbursement and, for the most part, not responsible for the field operations, where most of these resources are used. A somewhat more explicit indication is the actual allocation of appropriated funds to the Army operating agencies.

FIGURE 14

FUNDING PROGRAM OF THE ARMY, FISCAL YEARS 1952 AND 1953 [a]

	F. Y. 1952		F. Y. 1953	
	Millions	Per Cent	Millions	Per Cent
Technical and Administrative Services	$ 34,091	91.8	$ 13,449	88.1
Ordnance	$(16,629)	(44.8)	$ (5,706)	(37.4)
Finance	(3,769)	(10.1)	(3,601)	(23.6)
Quartermaster	(6,691)	(18.0)	(1,702)	(11.2)
Transportation	(897)	(2.4)	(646)	(4.2)
Signal Corps	(2,404)	(6.5)	(623)	(4.1)
Engineers	(3,050)	(8.2)	(873)	(5.6)
Others	(651)	(1.8)	(298)	(2.0)
Continental Armies and Military District of Washington	$ 1,228	3.3	$ 745	4.9
Overseas	1,249	3.4	823	5.4
Other Offices and Agencies	554	1.5	244	1.6
Total	$37,122	100.0	$15,261	100.0

[a] Based on data furnished by the Estimates and Funding Branch, Budget Division, Office of the Comptroller of the Army, August, 1952.

It is interesting that the Ordnance Department, procurer of weapons, vehicles, ammunition, and many other equipment items, is responsible for two-fifths of all Army funds in this two-year period, and more than 4 times the total funds available to all the armies and other using agencies put together (not including the other technical and administrative services). The Finance Corps funds for military personnel far exceed the funds available to all the armies. Yet it is the armies which, by and large, need and use the Ordnance weapons and equipment, the Quartermaster food, and the "G.I.'s" and officers paid by the Finance Corps.

BUDGET ESTIMATING: CENTRAL

Certain factors and influences outside of the military services may explain in part the high proportion of activities for which requirements and estimated costs are determined centrally. For instance, each of the services must deal continuously and realistically with the Department of Defense, the other military services, and the other government agencies sharing in its mission, and with the industries which supply its matériel. While progress has not been as rapid as some advocates of unification desire, the services are evolving a network of relationships for providing service to each other, standardizing operations, and avoiding duplication. These arrangements have usually been painfully worked out and made official only after negotiation at top organizational levels. All such cooperation under present procedures involves complicated financial transactions which come up in the budget process for scrutiny by the services themselves, the Department of Defense, the Bureau of the Budget, and the Congress. During its hearings on the 1953 budget the House subcommittee inquired repeatedly into the specific provisions of the Army's cooperative arrangements with the other services, or compared costs among the services.[7] As long as unification is in its developmental phases, it will not be surprising to find that the services consider central estimating of costs a necessary part of stabilizing and evaluating their relationships with the other services. It is but one aspect of the growth of centralization described in Chapter II.

If there were no other reason, the Army's relationship with industry practically forces it to handle most of its production and procurement program on a central basis. The Army no longer buys its major items as a "customer among customers" in the open market. In fact, the problem of maintaining the delicate balance between an overwhelming volume of military orders and the country's industrial resources has been such as to deprive the procuring services of a large measure of their independence in obtaining equipment. It has channeled their operations along lines laid down by the various coordinating agencies in the gov-

---

[7] For example, see the extended discussion of subsistence costs, in the hearings on *Department of the Army, Appropriations for 1953*, pp. 320-2 and 337-347. Coordination of the Army and Air Force in procurement and maintenance of aircraft is described on pp. 912-915. Army storage of ordnance for the Air Force is discussed on pp. 1168-69

ernment. Within the area of discretion which they retain, the services must seek out manufacturers who are willing to allocate plant resources to military rather than civilian production, able to make experimental models, or able to establish mass production in sufficient amounts. The Army's ability to obligate the funds made available to it since 1950 has depended heavily on plant schedules and capacity which it may influence but not control or predict with great accuracy. Even with firm contract arrangements, precise estimating of the costs of many items has been difficult, particularly of new models which are subject to test and redesign, and of long lead-time items which are affected by fluctuations in labor and material costs. Once production is established, a large proportion of contracts are subject to re-negotiation, a process upon which great emphasis is laid by the services and by Congress as a means of avoiding excessive costs. These complex processes of allocating scarce materials, of contract negotiation and re-negotiation, of scheduling, testing, and inspection, compel the services to establish relationships with industrial concerns which will reduce confusion and duplication. Centralization under these circumstances is almost a necessity for effective planning and operations. It makes relationships with suppliers simpler and more convenient, and it facilitates a degree of consistency and uniformity in the service's operations.

Another factor contributing to central budget estimating relates to the need for bringing about orderly change within the services. Since World War II the services have been under steady pressure to modernize, to meet new weapons with newer and better ones, and to utilize the latest developments of science and industry. Decisions to make changes in organization and equipment are normally based upon experimentation and experience in the field, but they are made or ratified centrally at higher levels of the organization. It follows that requirements for new programs or items must be projected centrally until they have existed long enough for the field to accumulate sufficient data for accurate estimating.

Another extremely important force toward central budget estimating and funding is that of past practice, tradition, and experience. The pay and allowances of military personnel, the purchases of food for subsistence, and the purchases of individual clothing are examples of practices which have proceeded under specialized and central direction for many decades. It may be noted that the practice of centralization under a specialized unit began when the services were of far less size, scope, and complexity than they are today.

Tables of Organization and Equipment

Another important reason for central budget estimating is that the armed services are virtually compelled to standardize their units and "bodies" in the field. It would be impossible to utilize such a large and mobile force of men in a mission of such complexity, if the organization, procedures, and equipment did not provide a large measure of uniformity. A basic tool of standardization in the Army is the authorization tables which include Tables of Distribution, Tables of Allowances, and, most importantly, Tables of Organization and Equipment (T/O & E's).[8] The T/O & E's have been called the "Bible of service requirements."[9] These tables are officially defined as "prescribing the normal mission, organizational structure, and personnel and equipment for a military unit."[10] They specify numbers of military personnel by rank and specialty, and equipment in terms of individual items for all organizational components on a service-wide, world-wide basis. Responsibility for development, review, and approval of the tables is assigned to the heads of the administrative and technical services for the types of units which pertain to their respective services, and to the Chief, Army Field Forces, for combat, combat support, and service support units which are normally part of a field force. The Assistant Chief of Staff, G-3, Operations, gives general policy direction in the development and modification of the tables, and, after obtaining concurrences from all interested parties, approves and authorizes them. The objective of the T/O & E's is "to reflect the most effective organization for combat, attaining flexibility of organization wherever practical."[11] Developing them involves technical military considerations and decisions, and the process

---

[8] In general, the T/O & E is the standard table authorizing personnel and equipment for combat and support units of the Army. There are several types, such as Fixed, Cellular, Flexible, Special, Standard, providing a variety of adjustments or modifications for units of different kinds. Likewise, modifications or changes in equipment requirements can be, and frequently are, authorized for individual units. The Table of Distribution (T/D) prescribes the organization and personnel distribution of organizations for which there is no appropriate T/O & E. Such tables apply particularly to the complements of installations in the United States. The Table of Allowances (T/A) prescribes "allowances of equipment for units and activities organized under tables of distribution; clothing and individual equipment; training equipment; expendable supplies and administrative equipment for use at posts, camps, and stations." See Department of the Army, *Special Regulations* No. 310-30-1, "Organization and Equipment Authorization Tables," August 1, 1949, especially pp. 2-4. The above quotation is from pp. 3-4.

[9] *Department of the Army, Appropriations for 1953,* Hearings, p. 799.

[10] Department of the Army, *Special Regulations* No. 310-30-1, p. 2.

[11] *Ibid.,* p. 9.

is distinct from the administrative processes of programming and budgeting.[12]

There is evidence that the most conservative review which the tables
receive in terms of potential cost and feasibility of procurement is that
of the Assistant Chief of Staff, G-4, Logistics. In testimony before the
House subcommittee of the Appropriations Committee concerning the
1953 budget request of Army, the Deputy Assistant Chief of Staff,
G-4, General W. O. Reeder, said: "It is G-4's interest to hold them
[T/O & E's] down. We have to produce the stuff and we have to fight
for the money to get it produced." [13] Justified or not, the questions of
the Congressmen on this occasion indicated their suspicion that the
provisions of the tables would tend to be generous rather than austere,
and that they were not subject to sufficiently critical examination by
economy-minded officials. The comptrollers have no regular role in the
development of T/O & E's, nor do the civilian secretaries of the services nor the Office, Secretary of Defense.

Changes in the T/O & E's are expected to grow out of the continuing work of the agencies which develop them and out of experience in
the field, and many revisions have been brought about as a result of
almost constant attention to the task since World War II.[14] Present
planning envisages a complete revision of the tables at least once every
four years, but there is no provision for their periodic revision as an
accompaniment of program adjustments or budgetary limitations. Once
the military mission is projected, the specific requirements of the organizational components which will carry it out are "given" as far as
budget estimating is concerned.

In budget terms, the standardization required by the T/O & E's
means that the Army projects costs for a soldier that are contingent
more on his rank and specialty than upon who his commanding officer
is or where his station is. Likewise, it means that a basis exists for estimating the requirements and costs of organizational components
equipped for and performing similar missions, irrespective of the location to which they may be more or less temporarily assigned. The system favors, and renders efficient, the practice of budget estimating at
the technical service headquarters level and at the General Staff level
on a world-wide basis.

---

[12] For a description of the development of T/O & E's for tank and vehicular
radio equipment see *Department of the Army, Appropriations for 1953*, Hearings,
pp. 937-8.

[13] *Ibid.*, p. 799.

[14] *Ibid.*, p. 800.

Factors Used in Central Estimating

We have referred above to the central estimating process as distinctive in its heavy reliance upon "factors." Descriptions of the process as it is applied in the various budget programs indicate that the most basic set of factors are derived from the *force program*—the projected strength of combat forces in terms of the primary tactical units, such as Army divisions, Air Force wings, and Navy warships, all classified by type, percentage of strength, deployment, degree of readiness, and year. These are initially determined by the Joint Chiefs of Staff. From the force program are derived the requirements of tactical and supporting units, or the *unit program* and the *troop program* for personnel. The troop program actually encompasses the unit program as well as the troop requirements of non-unit personnel. In the Air Force, it also includes civilian personnel. Standardized tables and formulae showing the different kinds of units required for support of a given tactical force provide a more or less statistical basis for computation.[15]

The unit projections provide, more or less directly, for the estimating of requirements that are determined on a unit basis, such as aircraft, weapons, vehicles, ammunition, and communication equipment. They also furnish the basis for estimating future requirements for the maintenance of installations, transportation, supply distribution, and some aspects of the training program.

The troop program projects military strength, classified by deployment, type of unit, or other assignment, status and grade. It becomes the basis for estimating most of the funds required for the appropriations for military personnel, including pay and allowances, subsistence, clothing, and travel. Directly or indirectly, it provides the basic factors for large parts of other budget programs, such as medical care, recruiting, training, and supply.

Other factors, varying with each budget program, derive from operating experience and reports and might be called "indices of operation." Such indices facilitate budget work because they make it possible to estimate costs of a whole complex of related operations on the basis of a simple workload indicator or unit cost item. In the Air Force, for example, the factor of "flying hours" has been found to be a reliable index to use in computing gasoline consumption, maintenance and replacement costs, and certain training costs.

---

[15] There is considerable room for debate about the supporting requirements for a given field force. Current practice is still to depend largely upon World War II experience, including the "Division Slice" (the total forces required to man and support a division) based upon that experience.

Other examples of such an index are the three interrelated factors used in estimating the costs of operating supply depots: tons received, tons shipped, and tons maintained in storage. There are many operations connected with the functions of receipt, storage, and issue such as inspection, identification of matériel, classification, packing and packaging, crating, processing, assembling, inventorying, and stock control. Yet on the basis of work and cost reports used by the Army depots, the chiefs of the technical services, and the General Staff agencies for the past ten years, it has been determined that the cost of the various operations is proportionate to the tonnage factors, and that it is possible to use only the tonnage factors for over-all comparisons and computations of the activity, for budget and other purposes.[16]

The Army also makes use of certain average cost figures which are based on its accumulation of experience data, modified when necessary by the anticipated trends of prices and labor costs. Examples are the anticipated cost of daily rations, and the per capita cost of travel to first-duty station.[17] Flat percentage ratios in relation to amounts of original issue are used as factors in computing replacement or maintenance requirements, including spare parts.[18] The application of such averages and percentage rates does not substitute an exact statistical operation for the "informed guess," for the figures may be modified to take into account the anticipated nature or intensity of future operations for which previous experience furnishes no parallel.[19]

Other factors used in central budget estimating are firm and relatively noncontroversial since they are derived from precise statutory provisions, from previous agreements among the services on uniform cost figures, or from military regulations which embody long-established custom or protocol. Most important for the amount of funds involved are the rates of pay for military personnel specified in the Career Compensation Act of 1949 (63 Stat. 802) and the rates of allowances established by the Joint Services Per Diem Travel and Transportation Allowances Board.[20] Other examples are the amounts provided under several laws to the dependents of military personnel who

---

[16] *Department of the Army, Appropriations for 1953,* Hearings, pp. 1161-63.

[17] The Army's estimated cost of the daily ration for fiscal year 1953 was $1.21 in the zone of the interior, and $1.35 overseas. Per capita cost of travel to first-duty station was $14 for an enlisted man and $130 for an officer. *Ibid,* pp. 253 and 259.

[18] *Ibid.,* p. 838. See also the application of an estimated 10 per cent reduction in the length of patient stay in hospital as a factor in computing the anticipated cost of operating medical treatment facilities. *Ibid.,* p. 1299.

[19] *Ibid.,* pp. 838-9.

[20] *Ibid.,* pp. 237-8.

die in service, severance pay for physical disability, lump-sum terminal leave payments, and interest rates on the savings deposits of enlisted personnel. Budget estimates for costs of medals and awards and for disposition of the remains of deceased military personnel are instances in which certain elements of custom and propriety are taken into consideration in computing costs.

Given agreement on the basic factors, the calculation of unit requirements and budget requirements is a nondiscretionary, statistical operation. Thus, if there is a firm statement of: the force program, the unit program, and the troop program; the operational and other factors upon which are based the rate of issue or use; and the unit prices of individual items or services; then budgeting becomes a fairly rapid process, criticizable only as to method and accuracy. This is in fact true of a considerable part of the centralized estimates. On the other hand, at a great many points in the process, as will be shown later, judgment considerations enter the determinations.

The procedure for central estimating varies somewhat among the services, but it follows similar outlines. In general, the requirements are initially developed one echelon below the top staff (the Air commands, the Army technical and administrative services, the Naval bureaus). They are based upon budget directives issued by the comptrollers and which normally include detailed logistical information and instructions. In the Army, most of the actual work is done in requirements or commodity units of the technical and administrative services. Before the estimates are submitted, they are normally reviewed and discussed informally by the army staff office concerned. But their basic substance comes from below.[21]

Estimating for Procurement—The Form DD 519

The largest and most important of the costs that are estimated centrally is procurement, whether it is included in the Procurement and Production appropriation or in others, such as that for Maintenance and Operations. The primary vehicle for budgeting in the procurement field, and itself an important outgrowth of unification, is the standardized form, DD 519, "Schedule of Materiel Requirements," required by the Secretary of Defense for each major item of equipment from all three military departments. In the Army, individual forms are required with respect to more than 600 different items. In addition, the

---

[21] A good description of Army procedure is that of the Office of the Quartermaster General, presented to the House Appropriations Subcommittee. *Ibid.*, pp. 307-8.

services have extended the use of the form to a large number of other, lesser equipment items and supplies. This form ensures the application to procurement estimates of uniform methods. Its use is tied in with the matériel form, DD 436, "Approved Production Schedule," likewise made for each individual item of equipment, and used primarily in the review and approval of procurement programs.[22] Both forms are used throughout the year; copies must be submitted for approval to the Office of the Secretary of Defense and one goes to the Assistant Secretary of Defense (Comptroller) every time a change is made in previously approved production schedules. In addition, the Defense Comptroller requires the submission of complete sets of the form DD 519 in connection with the annual budget estimates. They are the primary basis of review of matériel estimates within the services, the Department of Defense, and the Bureau of the Budget.[23]

The compilation of data on DD 519 proceeds as follows: [24]

1. The gross requirement for each item is calculated in five main categories: amounts for (a) combat consumption, (b) initial equipment, (c) peace-time consumption, (d) maintaining levels of supply, and (e) the mobilization reserve for the first year of war.

   a. For combat consumption the best obtainable factors are used, which vary somewhat from item to item. In the case of estimates for fiscal year 1953, the factors were those derived from 1951 operations in Korea, or lacking them, the World War II experience, adjusted if it appears desirable.[25]

   b. The amounts of initial equipment for the regular forces are obtained by cross-multiplying the allowances for the item for each organization by the number of organizations in the unit program to be newly activated. A 50 per cent allowance of the full T/O and E in terms of modern equipment is allowed for the civilian components who are in training during the period.

   c. Amounts for peacetime consumption are computed for the current fiscal year and the next two ensuing fiscal years by multiplying the

---

[22] This report was originally developed and used by the Munitions Board, prior to the elimination of that agency.

[23] The Department of the Army, in connection with its 1954 estimates, used an additional form for matériel budgeting, the so-called Budget Analysis Data Form, which provided considerably more detail about each item than DD 519.

[24] For a description of the procedure, see *Department of the Army, Appropriations for 1953*, Hearings, pp. 780-1, 836-43.

[25] Combat consumption for the budget year has not been included in the totals. As explained earlier, p. 44, Korean combat consumption was not included in annual estimates. However, it was entered for information purposes.

peacetime consumption rate per unit by the anticipated strengths for each year.

d. Amounts for maintaining levels of supply are determined on the basis that the services require a six-months supply of items for overseas and for combat support (or one-half the anticipated annual combat consumption rate) to keep a pipeline flowing without interruption from central depots to the hands of the troops. The length of the pipeline for peacetime consumption is figured at three and one-half months.

e. The computation for mobilization reserve for the first year of war covers several amounts, beginning with that for initial equipment for forces that will go into combat, over and above the existing active units. Some of these troops will be in civilian components previously in training. They receive a complete issuance of modern matériel and leave behind the training equipment computed under b above for use by newly mobilized troops. To this amount is added amounts to be consumed in combat and training, calculated as in a and c above, and amounts required for the supply pipelines, calculated as in d. Other amounts are added for the special items whose usage would depend on the anticipated locale of the war, such as earth-moving equipment for building roads and landing fields, landing craft, and prefabricated buildings.

2. From the total gross requirement are subtracted the amounts of stock on hand based on a world-wide inventory, and the amounts for which appropriated funds have already been made available toward meeting the gross requirement. This gives the net requirement for the item.

3. The net requirement is then divided between an amount which is budgeted and an amount which remains unbudgeted. The amount to be budgeted depends directly on the factor of reorder lead time, which is specified at the top of DD 519. It is assumed that all items having a reorder lead time of twelve months or over must be budgeted for and ordered before D-day, or delivery cannot be made during the first year of war. Items having a reorder lead time of less than twelve months are budgeted for to the extent that they cannot be ordered and delivered in sufficient supply during the first year of war. The amounts of the item which are estimated to be available from production or other sources during the first year of war are entered on the form.

4. Of the net requirement which is budgeted as in (3), the quantity of the items and their cost which might be chargeable to other appropriations and replacing funds for procurement are listed according to the appropriation so chargeable.

5. The remaining data on the form are a schedule of deliveries for the item in the amounts ordered, by quarters, for the current fiscal year and the two subsequent fiscal years.

An analysis of the factors used in compiling DD 519 indicates that it constitutes a bridge between planning and force programming and budgeting on the one hand, and budgeting and procurement planning on the other. More than that, it epitomizes, almost symbolizes, the "requirements" approach in military budgeting. Almost every DD 519 can be traced back, ultimately, to a force requirement, initially determined by the JCS. Likewise, most of them depend upon certain policy determinations, embedded in the troop program and the tables authorizing supplies and equipment for units, that are not normally subject to review during the budget process. But between these factors and the ultimate determination of the budget are a number of factors which are the products of judgment or are for other reasons debatable: the assumed rates of consumption; pipeline requirements; supply level requirements; stocks on hand; [26] and mobilization requirements.

It may be noted that an error or a miscalculation made at the initial stages of estimating tends to pyramid, because other requirements for the item are figured largely on a percentage basis from the initial figure. Thus, if a table authorizes a given piece of equipment for every soldier, wherever stationed, the requirement is ballooned by the various transportation, supply level, and mobilization factors. If the initial assumption were wrong, the budget requirement might be tremendously inflated.[27]

Production for mobilization reserves has raised special and extremely difficult problems. In general, the policies now followed provide that for items of standard commercial type the departments will build up little or no mobilization reserve. But for military-type goods, and particularly "hard goods," they are permitted to accumulate mobilization reserves to provide for newly formed wartime forces up to the time when wartime converted industries can start producing at a fast rate, usually stated in the Army as the first year of war. Actually, however, they have accumulated reserves only to the amount of a

---

[26] Inventory data in the Army and Air Force are generally considered inadequate. Below the depot level, particularly, information as to stocks in the hands of installations, units, or troops, is poor and, in a good many cases, nonexistent. Matériel sent into a combat area is often considered to be "lost" for future estimating purposes, and if it is returned it may not be brought back into the inventory figures.

[27] The almost "classic" example was the calculation in 1951 of the requirement for gas masks. In the review process, the figure was reduced from nearly 13 million to less than 3 million masks, following analysis of the formula provided in the tables. See Committee for Economic Development, The Research and Policy Committee, *Tax and Expenditure Policy for 1952* (New York, 1952), p. 14.

fraction or percentage of estimated mobilization requirements, after making allowance for continuing wartime production. But the approach to the "plateau" period, described in Chapter II, has introduced a new factor which probably will be of increasing importance. The requirement for mobilization reserve is not static but itself fluctuates greatly. As current monthly output increases, the requirement of reserve on the shelves decreases—and vice versa.[28] Thus, an all-out production program might actually result in a greatly increased need for reserves on the shelves because, at the end of the program, current output would drop off or be stopped. This has led to a policy against peak production, and, instead, the meeting of requirements over a longer period, primarily to maintain producing capacity rather than build up stocks on the shelves.

This situation gave rise to the provision by the Office, Secretary of Defense, that the services be guided in their procurement programs by what it termed "Minimum Industrial Sustaining Rates," sometimes dubbed "MISERY" rates. Basically, they are the rates of procurement required to sustain "warm" production lines in private industry, and prevent the accumulation of inventories which might encourage industry to convert to peacetime activities. Beyond this, however, the definition is very vague indeed, and its development and application to individual equipment items and supplies have been left largely to the services, subject of course to later review by the Secretary of Defense and the Bureau of the Budget. This introduces discretionary factors for an increasing number of items. How much industry must be sustained? How much production does it require to sustain it? How much additional unit cost, if any, should be permitted to maintain a production line?[29]

Finally, we may note about DD 519 that, like other aspects of cen-

---

[28] This was a point emphasized by W. J. McNeil, Assistant Secretary of Defense (Comptroller), in his testimony before the House Appropriations Subcommittee in connection with the 1953 appropriations for the Department of Defense. Using tanks as a purely hypothetical example, he said: "A year and a half ago, at the outbreak of Korea, it might have been very proper for us to have on hand 15,000 tanks, because we were 18 months away from production. Last fall perhaps 12,000 tanks would have served just as well, because we were much closer to quantity production. Next summer if we are producing tanks at the rate of 500 a month our mobilization reserve on-hand requirement should be much less than it would have been a year earlier." *Op. cit.*, pp. 149-50.

[29] A major revision and possibly a reversal of recent Defense Department policies on mobilization base seems to be in prospect or underway under the new Administration. Secretary of Defense Wilson is reported to favor concentrating production in fewer plants and closing down many of those not necessary for current needs. See particularly the *New York Times,* April 5, 1953, Sec. I, p. 1.

tral budget estimating, it takes little or no account of resources or of other economic and fiscal considerations in budgeting. The result was demonstrated in 1952 in the cutbacks of procurement estimates. General Reeder, Deputy Assistant Chief of Staff, G-4, for the Army testified to the House Subcommittee:

> Of the total money calculation which we made at that time [prior to review by OSD], 96% has been covered by the DD 519 process which I have just described. Although we made very liberal allowance for the production to be anticipated as a result of orders placed on D-day, the total estimate for this appropriation came to $8.6 billions. . . .
>
> It did not take into account the effect which the necessary peaking of production would have upon the country's economy, nor did it give effect to some slippages which have occurred. The size of the over-all budget request, the impact of the necessary procurement upon the country's economy and the fiscal problems involved, as well as many other considerations, caused a review of the Department of Defense estimates, and as part of the review, this request for appropriations has been reduced to $3.685 billion or less than half of the original request . . .[30]

The department proposed to deal with this reduction by reprogramming for procurement some funds appropriated in prior years and intended for the purpose of creating production base, and by stretching out over a longer period deliveries of certain items, providing only the minimum necessary to maintain a production line. New appropriations to maintain production lines were requested only for those items for which the fiscal year 1951–52 program funds were insufficient. The actual effect of this adjustment was to postpone until future fiscal years requests for appropriations to maintain production at sufficient levels to provide the projected gross requirements.

BUDGET ESTIMATING: FIELD [31]

As indicated above, the armies and, below them, most of the installations are responsible for preparing the estimates for budget requirements of funds to be obligated at the installation level. About 90 per cent of these funds derive from the appropriation, Maintenance and Operations, Army. Smaller amounts are estimated for certain elements of three other appropriations—Military Personnel, Army; Army

---

[30] *Op. cit.*, p. 782.

[31] Information in this section is based upon visits and inspections of the budget work at one field army headquarters and at a Class I post and a Class II post; and upon discussions with various officials of the Army, Air Force, and Office, Secretary of Defense.

National Guard; and Reserve Personnel Requirements. By far the largest budget program of all is that for Installation Support, which provides for maintenance, utilities, and similar expenses at bases. In one typical field army, this single program amounted to 72 per cent of the total funds requested.

From the standpoint of objects of expenditure, by far the largest category estimated by installations is salaries and wages of civilian personnel. This item runs well over half the total amounts estimated by the installations under the armies. Other objects of expenditure are locally purchased supplies, locally authorized travel and transportation, commercial communications, and locally contracted utility and maintenance services.

The armies are themselves intermediate echelons. They transmit and interpret the directives going down and review and consolidate the estimates coming up. The content of their budget estimates is thus a fairly accurate reflection of the content—and the omissions—of budgetary activity at the installation level. A study conducted in 1952 at Fort Knox, the armored training center, produced an estimate that it cost the Army $136 million per year to operate the post. Of this amount, only $18 million were allotted to the post for local expenditure, largely civilian salaries. This proportion of about 13 per cent is probably typical of the financing of military bases both in the Army and the Air Force. Estimates of officers in both services, made informally to the author, ran between 10 and 20 per cent. In other words, the typical operating installation is called upon to plan and estimate for less than one-fifth of its actual costs. The largest part of what is budgeted locally is for overhead or, in military parlance, "support" activities, necessary to the operation and maintenance of the installation. Costs directly attributable to "end-purpose" activities of the installations are in the main determined at other points. Thus, the fact that bands operate at installations is reflected in their budgets by requests for funds to purchase band music. Training activities at a post may be inferred from estimates for the pay of civilian instructors, or for the purchase of training supplies and literature not available through regular channels, or for salaries and wages for civilians engaged in the local manufacture of training aids. Medical activities appear, fractionally, in the salaries of civilians in the hospitals, infirmaries, and dispensaries.

Equipment and supplies that are locally estimated and procured include, generally, nonstandard items, construction materials such as lumber, standard items not in stock at depots, gasoline and oil, and certain other items such as ice and postage stamps. Perishable and other foods are likewise procured locally, but on sub-allotments from Quartermaster depots which do the budget estimating.

The major elements of most installation budgets are for repairs, utilities, supplies, and communications on the base, and repair and maintenance of equipment and vehicles. Largest of these in dollar amount is the budget project "Maintenance of Facilities" which covers fuel, light, water, and other utility services as well as the repair and maintenance of utilities, buildings, roads, and grounds, and minor construction and alterations.

Installation budgeting in the Army is greatly complicated by the dual system of field organization. The typical military training and operational bases, called Class I installations, are under the sole command of field armies; they submit their estimates to, and subsequently receive their allotments of funds from, the army headquarters exclusively.

The Class II installations, on the other hand, are field units of the specialized services such as the Quartermaster, Ordnance, Engineer, Chemical, Finance, and Medical organizations. These are under dual organizational and budgetary jurisdiction. For purposes of administrative and housekeeping support, they are under the appropriate geographic army; but their end-purpose functions are directed from the headquarters of the technical or administrative service. All of these installations receive two different budget directives, submit two separate sets of budget estimates (a so-called Class I budget and a Class II budget), and receive fund allotments from two sources. There are several hundred installations which fall in the Class II category, and they include some of the largest and budgetarily most important of Army activities —the depots, arsenals, general hospitals, procurement offices, specialized training bases, and research and development laboratories. Although efforts have been made to coordinate the budget activities between the army commands and the headquarters of the administrative and technical services, the general impression is that these efforts have been sporadic and ineffective. Basic problems arising at a single post must frequently be carried to the level of the Army Staff for resolution. The typical Class II installation receives its two budget directives at different times and with different deadlines; the Army command usually has little or no information as to the workload plans of the technical service on the installation; and there appears to be little systematic provision for the coordination of the dual sets of estimates from the individual installation short of the Department of the Army level in Washington. Although Army regulations have endeavored to be explicit as to exactly what kinds of costs should be estimated under the army command and what kinds under the technical service, "gray" areas of doubt and possible argument are inevitable under such an arrangement. It is not impossible, nor unheard of, that the installation play off one of its "bosses" against the other, budget-wise. The dividing lines between end-purpose equipment maintenance and administrative maintenance, or between local end-purpose travel and administrative travel, are examples of the distinctions which must be drawn.

Under the functional command system of the Air Force, this problem does not appear in so chronic a form. Each wing-base is for both command and budget purposes under a single command. However, a comparable problem does appear when an air base is used by two or more commands and its costs must be allocated to two or more budgets, a situation of fairly frequent occurrence.

The installation budgetary process is begun officially upon receipt of budget directives from higher headquarters. At some places, much of the work has already been started at the installation by what is called "pre-budgeting"—i.e. preliminary computations and estimates in anticipation of the budget directives. The budget directives arrive late in the spring and are usually delivered directly to the installation financial officer, the comptroller, the fiscal officer, or the budget and fiscal officer. The installation is usually given only a short period in which to compile its estimates, varying from one to two weeks.

The installation budgeting officer may at this stage discuss the budget with his commanding officer or chief of staff, and in some instances the commander may discuss budgetary policy at a staff meeting. Usual practice appears to be for the budgeting officer to proceed with the job with little if any policy guidance from the installation commander. His procedure is to prepare copies of instructions and necessary forms and distribute them to the units or "activities" on the post. He may at the same time hold meetings with the budget representatives of the units individually or collectively. Most of the budget estimates are prepared by these operating units and returned to the installation budgeting officer for review and consolidation. They may come back to him through the appropriate supervising staff officers (G-1, 2, 3, or 4, or S-1, 2, 3, or 4), or he may refer them to the staff officers following his own review. It should be noted that estimates for certain types of costs, not readily allocated to any organization, are normally made by the budgeting officer himself. The locus of responsibility for initial estimates among installation operating units is illustrated on the accompanying chart, Figure 15, based upon practice at

FIGURE 15

BUDGET PROJECTS AND ACTIVITIES RESPONSIBLE FOR ESTIMATING
AT A CLASS I ARMY INSTALLATION

Budget Appropriation, Program, and Project	Unit or Activity Responsible
MILITARY PERSONNEL, ARMY	
Subsistence: Commutation of Rations	S-1, S-4
Welfare and Morale Activities	Special Services
Troop Information and Educational Activities	Information and Education Officer
MAINTENANCE AND OPERATIONS, ARMY	
Forces and Facilities: Field Training Supplies and Equipment (band music)	Fiscal Officer
Forces and Facilities: Petroleum, Oil and Lubricants, Miscellaneous	Post Quartermaster
Training: Training Aids and other Training Costs	S-3
School Temporary Duty Travel	S-3
Medical Care: Dispensaries other than General	Post Surgeon
Commercial Transportation: Line-Haul Transportation	Transportation Officer
Installation Support	
Maintenance of Facilities: Normal Repairs and Utilities, Operating Expenses	Post Engineer
Maintenance of Facilities: Deferred Maintenance	Post Engineer
Maintenance of Facilities: All Other Repairs and Utilities Projects	Post Engineer
Maintenance and Repair of Equipment	Ordnance Officer and Post Quartermaster
Post Administration and Staff Activities	Fiscal Officer
Post Supply Activities	Post Quartermaster
Post Service Activities	Post Quartermaster
Rents	Post Quartermaster
Security Guards	Post Quartermaster
Salvage Activities	S-4
Local Communications: Operation and Maintenance of Fixed Wire Communications Systems	Post Signal Officer
Local Communications: Commercial Communications	Post Signal Officer
Local Transportation: Operation of Motor Pools	Post Quartermaster (for gas and oil) Ordnance Officer (for maintenance) Transportation Officer (for operation)
Storage and Stock Control	Quartermaster, Signal Officer, Ordnance Officer
Local Transportation: Movement Services	Transportation Officer
Purchasing and Contracting	Purchasing and Contracting Officer
Local Procurement of Installation Supplies and Equipment Not Otherwise Procured	Post Quartermaster

a Class I Army installation. The responsibility for initial estimating of the Class I budgets (i.e. the total budgets of Class I installations and the "housekeeping" parts of the budgets for Class II installations) is decentralized to the operating units on the posts. But it must be borne in mind, of course, that the items for which they budget are only a small fraction of what they consume or expend in terms of goods or services.

Practice varies widely from installation to installation and from command to command as to the factors, the classifications, and the detailed procedures used in estimating. The basis generally is the accounting and other financial records of past and current obligations and experience. Budget estimate forms require data on the last completed fiscal year (actual), the current year (estimated), and the budget year (estimated).[32] They also require detailed listings of all positions for civilian personnel by grade and salary for each of these fiscal years. Supporting justifications must be submitted in narrative and statistical form; and for fiscal year 1954, fairly ambitious supporting workload data were submitted, including work estimates on the basis of standardized units or indices of workload. Inasmuch as the various armies and services have authority to establish their own detailed budgetary classifications within the general framework of the performance budget program and project classification, the accounts are not kept, and the estimates are not submitted, on a strictly comparable basis among the various operating agencies. It should be noted that some of the technical and administrative services have also established accounting and cost accounting systems of their own, applicable to their counterpart units at the installations. These often necessitate duplicating sets of records and accounts, difficult if not impossible to reconcile with the obligation records required for budgetary purposes. There are said to be over thirty different accounting systems in current use within the Army, and as many as ten or a dozen may be carried on at the same time at a single installation.

In spite of the efforts to decentralize budgeting to the operating level, and the parallel efforts to put budget estimating on a performance basis, the budget estimates do not generally reflect a planning or programming approach. The author's impression from his own observations and from conversation with budgeteers and other observers is

---

[32] At the time the installations make up their original estimates all three figures must be estimates since the "last-completed" year still has two or three months to run.

that most of the estimates are in the nature of bookkeeping statements of the "current" projected into the future. Thus, the current list of authorized civilian positions or "spaces" becomes the budget requirement. It is modified to provide for automatic within-grade salary increases and for a few expected or hoped-for promotions. If the budget directive permits—and currently most of them do not—the list may be modified by adding a few new positions. Recommended decreases of positions are probably less frequent. With respect to civilian personnel, there is actually little discretion involved in the budget process because the determining decisions are made in the authorization and allotment of manpower through an entirely different control system under the jurisdiction of different organizations.[33] The Air Force now includes specific civilian manpower ceilings in its budget directive, and, in the Army, it is common practice to prescribe in the budget directive against any increase in personnel above current authorizations or current strength. The estimating of civilian personnel pay, which is by far the largest object in installation budgeting, is largely a process of carrying forward and costing current personnel authorizations.

Estimating of local supplies, of travel, and of many other types of items seems likewise to be largely a "historical" process. Past and current obligations for these objects become the basis of requests for the future. Like civilian personnel, they may be modified by changes, usually increases, in price and in some cases changes, usually increases, in quantity. These may be justified in terms of price or consumption trends or in demonstrable errors in previous estimates as to rates of consumption. Changes due to anticipated changes in program or in workload are less frequent, principally because the installation has little basis for predicting a change in program or workload for the budget year. As indicated earlier, its instructions are more likely to be to assume continuation of current programs and workloads.

One significant exception to these observations concerns the estimating of requirements for construction and maintenance of facilities, communications, and major equipment. Much of the work in these categories is planned on a project-by-project basis and estimates are developed from comprehensive cost accounting data. Repairs, re-

---

[33] Stemming from the Assistant Secretary of Defense (Manpower and Personnel), this authority comes down through G-1 in the Army to a manpower office at the operating agency level, either in G-1 or under the comptroller, and finally to a post manpower control agency, likewise usually attached to a G-1 or S-1 or to a post comptroller or fiscal officer.

placements, and new construction at installations are planned and carried out under the direction of the post engineers under the supervision of the army engineers, and, in the case of major projects, the district engineers. The planning, the determination of priorities among competing projects, and the estimating of costs are conducted through a process separate from, though complementary to, the regular budget process. The budgeting of requirements for these kinds of projects exemplifies the performance or program approach perhaps more than any other part of the installation budgets. It is of more than incidental interest that a large part of this process, and particularly its decision-making phases, is carried on outside of the normal budget-making, fiscal channels, and to some extent outside of regular command channels. The relations between the post engineer, the army engineer, and the district engineer are often close and continuous. With respect to much of the engineer work planned for and carried out at the post level, the army engineer maintains detailed and up-to-date records as to progress and costs. The projects and estimates which enter into the installation budget have already been determined or at least agreed upon by higher headquarters.

The remarks made so far apply primarily to budget estimating at Class I installations and to the estimating of the so-called "housekeeping" activities at Class II installations (except those under Industrial Funds). Practice varies widely with respect to estimating for the end-purpose activities at Class II posts. These include such items as procurement, storage, major maintenance, training of technical troops, operation of general hospitals, and research and development in technical fields. These estimates are prepared on the basis of instructions received directly from the headquarters of the technical or administrative service concerned and are submitted directly to it. But, as already noted, a very large proportion of the end-purpose activity depends upon nation-wide and world-wide workload requirements and is in fact estimated centrally. Some of the technical services operate work measurement and costing systems on a continuous basis and thus have up-to-date data upon which to develop their budget estimates. Thus, while the central services depend upon their installations for basic budgetary information and for some budget estimates, budgetary decisions generally are highly centralized in the headquarters offices of the technical and administrative services. The same is true of the Air Matériel Command of the Air Force.

As in the Class I installations, the pay of civilian personnel is a major element of Class II budgets. In fact, at posts engaged in supply, maintenance, industrial, research, medical, and like activities, the cost of civilian personnel is relatively far more important than at the typical military post.

An example of a large Class II installation is Fort Belvoir, a major unit of the Corps of Engineers. It is a tremendous establishment, including the Engineer School, the Engineer Research and Development Laboratories, the Engineer Officer Candidate School, the Engineer Replacement Training Center, an Army hospital, and a variety of attached units. The post operates on three fairly distinct budgets: a Class I budget for housekeeping services, which it prepares under the direction of the Military District of Washington; a Class II budget for research and development; and a Class II budget for engineer training. By far the largest of these in terms of dollars is that for research and development, which amounts to about two-thirds of the total funds estimated at the post. This budget estimate is largely determined by decisions on programs and projects made by higher authority, and the budget itself goes through dual channels—research and development and regular budgetary routes. Two-fifths of the research and development budget is for civilian salaries, the remainder being largely for procurement and contracts. Second largest of the Belvoir budgets is that for housekeeping. Nearly half of the Class I budget is for the activities of the post engineer, and it is a curious paradox of Army organization that this major element of the budget of a major engineering post is submitted not to the Chief of Engineers but to the Military District of Washington. The Class II budget for training is relatively small and covers primarily the salaries of civilian instructors and other staff, training materials and aids, and like items locally procured. It amounts to less than one-tenth of the total budget of the post in spite of the fact that training is by far its largest and probably its most expensive function. About half of the post's military population are in training status.

As in many other posts of both the Class I and Class II varieties, the funds estimated locally amount to only a fraction of the real costs of operating the installation. The military population of Fort Belvoir is nearly five times its civilian population; yet military pay and allowances and most other costs attributable to military personnel are excluded from the installation budget. It is probable that if the total cost of all goods and services could be determined, it would run between 150 and 200 million dollars per year, of which only about 35 million dollars are included in the three budgets described above.

The Class II budgets of some of the technical services are made up almost entirely at the headquarters of the services. For example, Camp Lee, a Quartermaster installation in Virginia, budgets only its house-keeping costs, which are transmitted to the Headquarters of the Second Army, and certain training and travel costs chargeable to Quartermaster funds. But those Class II units which are in the business of procuring, storing, supplying, and manufacturing are seldom in a position at the time of budgeting to predict what their workload will be more than a year hence, and it has already been noted that workload is seldom within the installation's control. For many of these organizations, advice as to programs and workload changes is received in the order of hours and days rather than years in advance. This being the case, it is, of course, entirely logical that the installation limit its estimating activity to those items that are more or less fixed and permanent—not dependent on fluctuations of workload. And where an installation does estimate for items that depend upon workload, its normal budgetary assumption is that it will operate during the budgetary year at full capacity; i.e. its workload will be the maximum it can handle.

It should be emphasized that, under the present budgetary calendar, the initial estimates prepared by installations must be submitted fourteen to fifteen months before the beginning of the period to which they apply, more than two years before the end of that period. This makes program budgeting at the average installation virtually impossible for the simple reason that it does not have program information that far in advance. Furthermore, the time distance is such that the installation can see little relation between its initial budget estimates and what it ultimately receives in the form of allotments when the budget year actually begins. Obviously, it is much more concerned with the latter than with the former. From the installation's standpoint, the preparation of budget estimates is an arduous and time-consuming activity, required by higher headquarters for the purposes of higher headquarters. It has little relation to post operations and post administration, for the post is much more concerned with the activities a year later when it is dealing with "hard cash" than it is with papers used primarily to "build up a case" for hearings before the Bureau of the Budget and the Congress. One local budget officer told the author that he had never even bothered to look at his budget estimates after he had submitted them, that he had never been advised how much of his initial request had been allowed or disallowed, and that he had never taken the trouble to compare what he received in terms of funds with what he had requested in his estimates a year previously. Indeed, there seemed to be little reason why he should.

A final observation about installation estimating is that it creates little incentive to seek or anticipate economies. If anything, the incentives are in the other direction. When the operating officer on a post makes up his estimates, his primary interest is to "play it safe"—that is, to make sure that he leaves nothing out and that he is protected against possible contingencies. In the absence of firm information as to what those contingencies might be, this motivation is likely to result in inflating his budgetary requirements above what he actually will need. A failure to anticipate and provide for his needs is much more likely to embarrass him than is an overestimate. This tendency may be accentuated also by the normal anticipation that his initial estimates will be reduced during the review and funding processes. So, to the extent that he feels that his initial estimates will have any effect at all upon the resources ultimately allotted to him, he will want to get "on the record" the strongest possible case for the largest possible amounts that he can reasonably defend. The services and the commands under them have, in varying ways and degrees, inhibited the drive for increases by flat and arbitrary prohibitions or ceilings. But rarely have they been able to substitute incentives to economize.

BUDGETARY REVIEW

In terms of the proportion of time and manpower and cost required, budgetary review is probably the most important step in budget development. It is a curious and significant fact that the effort and the attention given to the initial preparation of estimates are but a fraction of that given to the review of those estimates. In the Army and Air Force, for example, the installations are customarily allowed between one and two weeks for preparation of their estimates—and part of this time is dedicated to review at the installation level. From that point on, the work of consolidating and reviewing proceeds at various levels by various bodies over a period of about fourteen months, including the last six months of Congressional deliberations. This period is of course not one of continuous reviewing. It is punctuated by deadlines and feverish activity but includes fairly long periods of relative quiet. Nor is all the budgetary work strictly definable as "review," although a large part of it relates to, or stems from, review. It includes a great deal of arduous statistical and accounting labor; many communications up and down and across lines; the preparation of justifications and of the vast amount of documentation required for presentation of the budget at its various stages; and the making of an inestimable number of major and lesser decisions.

In the military departments as in most civilian agencies, budget estimating, as well as financial administration, is considered a function of command. Each echelon in the chain of command is held responsible by the next higher echelon for the estimates of all elements within its command. It must be prepared to support and defend *all* these estimates before its superior, and this, of course, means it must know and understand them and be itself satisfied that they are supportable. Budgetary review as a command function also has more positive roles. Insofar as budget estimates are an expression of plans and programs, the review process can serve an important purpose in the development and coordination of plans at each level of command. Budget review may serve a command purpose as a device for supervising and evaluating subordinate units, not only as to the soundness of their plans but also as to the efficiency and effectiveness of their past and current operations. There is a widely held assumption that successive reviews of budget estimates offer some assurance of greater economy in operations and of the elimination of "fat" from the budget. The review process in the military departments, to be described in succeeding paragraphs, may properly be considered from the standpoint of its effectiveness in accomplishing these various purposes.

Review at the Installation Level

The installation comptroller or budget officer, whatever his title, is responsible for accumulating the estimates and for conducting and/or coordinating their review locally. At some posts, though probably a small minority, local substantive review has been formalized through the establishment of budget advisory committees, consisting of the principal installation staff officers. Elsewhere, the budget officer and his staff review for conformance with instructions and for technical accuracy. They also see that the justifications are adequate. They may question the substance of estimates, particularly when they appear to be "out of line" or when they represent substantial increases. Few budget officers have sufficient status and knowledge to challenge substantive programs, nor does the budget calendar give them time to make a thorough review of the substance of the estimates.

The budget officer may refer to the installation commander's principal staff officers those parts of the estimates over which they have functional supervision. At any Army post, for example, the estimates of the various technical service officers such as the quartermaster, engineer, and ordnance officer may be referred to the G-4 or S-4. The extent and effectiveness of such review probably vary widely. At the installations visited by the author, the budget officers felt that these reviews were less useful than they should be for four major reasons: first, there was insufficient time for a thorough examination; second, the staff officers felt, with some justification, that the budget was a relatively inconsequential matter and did not deserve much of their time and effort; third, most staff officers were not trained or equipped for budget work and were unaccustomed to think in terms of dollars and to read and understand accounting reports; and fourth, because of their organizational position, they were usually inclined to support and accept without critical examination the estimates for the activities under their supervision. On the last point, the staff officers, like the line officers who initiated the estimates, have less incentive to economize in the estimates under their jurisdiction than to make sure that nothing has been left out and that the budget is large enough.

Final review at the installation is made by the commander or his chief of staff before the documents are signed and sent forward. Here again, the review is likely to be fairly superficial, and for similar reasons. One budget officer described his commander's budget review in about these terms: "He leafed through the papers; read over the highlight statement; asked me about two or three pet projects in which he was particularly interested to make sure I had not left them out; and then signed it. The whole business was over within fifteen minutes." This instance may not be typical. Many commanders probably take much interest in their budgets. But it is doubtful whether many, if any, make the annual budget estimates a focal process in post coordination and planning. In truth, the estimates probably do not merit such treatment. The commander has insufficient time to do much with them, even if he wants to. By the time the budget estimates reach him, they are often being "walked through" in order to meet the deadline of higher headquarters.

Review at the Command Level

At the intermediate levels of command—the field armies, the services, the air commands—budget work is somewhat more systematized. Focal point of responsibility is the comptroller's budget staff which must supervise installation preparation of estimates, consolidate the installation submittals, review and check them, and coordinate and monitor the review by the staff at their headquarters. Initial reviews may be made concurrently by the budget staffs of the comptroller and by the counterpart staff sections of the command headquarters. That is, the army engineer reviews the post engineer estimates of all posts, the army quartermaster reviews the estimates of all the post quartermasters, and so on. These special staff officers at the intermediate level may and often do communicate directly with their counterparts at the installation level on questionable items, and in some cases, specialist officers of the installations may be summoned to the command headquarters to explain and defend their estimates before their superiors in their technical field. It is not the usual practice, however, for post commanders to be called upon to defend the budgets of their installations as a whole, nor in fact for the installation budget officers to be asked to appear in person in behalf of the estimates of their posts.

The review of installation budgets at the command level is accompanied or followed by a consolidation of all of them into a single command budget and the preparation of a justification of the total estimate for the command as a whole. In this process, the estimates of the individual installations lose their identity with the exception of certain major work projects which must be supported on a project basis. However, the estimates of individual installations are sometimes forwarded to the departmental level intact for information purposes. Most questionable items or proposed changes raised by either the staff of the command comptroller or by the command functional staff concerned are resolved between them. Others are referred to higher staff officials of the command for decision. Some of the commands have established budget advisory committees, consisting of the chiefs or deputies of the general staff divisions and certain other top staff officers. These bodies review the entire budget of the command but direct their attention principally or solely to the questionable items and to issues that have not been resolved by the comptroller and the special staff officers concerned. It does not appear to be general practice to require the installations to defend and support their budgets before the budget advisory committees. Following the review and the determinations of the budget advisory committee, the command budget is put together in final form, submitted to the commanding general of the command for review and signature, and submitted to headquarters in Washington. The budgets of the continental armies run into very substantial sums of money—for most of them, between 100 and 200 million dollars.

At the command level, as at the installation level, the most significant substantive review is that conducted by the specialized functional officers of the installation activities in their own specialized functional fields. The extent to which these functional estimates are reviewed and coordinated among each other by officers with broader perspective and in terms of a total command program undoubtedly varies widely among commands. To a considerable degree, it depends upon the time and effort, the prestige and influence, and the knowledge and capacity of the comptrollers and their staffs.

Review at Service Headquarters

The most intensive budgetary activity of the military departments, as indeed of civil agencies, takes place during those warmest Washington months of June, July, and August. During this period, the budgets of the operating agencies are received, consolidated, reviewed in a series of informal and formal examinations and hearings, and shaped into a consolidated service budget. The process is particularly complex for the Army. In the Navy, the budgets submitted by the bureaus are, for the most part, self-contained and are approximately coterminous with the appropriations. The estimates as reviewed and approved become the basis for the Navy Department budget request with little modification. The Air Force must fit its command budgets into an appropriation structure which does not follow command lines, but it is not plagued by the dual organizational base of geographic armies and technical and administrative services. The Army Department must first review the estimates of its primary organizational units, the continental and overseas armies; consolidate them; then consolidate these estimates with the related requirements of the technical and administrative services; then review these on the basis of the budget classification; and finally bring forth a unified budget for the department as a whole which, outwardly at least, bears little relation to the organizational structure through which the estimates have been created. In the process, the armies and the services, in that sequence, lose their identity as budgetary entities.

In all three services, the responsibility for coordinating and supervising the review, and for bringing the whole budget together, rests upon the comptrollers and their budgetary staffs. But the main substantive influence on important decisions lies with the program staff agencies: in the Navy, the Chief of Naval Operations and the bureau heads; in the Air Force, the Chief of Staff and the Deputy Chiefs of Staff, particularly those for Operations and Matériel; in the Army, the Chief of Staff and the Assistant Chiefs of Staff, G-4, Logistics, and G-1, Personnel.

In the Army, the first estimates received and the first ones considered are those for the continental and overseas armies. Copies are sent both to the Budget Division of the Comptroller's office and to the budget program director, G-4. In addition, the various administrative and technical service headquarters receive copies and are called upon to review and make recommendations with respect to their subject-matter fields. Each of these units examines the submittals. Then the Comptroller budget analysts hold informal hearings with representatives of the field army as well as the headquarters offices. The review and the hearings at this stage are conducted by middle-grade officers and civilians, technically and functionally qualified for detailed review —the group known in popular Pentagon parlance as "Indians."

The next step is the hearing by the Budget Advisory Committee of the budgets of the continental and overseas armies, each considered as a whole and by itself. The BAC directs its attention primarily, though not exclusively, to the items which the "Indians" have not been able to resolve or which they feel should be decided by higher authority. At the BAC meeting, the representative of the army concerned is given an opportunity to make a statement in behalf of his army's budget and is called upon to support it and answer questions about it. It is noteworthy that the army representatives are usually comptrollers or members of the comptrollers' staffs, officers of medium rank and frequently with little information about the over-all programs and problems of their organizations. The BAC, after its hearing, goes into executive session and makes its decisions with respect to the items in question. These are recorded by the Army Comptroller staff and distributed to the various offices concerned.

The next stage in the process is the submittal and consideration of the budgets by appropriation and by budget program. The technical and administrative services have compiled estimates for their own programs and have also consolidated with them the estimates for the various armies that have already been approved by the BAC. These are reviewed and examined by the technicians of the Comptroller's office and by the appropriate staff section—in most cases, G-4 or G-1. The "Indians" hold hearings as they did in the case of the armies. The budget examiners of the Comptroller's office then make out detailed analysis sheets covering each budget item, including information as to the original request and the decision, or the disagreement, by the reviewers as to its merit. These sheets, together with the original justifications of the services, become the basis of the BAC review. The originating services are given an opportunity to consider, prior to the BAC hearings, the changes proposed by the staff section and/or the

Comptroller staff. They may accede, in which case the question is not raised before the BAC; or they may prepare appeals, called "reclamas."

In the main, the BAC operates on the basis of the "exception" principle. That is, it takes up for consideration those exceptional questions which the various concerned parties have not been able to resolve prior to the meetings. The major proceedings of the BAC, which are held at this stage, are a systematic review of the entire budget, appropriation by appropriation and budget program by budget program. These hearings occupy several hours every day for a month, normally in July and August. The usual procedure is about as follows: a representative of the staff office which has budget program direction for the program under consideration makes a brief statement about the content of the program and any special problems involved in it; he then introduces the chief of the technical or administrative service primarily responsible for the program; this officer, usually of high rank, makes a general statement concerning the items about which there is a question or which the BAC should consider. This is followed by questions and discussion of a fairly informal kind. Members of the BAC can and often do raise questions about items not on the Comptroller's agenda. The questions discussed are of both a technical and a program or substantive nature; and while most of them are directed toward the reduction or elimination of proposed items in the budget, the Committee has not infrequently added or increased items.

Following its open hearings, the BAC goes into executive session and reaches its decisions about the estimates under consideration. These are recorded and distributed by the secretariat, provided by the Comptroller's office. Though these decisions may be disputed and appealed by the interested offices to the Chief of Staff, they seldom are. The decisions of the Budget Advisory Committee usually stand as the budget of the Army which is subsequently submitted to the Chief of Staff and later to the Secretary of the Army.

The BAC is assisted by a so-called "Junior BAC," consisting of officers representing the same staff offices as the BAC itself does. This group meets prior to the BAC meetings, considers the principal budgetary questions, prepares proposed positions, and advises the senior body. Its individual members act as assistants to their seniors and brief them on the principal questions.

The Army BAC is an interesting institution in the American public administrative scene. It is in a sense an effort to achieve "representative government" within a highly corporate administrative organization. Each of its members is a representative of a functional organization or interest within the Army, and displays some reluctance to attack or even criticize the budget estimates which fall within the budgetary jurisdiction of his fellows. Yet a BAC member not infrequently questions the estimates of his own subordinates when they appear before the body. The individual members are vastly unequal in their influence and forcefulness. This is partly because of individual capacity and interest in the subject matter, but far more importantly because of the strength and budgetary importance of the offices which they represent.

The BAC has steadfastly maintained the position that it is not a policy-determining body but only a reviewer of fiscal estimates. Questions of major policy and program it refers to the Program Advisory Committee, to appropriate members of the staff, and on occasion to the Chief of Staff. During its consideration of the 1954 budget, it interrupted its deliberations to meet with the Chief of Staff and to obtain from him decisions on policy questions raised during the course of its hearings. Many of its decisions involve policy and program.

Finally, it may be observed that, like that of the other units involved in budgetary review, the BAC review is oriented more toward succeeding reviews at higher echelons than to the supervision and coordination of activities below. Its aim is to produce an Army budget which is defensible and persuasive to the Secretary of Defense, the Bureau of the Budget, and the Congressional committees. Indeed, its own members will later be largely responsible for presenting the Army case before these bodies. It is little wonder that they want the case to be as solid as possible. But the BAC is still an Army organization; it will not sell its "parent" short. At a time when drastic budget cuts seemed to be called for in the Defense Department, the BAC's reductions were relatively minor, and it made some significant increases.

The BAC review of the budget, however, serves an important purpose as an informational device for the top staff. It provides the first opportunity for the entire budget of the service to be brought together and considered as a whole. Through the hearings the top staff of the Department are educated as to the content of the estimates, the methods and policies by which the estimates have been built, and the problem areas which should be re-examined or for which the Department should be well prepared for the later defense of its budget. It should be noted that the BAC itself is composed entirely of high-ranking military officers, and its determinations, made in executive session, are thus strictly military decisions. However, the Office of the

Secretary of the Army has one or more civilian representatives present at the regular hearings who may and do raise questions during the proceedings. The Secretary and the Under Secretary thus have a mechanism to keep currently informed as to the progress of the budget and can be acquainted with the issues involved before the document itself is brought to the Secretary for final departmental review. Likewise, civilian representatives of the Assistant Secretary of Defense (Comptroller) attend most of the hearings and may raise questions. They do not attend the executive sessions at which final decisions are made.

Following the BAC review, the Budget Division of the Comptroller's office supervises the revision of the estimates and the supporting materials. The budget is then presented to the Chief of Staff. His review is rapid but fairly penetrating; it sometimes results in substantial changes. A few days later, the budget is presented to the Secretary of the Army, who, with the Under Secretary and others from his staff, reviews its major elements rapidly but with some care. These final Army Department reviews occur in the latter part of August under the current budget calendar (applicable in 1952). The Comptroller's budget office spends the last few days of that month making the final revisions in the documents and submits the Army budget to the Office, Secretary of Defense, at or near the beginning of September.

It may be noted that it is not until very late in this process that the Army budget can be looked at as a whole in terms of its total fiscal, economic, and political impact. The budget is presumed to be a direct dollar translation of programs previously approved for the Army by higher authority, and the decisions made in estimating and review are intended to involve interpretations but not modifications of those programs. No dollar ceilings or even targets are applied at any stage until near the very end. However, when each of the services was almost at the end of its work in preparing its fiscal year 1953 budget, the Secretary of Defense gave it over-all target figures. The Army BAC was in the midst of its regular hearings on the 1953 budget when Mr. Lovett's letter arrived, asking that the Department submit, with its regular budget request, another budget based upon a total figure of fourteen and one-half billion as a "point of departure." This figure represented about a 30 per cent reduction of the budget on which the BAC was completing its review. The "Point of Departure Budget," as it was called, was, in fact, developed in the course of a few days by ranking members of the BAC, their immediate assistants, and staff members of the Comptroller's Budget Division, principally by lopping off huge amounts of procurement and supply. This entire budget was rushed through the BAC in one day; then the Committee proceeded with its laborious review of the regular budget. The Army, like the other services, in effect submitted two budgets, and both were considered in subsequent Defense Department reviews; but it is apparent that the "Point of Departure Budget" became the true point of departure for the President's budget. The request which was subsequently sent to Congress was actually under the limiting figure which Lovett had proposed. Similar events had taken place in the spring of 1951 with respect to the 1952 budget—a drastic cut at the end of the regular estimating process.

There is no mechanism within the Army's budget process to take into consideration the limiting factors of probable availability of resources, not even at the level of the Budget Advisory Committee itself. In spite of the tremendous care and work which went into the calculation and review of detailed estimates, the *real* budget was put together on a "crash" basis by a few individuals in a matter of days and hours. If the long process of programming and budgeting were successful in bringing forth a budget internally coordinated and balanced, the hurried slashes made at the end must inevitably result in "unbalancing" it. This is particularly true because different elements of the budget are unequally resistant to sudden changes. Some are so fixed by prior commitments that they can hardly be changed at all. Cuts are made where they can be, even though the items reduced may be badly needed in terms of the total program.

A second effect of this procedure lies in the minds and attitudes of the personnel concerned in budgeting. Following the experiences of recent years, the budgeteers would be blind indeed if they did not anticipate a fairly violent slash in their requests. This results in a feeling by many of futility and frustration. More important is the potential loss in the sense of responsibility with respect to the initial budget and the program it reflects. Particularly at higher levels, decisions on elements of the budget may be made with a view to setting forth a case for maximum funds, even though it is realized fully that the request is not feasible. But the onus, and the accompanying responsibility, for reducing the estimates is pushed off to the reviewers at higher levels. Under these circumstances, the budget can become less a reasoned plan than a "white paper," made for the record, having slight relation to reality. If carried to its dangerous extreme, this attitude might result in completely irresponsible behavior within the service. It is an attitude which might be expressed: "This is what I need, even though I know it is impossible for you (Secretary of Defense, Bureau of the

Budget, President, or Congress) to give it to me. However, it will not be possible to do my job without all of it. If you make any cuts, you assume full responsibility for any dire consequences which may result."

The Army Medical Budget—An Example

The progress of the estimates covering Army medical activities through the Headquarters review process is illustrative both of the nature of the process and of the complexities involved in converting estimates from an organizational base to the performance budget classification. The medical budget is, in fact, simpler than most other parts of the Army budget because almost all the costs involved in medical activities are included in a single budget program, Medical Care, which is part of the appropriation, Maintenance and Operations, Army. Unlike most of the other functional budget programs, this one includes medical procurement and supply, but it does not include military personnel costs. A second reason for the relative simplicity of this part of the budget is that one and only one technical service organization, that under the Surgeon General, has a clean-cut functional jurisdiction over virtually the entire budget program. There is very little overlap with the Signal Corps or the Chief of Ordnance or the Quartermaster General.

The first step is the receipt and the examination of the estimates from the continental armies and the overseas commands. Medical care is a relatively small fraction of the total fund requirements of these organizations. These estimates cover the operations of station hospitals, dispensaries, infirmaries, and laboratories; travel of medical personnel to and from medical schools; physical examinations at recruiting stations; food and sanitary inspections; etc. The estimates for medical care of the armies are reviewed by representatives of the Surgeon General's Office and the Budget Division of the Comptroller. After the preliminary meetings with the representatives of the armies concerned, the entire budgets of the armies and overseas commands are then taken up, one by one, by the Budget Advisory Committee. Included in the review is, of course, the estimate for medical care. The BAC determinations with respect to medical care for each of the armies are then referred back to the Surgeon General's Office. It is now his responsibility to prepare a complete budget estimate for the entire budget program for medical care, incorporating within it the approved requirements of the field armies as well as the direct requirements of his own Medical Department. In addition, he must include amounts requested by the National Guard Bureau and the Quartermaster for certain depot supply services. Well over one-half of the total budget for medical care is estimated and subsequently obligated directly under the Surgeon General's own command for procurement of medical supplies and equipment, storage and distribution, operation of the general hospitals, medical training, and related program elements.

The consolidated estimates for medical care are first examined by the budget program director, G-4, and the examiners of the Comptroller's office. Hearings are held at this level with representatives of the Surgeon General's Office, and the Comptroller "marks up" the estimates. The Surgeon General may then appeal, or "reclama," these mark-ups back to the Comptroller, and the majority of the questions are resolved or compromised at this level. Those that are not go on the agenda of the Budget Advisory Committee.

Prior to the BAC meeting on the medical care budget, the assigned examiner of the Comptroller's Budget Division is required to furnish each member of the Committee with a copy of the budget justification book, prepared by the Surgeon General's Office, which contains the detailed estimates and supporting data. He must furnish a copy of the analysis sheet, a standard form developed by the Budget Division for purposes of setting forth in detail the changes and comments of the analyst. He also may furnish a copy of the general statement to be made by the Surgeon General and also his own statement about questioned items.

The BAC hearing on medical care for fiscal year 1954 lasted about two hours. First, a representative of the program director, G-4, made a brief general statement concerned primarily with the review procedure up to that point, and closed by introducing the Surgeon General of the Army. This officer then delivered a brief prepared statement about his budget, pointing out some of its salient and new or markedly changed features and referring to some of the accomplishments of the current year and major programs for the future. His statement was followed by a discussion in informal, conversational tone with members of the Committee on various subjects, of which the following are representative:

Construction plans for new hospitals—standard plans utilized by all the services for expansible hospitals.

The beginning date of the Medical Stock Fund and its effect on the budget.

The effect of the budgetary assumption that the Korean War would be over by June 30, 1952, upon the budgeting of medical supplies, and the consequent requirement of supplemental appropriations to cover both current war consumption and replenishment of the pipeline.

The question as to whether television sets for Army hospitals should be charged to Medical or Signal Corps funds.

The budget analyst, a civilian from the Comptroller's office, then made a brief statement in which he praised the soundness of the medical budget and said there were few things with which he could find fault. He then raised certain specific points for the attention and information of the BAC. These included such matters as:

The average ratio of hospital staffs to hospital beds, which was above the Bureau of the Budget approved yardstick for Federal hospitals.

The value of hospital rations.

An increase in the civilian personnel costs for maintenance and operation of hospitals, due in part to the assumption by the Army of other salary costs in Germany.

An increase in civilian personnel costs at Medical Department schools in order to relieve students of KP duty.

The BAC discussed each of the above points, along with some others, briefly, but more from the standpoint of exploration and information than from that of action to change the estimates. On one item, the budget analyst had cut the estimate of the Surgeon General. He stated what the cut was and the reasons for it. The Surgeon General then read a "reclama" statement arguing for a restoration of the cut by the BAC. The request was for an increase in civilian staff of the Surgeon General's headquarters. The analyst had reduced the requested increase by about one-half. It is interesting that he did not question or doubt the real need for the additional staff, which was justified on the grounds of increased workloads for management purposes imposed by higher headquarters. The problem was not dollars but "spaces"—that is, positions available within personnel ceilings. In fact, it developed during the ensuing discussion that the cut had actually been forced upon the budget analyst by the manpower control officers in the office of Assistant Chief of Staff, G-1.

It is apparent that no significant changes in the medical care budget were made or even considered by the BAC. It was a pleasant, friendly meeting, carried on in a spirit of cordiality and mutual respect. The BAC and the budget examiners obviously have a high degree of confidence in the Surgeon General, his staff, and his budget; furthermore, they lack detailed acquaintance with the relatively technical aspects of the medical care budget.

In the hearings on military matters in which the Committee members are themselves knowledgeable, they are likely to be "rougher." But even then, the changes of the BAC are seldom drastic. It must be borne in mind that by the time a budget program is ready for BAC consideration, it has already been approved by the responsible staff agency (the budget program director). And the representative on the BAC who is best equipped to take the lead in questioning the estimates for that program is a representative of the same staff office. It is not likely that a deputy to one of the Assistant Chiefs of Staff would permit a program to be presented which he thought to be unsound or which he himself intended to attack in a fundamental way. One's general impression is that the BAC hearings are not very effective as an objective and searching examination of budget estimates. But they are useful to the Army in bringing out weaknesses in its position; in informing top officials about the content of the budget; in keeping the budgeteers and examiners on their toes. Perhaps most of all, they are a good dress rehearsal for the main actors in the later and more crucial scenes of the budget show.

Headquarters Review in Other Services

The conduct of review and consolidation of the Air Force budget is similar in essential respects to the Army process. Here again, the estimates come up from the commands, where an intermediate review and consolidation has taken place. Budget examiners of the Comptroller's office as well as officers from the appropriate functional divisions of the Air Staff conduct detailed reviews and hold informal meetings and hearings. The Budget Advisory Committee of the Air Staff then holds intensive hearings over a period of about two weeks in which it reviews and discusses the entire budget. Basic policy questions may be raised by the BAC to the Air Council for resolution. The budget is then consolidated and submitted to the Chief of Staff and finally to the Secretary. In the case of the Air Force, a very large part of the budget, in terms of dollars, is under the command jurisdiction of the Air Matériel Command, located at Wright Field in Dayton. Therefore, a large share of the budgetary work is, in fact, carried on outside of Washington by a subordinate command. The Air Staff has less of a problem than the Army of bringing together and coordinating the data and the estimates of a large number of unitary organizations. On the other hand, there appears to be somewhat less discretion and control over

Air Force estimates at the staff level than in the Army for the very reason that so much of the data and the process are concentrated in a single fairly independent command.

In the Navy, the greatest part of budget preparation and consolidation takes place within the several bureaus. Each bureau has one or more appropriations over which it has almost complete jurisdiction. The bureaus submit their estimates to the Comptroller's office and to the Chief of Naval Operations. Budget examiners under the direction of the Deputy Comptroller, a vice admiral, examine the estimates in detail. Then a series of hearings are conducted in the Comptroller's office at which the principal officers of each bureau present and defend their estimates. Representatives of the Chief of Naval Operations also participate in these meetings. Following the hearing, the Comptroller staff "mark up" the budgets and notify the bureaus of their allowances. The bureaus then have an opportunity to appeal the decisions back to the Deputy Comptroller and, if not satisfied by his action, to the Chief of Naval Operations, whose decisions are normally considered final. After the budget has been "firmed up," a meeting of the Budget Advisory Committee is held. This session usually lasts not more than one day and appears to be largely for the purpose of presenting and explaining the budget to the "top brass."

Review by the Office, Secretary of Defense and the Bureau of the Budget

In one sense at least, the situation of the Office, Secretary of Defense in relation to the budget process typifies a common problem in Federal administration: the role of a top echelon interposed between strong, unitary operating organizations and the Executive Office of the President. There appear to be four possible courses it may follow in the budget process:

First, it may perform no substantive functions at all except as a transmitting agent—that is, simply receiving the estimates from subordinate units and passing them on to the Bureau of the Budget. This has been the traditional practice of the so-called holding-company departments and agencies. For many, many decades the Departments of War and Navy operated in much this way, exercising little influence upon the budgets of their services and bureaus.

Second, it may exercise a general review function over the total amounts and the basic programs and policies of its constituent units, attempting to pare the total estimates down to reasonable ceilings but leaving the details of the cuts to the units affected. The review process in this situation is brief in duration and fairly general in nature. The practice, now followed by a number of Federal agencies, was essentially that employed by the Defense Department before passage of the National Security Act Amendments of 1949. Thorough examination of the content of the unit budgets was left to the Bureau of the Budget.

The third possibility is for the top echelon to staff and equip itself for a complete review of all the estimates and to assume leadership and responsibility for the budget before higher echelons. This adds another fairly extended review process between those of the constituent units and of the Bureau of the Budget.

The final possibility is a variation of the third: to conduct a complete and thorough review by combining its review process with the reviews of other echelons, either above or below it. For example, the Secretary of Defense might have his staff attend and participate in the departmental reviews of the Army, Air Force, and Navy, maintaining independence of decision after the estimates have finally been submitted by those departments. Or he can combine his review with that of the Bureau of the Budget. Clearly this is an alternative of economy and convenience. It saves the cost and time of a complete additional review while theoretically retaining for the Secretary the authority over, and the responsibility for, the budget of the entire organization.

Following the passage of the National Security Act Amendments of 1949, which clearly defined the responsibility of the Secretary of Defense in the budgetary process, his office was faced with the necessity of building up a competent budgetary staff. The recruitment, training, and familiarization with defense budgeting problems obviously required a considerable period of time; these processes are, in fact, still going on although the present budgetary staff of the Assistant Secretary of Defense (Comptroller) is a sizable one of considerable and increasing competence. At the start, however, the staff was inadequate for a comprehensive review of all the service budgets. Furthermore, there was a shortage of time in the recurring budgetary crises following the start of the Korean war. It was fundamentally for these two reasons, inadequacy of staff and shortage of time, that the Secretary called upon the Bureau of the Budget to join in a combined review of the service budgets. All the annual budgets for fiscal years 1952, 1953, 1954, and 1955 have been reviewed jointly by the Office, Secretary of Defense and the Bureau. The Bureau has not forfeited its opportunity for a short further review of questioned points after the Secretary of Defense has completed his action on the budget; nor has it refrained from making its own decisions, often divergent from those of the Secretary of Defense. But the bulk and core of the review process itself is a combined operation—a practice which, to the writer's knowledge, is unique in current Federal budgeting practice. With the growing competence of the Defense Comptroller's staff, one of the initial arguments for the practice is weakening, perhaps vanishing. But the problem of time remains. The combined review now runs over a period of six to eight weeks, and the addition of any such period for a separate complete review would appear almost forbidding in time and expense. The additional fraying of nerves and exasperation might also be a factor of more than parenthetical importance.

The analysts of the Office, Secretary of Defense (OSD) and the Bureau of the Budget actually begin their review of the estimates before the official submission of budgets by the three services. During the summer of 1952, for example, the estimates for various items of supply, together with supporting data, were submitted and considered as they were completed in the services. The analysts held informal meetings during this period with the officers of the services responsible, at the working level, for the items considered. Officially, the review began after submittal of the budget, which was set for September 2, 1952.

The staffs of both the Bureau and the OSD are organized so as to permit specialization of the examiners according to the basic elements of the budget. Primary specialization is according to the category of cost system—i.e. a group on matériel, a group on personnel, a group on maintenance, etc. In addition, there is a cross-specialization by service—i.e. Army, Navy, Air Force. The estimates when received are distributed among the groups and the individual examiners on the basis of their specialization. Their analysis and, in fact, their hearings can thus be carried on simultaneously. At the hearings, which are conducted informally in the offices of the OSD examiners, the representatives of the services are invited to make statements about their requirements and particularly about how they were determined. The Bureau and the OSD examiners, who have previously analyzed the written data in detail, then raise questions about the individual items, justifications, and assumptions. Frequently, data are requested that are not readily available and the service representatives must call upon their organizations for further information and tabulations. It may be noted that, while some of the hearings are attended by the "top brass," a large proportion of the participation is by the "Indians" at the working level of the services.

The joint hearings are carried on daily, or almost daily. Between the sessions, there are frequent meetings among the examiners within the OSD and within the Bureau of the Budget as basic problems are thrashed out and policy questions are raised to higher levels for decisions. There is also frequent communication between the examiners of OSD and their counterparts in the Bureau. Each group, however, "marks up" the estimates independently. Then they meet to compare notes, discuss their differences, and see if they can arrive at agreement. They do arrive at consensus on many questions but there is no compulsion that they should. There have been, in each year, important and sizable differences totaling some billions of dollars. In the majority of such instances, the Bureau's figures are lower.

Following the review, the OSD sends its "mark up" to the three services. This is a statement of the changes and the allowances on an item-by-item basis with brief explanations of major reductions. The services have a brief period to study these determinations and to prepare "reclamas" or appeals for the restoration of part or all of the individual cuts. The climax of this entire process is a series of "reclama" meetings in the Defense Secretary's own office, at which the services present and argue their cases for the important items which they are appealing. These meetings are conducted on successive days for each of the services. They last all day and sometimes well into the night. They are attended not only by the principal budgetary examiners and authorities of the departments, the OSD, and the Bureau of the Budget, but also by the top civilian and military officials—the secretaries, assistant secretaries, chiefs and assistant chiefs of staff. At these sessions, the Secretary of Defense in some cases makes his decision personally and on the spot; in others he hears the arguments on both sides and reserves his decision for further consideration or information. Following these meetings, the services, working with the OSD, make the necessary changes in their budgetary documents. Early in November, in 1952, the 1954 budget request for the entire Department of Defense was submitted to the Bureau of the Budget. It may be noted that while the Bureau participated in the OSD review and the Secretary's "reclama" session and had an opportunity to raise questions and express its views, it did not commit itself throughout the process and it still reserved the right for further review and decision.

The Bureau does study the budget further and conducts additional hearings. These are primarily for the purpose of developing further information on questionable parts of the budget that have been identified at earlier stages. The Bureau notifies Defense and the services of its cuts and they are given an opportunity then to appeal on these additional reductions. Final stages of the executive review process during November and December lead to Presidential decision on the items still in dispute between the Bureau of the Budget and the Department of Defense. The meetings and negotiations during this period include a widening circle of the top executive officials of the government. In these, the Director of the Budget, the Secretary of Defense, and the President undoubtedly play the key roles, but leaders and representatives of the Council of Economic Advisers, the Departments of State and Treasury, and others participate. For both fiscal years 1953 and 1954, the President made certain last-minute decisions in response to the pleas of Defense representatives which resulted in substantial modifications of the Budget Bureau recommendations. The estimates finally appearing in the President's budget were considerably above the Budget Bureau recommendations but still considerably below the budget proposed to the Bureau by the Secretary of Defense.

Evaluation of the Review Process

At present, the most important and effectual part of the review process, prior to Congressional review, is the joint review of the Secretary of Defense and the Bureau of the Budget. It is distinguished from the prior reviews within the service departments in several ways:

First, it is the first stage in review in which the total budget is viewed from the standpoint of the financial situation of the government and its over-all economic and political impact. Until this point, the budget preparation has been largely from the perspective of military requirements with relatively little systematic attention to the demands these requirements will make upon the resources of the nation.

Second, it is the first point at which the basic military assumptions and policies are really challenged. Prior reviews have largely been based upon a set of assumptions within a chain of command in which both the justifiers and the reviewers are conditioned by a common system of authority and thinking. The basic strategic and force programs are largely accepted, but the interpretations of these objectives in terms of specific requirements offer a wide range of latitude, not only as to amounts but also as to the time period within which the requirements must be satisfied. Participants in the OSD—Bureau review look at these interpretations critically and may fundamentally modify them. Prior discussions and reviews, it is true, direct attention to similar questions, but their aim appears to be primarily to develop a strong and defensible position for the service.

Third, the review is quite surprisingly thorough and detailed. It involves a fairly searching examination of the estimates on an item-by-item basis for hundreds and hundreds of items of matériel, including reviews of all the assumptions and the arithmetic calculations. The examiners of the Bureau have fortified themselves with first-hand information derived from field trips to military posts. They come to the meetings probably better informed about military operations and budgeting than do the examiners on the Comptroller staffs of the services.

Fourth, this review is the first complete and systematic examination of the military budgets by civilians, under civilian authority. The customary separatist attitude of the Bureau of the Budget is augmented by the civilian-military dichotomy, and it serves as an obstacle to effective communication and to mutual trust. Some of the examiners in both OSD and the Bureau feel very strongly that review of the budget is one of the most important, if not *the* most important, guarantee of the democratic principle of civilian control. This view seems to encourage attitudes and behavior on the part of the examiners that are aggressively critical, even hostile, and perhaps even a feeling that budget cuts must be made for their own sake—i.e. as an expression and reminder of civilian authority.

One further aspect of the civilian-military relationship in budget review is the question as to the proper scope and depth of civilian examination in exploring military affairs. This problem is exactly the same as that found in other agencies between the administrative examining group, nonexpert, and the professional experts of the operating staff. Like other professional groups, the officers can withdraw behind their professional armor when necessary and refuse to discuss questions of an operational military character on the ground that such matters are not within the relevant bounds of budget examination, and not within the area of competence of the budget analysts. A very large part of the military budget represents directly, or at least hinges upon, policies, criteria, and factors of a military-operational nature. To the extent that such items are exempted from consideration in OSD-Bureau review they are virtually immune from any budgetary examination.

In point of fact, this is one of the basic weaknesses of the entire budget review process. Many of the basic program factors are not at any stage systematically studied from the standpoint of the limitations imposed by, and the allocation of, scarce resources. The force program is taken as gospel—before there is an estimate on its cost. The unit program and other subsidiary programs likewise are little questioned, once developed; and a large part of their development hinges upon standard tables, ratios, and factors. The bulk of manpower budgeting is really carried on outside the financial budget process under the aegis of specialists in manpower utilization and control. But the biggest part of the budget—equipment and supply—hinges upon tables of allowances and equipment, formulas for issuance, and supply levels. These tables are not systematically examined during the budget process; in fact they are seldom examined at all from a truly budgetary standpoint. Budget reviewers, particularly at the OSD-Bureau level, raise questions about allowances of certain types of supply and equipment, particularly vehicles and supplies of a standard civilian nature. But, for the most part, the bases of the requirements for military equipment go unchallenged throughout the entire budget process.

FUNDING

The process of budget preparation described in the foregoing pages of this chapter covers a period, in "normal" times, of nine to eleven months. It culminates in the presentation of the President's Budget the middle of each January. During the succeeding five or more months, the services and particularly their budget officials are engaged in justifying and defending their approved estimates before the committees of Congress. By or near the first of July the Congress passes the Department of Defense Appropriation Bill as well as one or more supplemental bills providing appropriations for the military departments.[34]

In the meantime, the services launch what amounts to a new budget planning procedure which covers approximately the same content as the original budget and applies to the same fiscal year, but which is carried on about one year later. This process is known in the Army as the development of a funding program; in the Air Force, as the development of a financial plan. It is begun usually in April or about the same time that the estimating process for the fiscal year next following is getting under way. It is completed near the beginning of the fiscal year. The funding or financial program comes together with the original estimating and appropriating processes near July 1 in the consideration of apportionment requests by the Bureau of the Budget. The apportionments may be considered the first stage of budget execution.

---

[34] The annual appropriation should pass and be signed prior to July 1, the beginning of the fiscal year. In practice, the Congress has not met that deadline and has sometimes run several weeks into the new fiscal year. The Department of Defense Appropriation Act, 1953 (P. L. 488, 82nd Cong.), was approved July 10, 1952. A major item of the military budgets which is carried in a supplemental appropriation is military public works. The Supplemental Appropriation Act, 1953 (P. L. 547, 82nd Cong.), which includes funds for this purpose, was approved July 15, 1952.

A funding program is designed to provide an operating plan for the execution of the budget, as finally approved and expressed in appropriations. A separate planning process to develop such a program is particularly needed in the military departments for two reasons: first, to reflect up-to-date and more accurate information about conditions and program requirements, and more dependable forecasts; second, to reflect in operating financial plans the actual or probable dollar resources that will become available for different purposes. At the time the funding program is developed, there is, of course, complete knowledge as to what the President has allowed in his budget and there is usually a fairly accurate indication as to what the Congress will finally approve. Unlike the original budget estimates, the funding program must be realistic and must be feasible. It must be a capabilities plan, whereas the budget itself can be a statement of requirements. They differ in one other important respect. The original budget is designed to provide a basis of review by higher bodies—the Bureau of the Budget, the President, and the Congress. The funding program provides the foundation for apportionment requests and these are likewise reviewed at the Department of Defense and the Bureau of the Budget levels. But it is also, and perhaps more importantly, a tool for internal management and control of operations. At intermediate and lower echelons, the funding program is a matter of much more obvious and immediate concern than the budget. Only a step behind it are "hard dollars."

The procedure for the development of an annual funding program in the Army is as follows: In April, the Estimates and Funding Branch, Budget Division, Office of the Comptroller of the Army, prepares and sends to each of the budget operating agencies (the field armies, technical and administrative services, and others) a directive instructing them to submit a requested funding program. Each operating agency then prepares such a program for its entire command and returns it early in June. The operating agencies normally do not go below their headquarters level in the preparation of such programs, and few installations participate in the process. The development of the program at the operating agency level is coordinated and supervised by the budget staffs of the comptrollers' offices. As in the case of the original budget estimates, however, much or most of the actual planning is done by the substantive or functional units in the service headquarters. The operating agency may carry out a formal review of the funding program, but most of them do not.

The requests for funding programs are received and analyzed in the Army staff along much the same lines as the original budget estimates, under the direction of the Comptroller's Budget Division. However, the analysis is quicker and less intensive. The BAC reviews briefly the programs recommended by the Budget Division and the request for apportionments which it prepares for the Bureau of the Budget.

The Bureau holds brief, though sometimes searching, hearings on the requests for apportionment. Representatives of the Office, Secretary of Defense, attend these hearings. Following the hearings, the Bureau issues advices of apportionment, usually authorizing the obligation of funds for each of the first three quarters of the fiscal year within each appropriation. The Bureau can apportion in detail by budget program or project but so far has done so on an appropriation basis. The apportionments are made to the secretaries of the three service departments, but reach that point only after they have been reviewed and certified by the Secretary of Defense who may himself limit or reserve the use of funds.[35]

On the basis of the approved apportionments, the Secretary of the Army, through the Budget Division of the Comptroller's office, issues funding programs to each operating agency *and* an approved allocation of funds. These funding programs constitute planning figures covering the entire year, based upon appropriations and apportionments. They do not constitute authority to allot or obligate funds. The allocations, on the other hand, are issued on a quarterly basis and constitute authority to allot funds. The funding programs are broken down by appropriation and budget program. In addition, certain budget projects are specified as are a very few sub-projects.[36] Also, ceilings are

---

[35] The National Security Act Amendments of 1949 provided that ". . . appropriations made to the Department of Defense or to the military departments, and reimbursements thereto, shall be available for obligation and expenditure only after the Secretary of Defense shall approve scheduled rates of obligations, or modifications thereof. . . ." P. L. 216, Sec. 404.

[36] Budget projects earmarked in funding programs for 1953 included items for which the Army centrally, or the Congress, previously indicated a special interest, such as:

Maintenance and Operations, Army:
   1142–Local Command and Technical Service Exercises;
   1221–Training at Civilian Institutions;
   1230–School Temporary Duty Travel.

They also included funds reserved at the installation level for the Corps of Engineers, notably:

Maintenance and Operations, Army:
   2911–Normal Repairs and Utilities Operating Expenses, Continental United States and Overseas;
   2915–All other Repairs and Utilities Projects, Class I Continental United States and Overseas Installations;
   2916–All other Repairs and Utilities Projects, Class II Installations

provided within each budget program as to expenditures for objective classification O1-Civilian Personnel.

On receipt of their Funding Programs, the operating agencies prepare Field Funding Authorizations, one for each installation under their jurisdiction. These show the amounts authorized for obligation by the installation for each budget program, project, and sub-project for the year. Like the Funding Programs, they break out separately the objective classification for civilian personnel, O1. The installations in some commands have an opportunity to specify the amounts they require as allowances in the Field Funding Authorizations; in others, the amounts are arrived at entirely at operating agency headquarters. In either case, however, the installations may make appeals or "reclamas" back to the command level with respect to their authorizations.

The Field Funding Authorizations, like the Funding Programs at the higher level, are planning figures, not authorizations to obligate funds. This latter authority is delegated by the commands by issuing allotments on the basis of the Funding Programs and the allocations of funds which they themselves receive from higher levels. The allotments are made to individual installations, showing separately the civilian personnel objective classification, and to the level of budget projects and sub-projects. Advices of Allotment (WD14-127) are issued at least quarterly during the fiscal year by the army and technical service commanders, normally through the heads of their budget divisions, to the commanders of installations, normally through their comptrollers or budget and fiscal officers. In addition, changes in allotments may be made from this level at any time during the course of the fiscal year. The allotments are based upon the Field Funding Authorizations and they alone constitute authority to obligate appropriated funds.

The local budget officers, receiving the allotments, divide the authorized funds among the installation units on the basis of station operating accounts, usually numbering more than one hundred. It will be recalled, however, that these local accounts are normally standardized at the operating agency level. They differ among the various armies and technical services. Commitments and obligations, though not necessarily expenditures, are recorded at the level of detail of station operating accounts. The objective classifications of civilian personnel, O1, and travel, O2, are normally recorded separately.

Once a month, each installation reports to its operating agency (or agencies) the status of its allotments and obligations for the month and cumulatively to date, by station operating account. These become the basis for the operating agency cumulative reports to Washington of obligations for the month and cumulatively, and of unobligated balances by project and sub-project. And these reports, in turn, form the basis of the Army's monthly report on the status of obligations and funds.

The formal level of delegated flexibility in this system is as follows:

By Congress: to the Army by appropriation, by year;

By the Bureau of the Budget: to the Army by appropriation, by quarter (apportionment);

By the Secretary (Comptroller) of the Army: to the operating agencies by budget programs and a few budget projects, by the year and by quarter;

By the commanders of the operating agencies: to the commanders of installations by budget program, project, and sub-project, and by quarter;

By the commanders of the installations: to the station operating officers by station operating accounts, by quarter.

Both Congress and the Bureau of the Budget have, however, expressed interest in certain other detail, such as civilian personnel; and the Army and the other services have additionally controlled to greater detail some other parts of their budgets. Likewise, the Secretary of Defense has participated, through his Assistant Secretary (Manpower and Personnel), in the imposition of civilian personnel ceilings, and these have become a part of budget authorizations at the Army level.

The Bureau of the Budget in its apportionment process commonly divides the amount appropriated for various programs on a 30 per cent, 25 per cent, 25 per cent, and 20 per cent basis by quarters through the year, thus permitting greater flexibility than an even apportionment for each quarter would permit. A similar pattern is followed by the Army Comptroller in his issuance of allocations and by the armies and technical services in making allotments. In addition, the Comptroller of the Army and the comptrollers at the operating agencies customarily keep out a small reserve of most of their fund authorizations to permit greater flexibility as the year progresses. This amount probably seldom exceeds 5 per cent. It should be noted also that a very substantial dollar amount of appropriated funds is not in fact apportioned or allocated in this way. Most of the money for major procurement, for example, is apportioned and allocated in a single lump at the beginning of the year in order that contracts may be negotiated. Major engineering construction, on the other hand, may be held up by the Bureau of the Budget until plans are made final and approved, at which time the entire amounts may be apportioned. Similarly, the Secretary of Defense or the Army staff may hold up funds pending approval of program plans.

In general, the reporting of information upward is to a much greater level of detail than the granting of funds downward. The stations report to the armies and technical services their obligations and balances monthly to the level of station operating accounts. The commands and technical services report monthly to the Headquarters their obligations to the level of sub-projects. In fact, the information which goes into the annual budget is to this level, but normally installation information is not provided.

Finally, it should be noted that in connection with funding, the scope of the installations' control is limited in a fashion similar to that of the original budget estimates. That is, they receive and obligate funds for approximately the same things that they estimate their needs for; and they receive their funds through the same channels. Thus, they do not budget for goods and supplies that are issued; for military personnel that are paid on open allotment; nor for goods and supplies that they may purchase locally on a sub-allotment from a technical service, such as one for food for their local commissary. Likewise, Class II installations normally have at least two funding programs and budget allotment systems; one from their army, another from their technical or administrative service. The two may and often do have different systems of station operating accounts, thus requiring differing accounting systems at the same installation.

chapter VI

military comptrollers and the budget[1]

> *Reference (a) [the comptrollership provisions of the National Security Act Amendments of 1949] and its statutory history, as well as the Hoover Commission hearings which led ultimately to the enactment of reference (a), show that it was the intent of the Congress to have the fiscal system of the military departments resemble that of private business as closely as the fundamental differences between them would permit.*
>
> SECRETARY OF THE NAVY FRANCIS P. MATTHEWS.[2]

> *All goddam auditors ought to be in the bottom of hell!*
> Attributed to General George S. Patton.

One might well question the need for a chapter on comptrollers in a study directed primarily to the process and effectiveness of budgeting. For comptrollers are organizational entities whose functions in connection with the budget process have already been treated in the preceding chapter.

Yet the comptrollers, and the concept of management which they represent, have an importance now and a greater potential importance to military budgeting than is suggested by the mere statement of functions in the process. Their significance is partly structural, partly symbolic and psychological, and partly substantive. The comptrollers rep-

---

[1] "Comptroller" is now considered to be synonymous with, and a variant spelling of "controller," the spelling widely used in business and increasingly in government. The former spelling, which is the official one in the Defense establishment, is used herein in reference to those offices; the latter is used in references to the office in businesses.

[2] In a memorandum to the bureaus, boards, and offices of the Navy Department, "Comptroller of the Navy, Functional Authority and Responsibility of," November 13, 1950 (processed).

resent and even epitomize several related basic motifs in the ethos of military management since the war: the rise to eminence of the fiscal and financial factors, functions, and organizations; the struggle of the principles and techniques of scientific management with those of traditional military and Federal management; the emulation of, and growing dependency upon, business and business practices; the establishment of the phrase "economy and efficiency" as a commandment, not merely a slogan; and, in a still confused way, the search for a formula (or perhaps merely a wedge) for more effective civilian control of the military. All of these have their effect upon the way the budget job is done, and, probably more importantly, upon the directions it may take in the future.

To those concerned with administrative management in the government, the comptrollers of the Defense establishment are a matter of considerable interest in their own right. Use of the concept and title marked a step in a different direction from that being followed by other departments during recent years. At the risk of overgeneralization, it may be stated that the trend in Federal departments and other large Federal agencies has been toward the grouping of a variety of administrative functions under an administrative assistant secretary or assistant administrator. This arrangement was greatly stimulated by the Hoover Commission, which proposed such a pattern for all the executive departments.[3] The plan provides generally for an experienced career administrator operating directly under the secretary or top administrator and responsible for most of the common administrative services and controls including budget, finance, personnel, organization and management, supplies, mail and communications, property management, and others. This theme, or variations on it, is followed in the Departments of Treasury, Interior, Commerce, Labor, State, Justice, and the Post Office. Among the non-cabinet agencies, one finds officers with comparable responsibilities in the Housing and Home Finance Agency, the Foreign Operations Administration, the Civil Defense Administration, and many others.

No executive department except those in the Defense establishment and the Post Office has a comptroller at the department level. On the other hand, many of the government corporations and so-called business

---

[3] "In addition, there should generally be an administrative assistant secretary who might be appointed solely for administrative duties of a housekeeping and management nature and who would give continuity in top management." The Commission on Organization of the Executive Branch of the Government, *General Management of the Executive Branch* (Washington: Government Printing Office, 1949), p. 37.

enterprises have such officers, as do a number of important agencies which operate extensively through contracts and other commercial relationships with business and with other governments. Among these are the Tennessee Valley Authority, the Atomic Energy Commission, the Foreign Operations Administration, and the General Services Administration. It may be noted that in many of these agencies the controller activities emphasize the external and commercial-type operations of the agencies rather than internal management. The functions commonly attributed to such controllers include the supervision or review of financial transactions, accounting and auditing, and sometimes budgeting. But it is noteworthy that in several of these agencies, budgeting has been segregated from the controllers and placed under general management officers. For example, in the TVA, which was among the first Federal agencies to establish a controller in recent times, the budget function is supervised by a Chief Budget Officer who is part of the General Manager's Office.

The Business Background [4]

It is apparent that the initiators of comptrollership in the Defense establishment were deriving their ideas from business rather than governmental precedent; they were, in fact, turning their backs upon the organizational trends in sister departments in the government. It is therefore pertinent to examine briefly the development and the role of controllers in private business.

The growth of business controllership is a fairly recent phenomenon, most of which has taken place since the First World War. It is somewhat paradoxical that business derived the title and the idea from government. Use of the title, variously spelled, actually goes back to the fifteenth century and even before in the English government.[5]

---

[4] For the ensuing discussion of business controllership, the author is heavily indebted to *Controllership in Modern Management,* edited by Thornton F. Bradshaw, Assistant Professor of Business Administration, Harvard Graduate School of Business, and Charles C. Hull, Director of Education, Controllers Institute of America (Chicago: Richard D. Irwin, Inc., 1949). This collection of essays sponsored by the Controllership Foundation, Inc., appears to be both authoritative and representative of the views of leaders in the field. Its authors include a number of outstanding controllers, business executives, and leading educators in business administration.

[5] One of the early offices using the title was the Countroller of Accounts in the Lord Chamberlain's office. Later appeared the Comptroller and Auditor-General, head of the Exchequer and Audit Department; the Comptroller General, head of the National Debt Office; the Comptroller General of Patents; the Controller of the Navy; etc. J. Hugh Jackson, "The Growth of the Controllership Function," in Bradshaw and Hull, *op. cit.,* pp. 17-18.

The title appeared in the United States in 1778 when the Continental Congress, obviously borrowing from the British, created a Comptroller along with several other financial officers—an Auditor, Treasurer, and six Commissioners of Accounts.[6] The office was dropped a few years later but reappeared in 1789 as part of the newly established Treasury Department.[7] This office, after a long and sometimes turbulent history, became the present Comptroller General of the United States. Other government comptrollers appeared during the late eighteenth and the nineteenth centuries in the states and local jurisdictions.[8]

Comptrollers had been familiar offices in American government for about a century before they first appeared on the business scene. Apparently the first business controller was established by the Atcheson, Topeka, and Santa Fe Railway System in 1880.[9] During the two succeeding decades, a number of other railroads and utilities followed suit, though the functions and roles of those officers were somewhat different from those now associated with business controllers. However, the office did not really come into its own until the twenties. Since then the growth has been rapid and widespread among large concerns until now it may be said to represent the general pattern in top organization of big business, and it is becoming increasingly common in middle-sized businesses.[10]

The growth and spread of controllership in business has been accompanied and stimulated by a drive toward its recognition as a profession, distinguished from, though part of, general business management. The Controllers Institute of America was formed in 1931. It has been an articulate and effective spokesman for the calling as well as a stimulator of professional self-consciousness, education and standards, technical development and research, and responsibility.[11] It publishes *The Controller*, a professional periodical, as well as frequent bulletins and reports, and through its research organization, The Controllership

---

[6] *Ibid.*, p. 19.

[7] It was provided in the Act of September 2, 1789, which created the department (1 *Stat.* 65; 5 U.S.C. 241).

[8] For example, New York State established its comptroller, who is now the chief fiscal officer of the state, in 1797. Another Federal comptroller, the Comptroller of the Currency, was created in 1863 (12 *Stat.* 665).

[9] Bradshaw and Hull, *op. cit.*, p. 16.

[10] A survey reported in 1949, of 195 corporations, revealed that 143 had the office of controller. The average age of the offices in those firms having them was 22 years. *Ibid.*, p. 15.

[11] Arthur R. Tucker, "Organized Cooperation Among Controllers in the United States," in Bradshaw and Hull, *op. cit.*, pp. 29-44.

Foundation, Inc., has conducted and supervised significant studies and publications.

"What's in a Name?"

Certainly the controller has "arrived" in the world of business. He is widely and firmly established. Yet one may properly inquire: What is he? What does he do that is distinctive and new? Is this merely a new kind of grouping of well established functions? Has he really modified the structure and method of business management? The literature in the field reveals that the actual rôles and the duties of controllers vary widely, both in business and in government. The concept itself is elusive and subject to a broad range of interpretation. Mr. J. Hugh Jackson, Dean of the Graduate School of Business at Stanford University, wrote in 1949: "In fact, in American business today the controller's duties vary all the way from simple responsibility for the accounts and records to those of a senior operating executive of the corporation. . . . There is still a large degree of indefiniteness and uncertainty as to the position of the controller and the responsibility which should be accorded him." [12]

Nevertheless, there are certain significations of the title which reflect both its general usage and the profession's own understandings and aspirations. Some of these have particular pertinence when transferred to the environment of military management. First, and self-evident, is the association of controllers with financial management—with affairs having to do with money. Historically, controllers have almost universally developed around some aspects of the management of financial transactions. The first ones, in fact, sprang up in agencies with exclusive or predominant concern in money matters such as the Department of the Treasury. And while the functions of some controllers today include activities not strictly financial in character, these other functions are usually those that can be, and it is felt should be, translated into monetary terms.

The second and third connotations of the title of controller, though significantly different, must be considered together because they are keys to the problem. The second is the association with the role of

---

[12] Bradshaw and Hull, *op cit.*, pp. 14-15. The more recent views of a reporter outside the controller profession are contained in an article by Perrin Stryker, "P & C for Profit" in *Fortune*, April, 1952, p. 128 ff. Dissatisfaction with Mr. Stryker's presentation of the role of the controller and a further effort to refine the concept are expressed in articles by T. F. Bradshaw and John V. Van Pelt, "The Place of the Controller in Management Planning and Control," *The Controller*, October, 1952, p. 472 ff.

checking or *checking up* on the activities or transactions of others by comparison with some official record or roll. The third is the association with the function of accounting. The difference between these two functions is reflected in the manner in which they are commonly placed in separate organizational units, which, instead of working harmoniously together, may be administratively antithetical. In actual usage, however, the term "controller" is used to refer to someone who may perform either or both functions. This reflects the curious and paradoxical derivation of the word itself.

The dictionary informs us that the preferred spelling is "controller"; the bases of the word are the Latin *contra* (against) and *rotulus* (roll), which is itself derived from *rota* (wheel); this became late Latin *contrarotulator* (counter-roll keeper), and the French *controleur*. During the medieval period, the term referred to an official whose primary function was to keep a copy of a document to check against the transactions of a treasurer or other official. The correct and direct derivation therefore is to "controller," the spelling now officially endorsed by the Controllers Institute. Interestingly, its derivation is parallel to that of "control."

For several centuries, nonetheless, the approved spelling among English speaking peoples was "comptroller," although the pronunciation remained the same. This the dictionary attributes to an etymological error when the French word was adapted to English. The prefix was confused with the French stem *conte*, or simply misspelled and subsequently confused. *Aconte* is the French ancestor of "account," itself deriving from the Latin *ad* (to) plus *computo* (compute). The anglicized version of "conte" is "compt." The alleged error resulted in a different connotation in which the accounts became primary, whether the function were one of checking or of keeping them, or both.

The examining or checking connotation has clearly been an important, even dominant, factor in the development of controllers in the United States government. The functions of our first Comptroller in the Treasury Department included: the examination of accounts settled by the Auditor; the certification of balances; and the countersigning of warrants drawn by the Secretary. The function has always been closely related to, and sometimes identified with, that of auditing. The controller thus has some of the role of an inspector; he is the protector against fraud, dishonesty, and irregularity. This kind of role has long been recognized to require a degree of objectivity, an independence from the hierarchy, and a channel of reporting and responsibility outside the regular administrative structure. For these reasons, governments have long provided that their controllers (and auditors) be made directly responsible to the legislature (as in the case of the present Comptroller General of the United States), or to the people (by making the office elective).

Similarly, the development of business controllership has reflected an emphasis upon objectivity and independence for the office and, for this purpose, the establishment of direct channels outside, and of a sense of responsibility outside, the administrative hierarchy. This is indicated by the fairly widespread practices of: making the controller appointive by the board of directors of a company rather than by its general manager; providing that he report directly to the board on affairs of the company; and making him responsible to the board on policy or other specified matters.[13] The latter is reflected in the "Declaration of Principles" adopted by the Controllers Institute:

The Controllers Institute of America stands for the observance of the highest ethical standards in corporate accounting practice and in the preparation of reports of financial and operating conditions of corporations to their directors, stockholders and other parties at interest, in such manner that all concerned may know the actual conditions insofar as such reports may assist in the determination thereof. To that end, the Controllers Institute of America offers its advice and assistance in connection with any movement which has for its purpose the establishment of better safeguards for the protection of the investor.[14]

Here clearly is a statement of responsibility going beyond that to management and encompassing the board of directors, the stockholders, and even the investing public.

We have seen that the "comptrollers" may have acquired the accounting function by accident or error. But actually and historically, accounting and the supervision of accounting have been their *pièce de résistance*. The association of accounting with the checking or auditing role has been a source of confusion and dispute for a very long time.[15] In business, there may be wide variation in the other functions of the controller, but virtually all have to do with keeping accounts and making accounting reports. "He is the lineal descendant of the 'head bookkeeper' of the gas-light era and the 'chief accountant' and 'auditor' of

---

[13] In the survey referred to above, 49 per cent of the controllers were reported to be chosen by the board of directors. Bradshaw and Hull, *op. cit.*, p. 25.

[14] Quoted in Bradshaw and Hull, *op. cit.*, p. 37.

[15] The long-standing argument about the Comptroller General of the United States concerns essentially this issue. See, for example, the Hoover Commission report on *Budgeting and Accounting*, and for a scholarly analysis, Harvey C. Mansfield, *The Comptroller General* (New Haven: Yale University Press, 1939).

the pre-World War I generation, who were primarily concerned with keeping records. . . ." [16] "The controllership function historically began with responsibility for the record keeping for the company, and this is probably still the primary obligation of the office." [17] "First and foremost in the arsenal of skills for the controller is a thorough groundwork in accounting." [18] There is no question that the accounting background is heavily represented among the controllers and that training in, and understanding of, accounting is a *sine qua non* for aspiring controllers. The central function, as well as the organizational position, is illustrated in the following excerpt from Article IV of the Bylaws of the International Harvester Company, which is described as more or less typical:

Section 9. *Comptroller*. The Comptroller shall be the principal officer in charge of the accounts of the Company. He shall be responsible to the Board of Directors for the maintenance of adequate accounting procedure and records of the Company and of subsidiary companies and for the preparation of financial statements and reports on the operation of the business. He shall be responsible to the President or to the Chairman of the Board with respect to the administration of his office . . . . [19]

A fourth association of the word controller is symbolized in, and perhaps a reason for, the revival of the spelling of the word with an "n" rather than an "mp." It is that the office is something *broader* and *higher* than a chief accountant or even of an auditor or inspector. In fact, this meaning is a clear reaction against the rather narrow and limited roles and the mediocre status connoted by those titles. This aspect of controllership has only a brief historical precedent and is almost entirely a contribution of business management in the past thirty years. The modern business concept of controllership "jumps off" from the checking and the accounting functions into the realm of top management services, policy development, and planning. "From the standpoint of sound business organization it would seem almost self-evident that the chief accounting officer is the logical person to assume responsibility for providing management with the information it needs to plan and control operations. It is his duty to construct and maintain the basic records of the business, in which the results of all operations

---

[16] David R. Anderson, "Controllership's Contribution to Executive Management," in Bradshaw and Hull, *op. cit.*, pp. 47-8.

[17] Richard L. Koselka, "Education for Controllership," in Bradshaw and Hull, *op. cit.*, p. 169.

[18] *Ibid.*, p. 173.

[19] Quoted in Bradshaw and Hull, *op. cit.*, p. 26.

are recorded and summarized; and, because he has no line-operating responsibility, he is in a position to report and interpret objectively the data available in those records." [20] "In other words, the need of modern management for information service has given the accountant who can demonstrate executive ability the opportunity to step out of his specialized and somewhat narrow field and become an active member of his management group—that is, a controller in the full sense of the word." [21] The leap from the accountant to the controller, in the eyes of some writers at least, is a considerable one. For example, Arthur R. Tucker, Managing Director (Retired), Controllers Institute of America, wrote that, ". . . accounting and the supervision of it by the controller constituted only about one-fifth of the fundamental responsibilities of a controller and that there were many others which ranked at least as high. . . ." [22]

At the risk of overgeneralization and misplaced emphasis, it may be useful to attempt a synthesis of the controller concept, as it is reflected in the writings of controllers and students of controllership:

1. Decisions on business policy and management can be wise only if they are based upon a knowledge and understanding of the relevant *facts and figures* (terms which are virtually synonymized), intelligently and objectively interpreted. This, it may be noted, is perhaps the fundamental principle of the philosophy and movement commonly known as scientific management.
2. The basic and ultimately the only criterion of business success and failure is profit or loss, which, in the last analysis, can be measured only in monetary terms. Financial data must therefore be the core of information essential to business management.
3. Such data, however, are meaningful only to the extent that they are related to measures of operations and work. Therefore, the financial reports and the accounts must be tied in with program and work reports, i.e. statistics.
4. The controller is the logical, if not the only, officer equipped to bring together all these types of information and to interpret the information for top policy and management officers. This is in part because of his and his staff's background and technical ability; in part because of his already established command of the "core" information on the accounts and finances; in part because, having no line responsibility, he can be completely unbiased and objective; and, finally, because he is in a posi-

---

[20] David R. Anderson, in Bradshaw and Hull, *op. cit.*, p. 48.
[21] *Ibid.*, pp. 49-50.
[22] Quoted in Bradshaw and Hull, *op. cit.*, p. 34.

tion to provide information with regard to the *whole* organization, his scope is total.

5. In order to carry out this role effectively, it is essential that the controller operate as staff to, or preferably as part of, top management with direct and frequent access to the principal manager, as well as to the policy-making board. His unique mastery of factual information equips him, at this level, not alone to *provide* the information, but also to *interpret* it, and, according to some, to *advise* on policy and action based upon it.

6. The controller should provide appropriate information, services, and advice to other departments of the organization. But he must also act as *coordinator* of their operations insofar as they perform functions for which the controller is responsible—that is, finances, accounting, reporting, and others. This responsibility necessitates that the controller operate at a level above the regular operating departments.

7. Forward-looking plans and budgets rest upon intelligent forecasts which in turn depend upon an understanding of past experience, the present situation, and trends. With regard to budgets in particular, such information is very largely financial, accounting, and statistical in nature. It is therefore appropriate or essential that the controller have primary responsibility for supervising the development of the budget, for coordinating its content, for presenting it, and for coordinating its execution.

In more precise terms, the functional areas of controllership in which there appears to be basic agreement now include the following: accounting, which is still the core, including general and cost accounting and accounting policy; budgeting and budgetary control; internal auditing (though some feel this should be segregated from controllership); reporting, statistics, and forecasts; office service functions; tax returns; and legal work in the financial field.[23] But these specific functions form only a platform for the broader role in the areas of coordination, planning, and control. The dimensions as well as the level of controllership are suggested in the following statement of functions of controllership which was developed by the Controllers Institute on Ethics and Eligibility Standards and approved by the National Board of Directors on September 25, 1949:

1. To establish, coordinate, and maintain through authorized management, an integrated plan for the control of operations. Such a plan would provide, to the extent required in the business, cost standards, expense

---

[23] Based upon a list of duties approved some years ago by the Controllers Institute of America as reported by Christian E. Jarchow, Vice-President and Comptroller, International Harvester Company, in Bradshaw and Hull, *op. cit.*, p. 115.

budgets, sales forecasts, profit planning, and programs for capital investment and financing, together with the necessary procedures to effectuate the plan.

2. To measure performance against approved operating plans and standards and to report and interpret the results at all levels of management. This function includes the design, installation, and maintenance of accounting and cost systems and records, the determination of accounting policy and the compilation of statistical records as required.

3. To measure and report on the validity of the objectives of the business and on the effectiveness of its policies, organization structure and procedures in attaining these objectives. This includes consulting with all segments of management responsible for policy or action concerning any phase of the operation of the business as it relates to the performance of this function.

4. To report to government agencies, as required, and to supervise all matters relating to taxes.

5. To interpret and report on the effect of external influences on the attainment of the objectives of the business. This function includes the continued appraisal of economic and social forces and of governmental influences as they affect the operation of the business.

6. To provide protection for the assets of the business. This function includes establishing and maintaining adequate internal control and auditing, and assuring proper insurance coverage.[24]

The higher and broader sights of controllers are perhaps best reflected in the qualifications and preparation now considered necessary for the job. Here we find a recognition, though a somewhat reluctant one, of the necessity of a sound grounding in the tools of accounting, statistics, and reports. But increasingly there is emphasis upon competence in general business management, broad social understandings, salesmanship, public relations, and human relations. One author lists four basic categories of qualifications for controllership as follows (paraphrased):

1. Technical competence, but with emphasis upon judgment and imagination in applying techniques.
2. The faculty of cooperating and enlisting cooperation.
3. Emotional stability, objectivity, patience.
4. "Inner drive." [25]

Another writes: "Thus the primary function of the controller is in the realm of business judgment and not in the area of slide-rule com-

---

[24] As quoted by James L. Pierce in "The Controllership Function: A Modern Concept," *The Controller*, September, 1952, pp. 419-22.
[25] David R. Anderson, in Bradshaw and Hull, *op. cit.*, pp. 108-9.

putations." ". . . controllers have no business of their own but that every-body's business is their business." "If there is confusion in objectives and organizational weakness—and this is by no means infrequent—then the controller's task is one which, even more than in ordinary circumstances, demands skills other than technical proficiency in accounting. It demands tact, vision, aggressiveness, and the ability to give directional influence to the entire business unit. Controller's men cannot and must not be mere accounting craftsmen. . . ." "Controllership requires men who are as broad-gauged and as well endowed with and trained in the skills of human relationship as are executives in the operating departments of the business—in sales and production. The task requires salesmanship of the highest order and demands aggressiveness and organizational ability." "However, the important point to keep in mind with respect to training is that it should be directed primarily toward the development of social and administrative skills rather than toward the development of mere technical proficiency in accounting." [26]

BACKGROUND OF MILITARY COMPTROLLERS

The "controller" who returned to the government from business was a wealthy big brother of the "comptroller" government earlier had bestowed upon business. The Defense Department chose to return to the old fashioned spelling, but in other respects its comptrollers reflect a quite faithful effort to transplant the full business concept.

Many of the activities which now are included among comptroller responsibilities of course go back many years in each of the military departments. Accounting and fiscal functions are about as old as the services themselves. Army and Navy have had budget officers since 1921, and the Air Force had a budget office with limited responsibilities well before it became a department. The Army's Chief of Finance and the Finance Corps which he heads constitute a long-established financial service whose duties at the time of establishment in 1920 were quite comparable to those of the present Comptroller. However, a large portion of the discretionary or general management functions of the corps were never developed, and the Chief of Finance lost the budget responsibility in 1942. The functions associated with the Finance Corps and its officers in recent years have been largely the routine jobs of management of disbursements and collections, and certain other accounting and financial services.

---

[26] Keith Powlison, Vice-President and Controller, Armstrong Cork Company, "Selection and Training of Controllership Personnel," in Bradshaw and Hull, *op. cit.*, pp. 147-63.

Likewise, Army and Air Force had developed central statistical and reporting offices before the end of World War II, and Navy had grouped certain reporting activities with budget in its Office of Budget and Reports. The comptroller offices in all the services included as charter members the central units having to do with budget, reports and statistics, and certain fiscal activities. Insofar as they were developed, all these units anteceded the comptrollers by many years.

During the war, each of the three services (the Army Air Forces for convenience being treated as a separate service) developed a new management organization. In the Navy, it was the Office of Management Engineering, attached to the Secretary. In the Army, it was the Army Service Forces Control Division, attached to the Commanding General, ASF; in the Army Air Forces (AAF), it was the Office of Management Control, attached to the Chief of Air Staff. All were staffed heavily by "civilians," whether in uniform or out—that is, by people trained and experienced in private or nonmilitary government organizations, most of whom left after the end of the war. The functions of the AAF and ASF control units included management engineering, statistics and reports, and certain others. They were roughly comparable to staff units in other Federal agencies, and their development was stimulated by the Bureau of the Budget. Both of these organizations became influential and unpopular. Both were promptly eliminated by the returning regulars at the end of the war. Vestiges of control divisions remained (and still remain) in some of the technical services of the Army. But at headquarters, the principal residual was a bitter memory and a distaste for anything that smacked of "management" or "control." This experience in Army and AAF has had an important effect upon the way the comptroller offices developed in these two departments. The Navy Office of Management Engineering appears to have made a lesser dent on Navy practices and therefore aroused less antipathy.

It may be noted that none of the three organizations had anything to do with "dollar-sign" activities, and none was responsible for budgeting. However, dollar budgeting was of relatively small managerial importance in the war. In the AAF, control and authorization of manpower was actually the important budgeting function. In the Army, manpower work was performed by the War Department Manpower Board (Gasser Board), which continued in operation until the Army Comptroller was established. In the Air Force, this function as well as almost all the other functions of Management Control except statistics were scrapped, along with the office that performed them. The Air

Force thus was compelled (or enabled) to rebuild its management organization pretty much from scratch after 1945.

The thinking that culminated in the establishment of comptrollers in the AAF and later the Army began almost immediately after the war. One of the factors favoring the new concept was the management "vacuum" left by the hasty elimination of the predecessor control organizations. But the comptroller idea was not founded on the previous management organizations and experience—in fact, quite the reverse. There was an effort from the beginning, which is still evident, to distinguish the new units from the old ones. Rightly or wrongly, the wartime units were disliked because of alleged high-handedness in the exercise of their power, which was considerable. There is no question that they trampled on a good many traditions and feelings. The business controller concept could be marketable in the services if it did not involve "control," as the services had grown to understand the word. Therefore, heavy emphasis was laid upon the service functions of the controller, upon his objectivity, upon his reliance upon facts and figures, and upon his association with dollars and dollar economy. Obviously, the old spelling of comptroller was preferable in order to establish that the new offices had no relation with the old, either geneological or conceptual.

Other general factors favorable to the adoption of the new concept included the fact that the military services were at the time undergoing criticism for alleged waste and mismanagement. Furthermore, they were entering a peace or at least a semi-peace situation in which, suddenly, dollars were scarce after a war period of abundance. To the necessity for increased emphasis upon costs, dollars, careful planning and allocation of resources, and economical practices, the business controller concept provided a made-to-order answer. Finally, this was a period when American industry was riding particularly high in popular and military esteem, hailed widely for its enormously productive record in the war and its ability to reduce unit costs.

THE COMPTROLLER OF THE AIR FORCE

For the Air Force, "unification" meant the exact opposite of its dictionary meaning—it meant separation. And though much of the Air Force was already "unified" in this sense in its psychology, its operations, and its organization, the legal "unification" of 1947 gave it new areas of responsibility as well as new scope for innovation. Particularly in the field of financial management had the old Army Air Forces been reliant and dependent upon the Army. The Army had supervised and defended its budget, had paid its bills and audited its accounts. The AAF had a small budget office, roughly comparable to the budget offices of the other branches of the Army, and a small liaison office to negotiate with the Army Finance Department on finance problems. The new service was therefore relatively free of the restrictions of tradition and habit and could develop new practices and organizations, taking the leadership in innovation.

And it did. It was the first to establish a comptroller, first to go on a performance budget (though Navy had tried two years earlier), first to develop a service-wide performance-costing system. Some of its managerial systems it inherited from the AAF. Notable among these was a highly developed statistical reporting system. But most of the functions of the comptroller organization have developed from the ground up since the end of the war.

The work which culminated in the establishment of a comptroller began almost as soon as the war had ended—and perhaps even earlier. On October 5, 1945, Robert A. Lovett, then Assistant Secretary of War for Air, addressed a memorandum to the Chief of Staff directing his attention to the peacetime control problem of the AAF. He wrote:

The complexity of a modern Air Force, coupled with its global field of operations, has been great; the complexities which face a smaller Air Force in physical size will be even greater in the future because the limitation of funds and of personnel will not permit of the margin of safety against error given by multiple projects but will require a more accurate selectivity of projects and a more intense follow-up of the application of the limited funds allocated to such projects. In short, we must be sure that every dollar allocated goes to the most needed project and we must get a full dollar's worth out of every dollar expended.[27]

This memorandum led to a series of studies of Air Force organization by the staff and by consultants, culminating in the establishment of the Air Comptroller on June 7, 1946. These studies included examination of the managerial organization of some large business enterprises, and their product was pretty clearly an effort to treat the Air Force as a business proposition. Five years later, the retiring Comptroller of the Air Force introduced his account of the history of his office as follows: "This is a brief story of the development of a modern business concept." He wrote: "The general concept was to centralize the collection and recording of operating information under a Comp-

---

[27] Quoted in Department of the Air Force, "Deputy Chief of Staff, Comptroller, USAF" (undated, processed).

troller who would insure that the various 'managers' of the Air Force had the best possible facts in the best possible form to guide their decisions." [28] The Air Force concept then, and now, focussed on the obtaining and furnishing to management of facts and figures. The original Comptroller's office was formed by grouping three existing units, the Office of Statistical Control, which supervised the AAF reporting system; the Budget and Fiscal Office; and the Office of Program Monitoring, a unit developed during the war to review and make recommendations concerning Air Force program progress. The Air Comptroller was a Brigadier General directly responsible to the Deputy Commander, AAF. The subsequent development has been one of steady growth in functions, scope, and prestige. Some of the major events were:

March, 1948: The Finance Division, theretofore under the Deputy Chief of Staff, Matériel, was transferred to the Comptroller and established as the Directorate of Finance.

July, 1948: The Office of Auditor General was established under the Comptroller to take over responsibility for all auditing, formerly performed by the Army Audit Agency (*Air Force Regulation* 20-40).

October, 1948: All major air commands and air forces throughout the world were required to establish comptrollers (*Air Force Regulation* 20-34).

July, 1949: Comptroller organizations were required in all wings, worldwide (*Air Force Regulation* 170-10).

August, 1949: The National Security Act Amendments of 1949 were approved (P.L. 216).

September, 1949: The Comptroller was redesignated as Deputy Chief of Staff/Comptroller, USAF (*General Order* No. 66).

June, 1951: The Comptroller established a new Directorate of Accounting, responsible for developing plans, policies, and methods on all accounting problems.

The Office of the Air Force Comptroller, the earliest in the military, is in some ways the most developed and most extensive. Its functional scope is limited in comparison with that of the Army, and it must share the role of general management office with the Directorate of Manpower and Organization, which is under the jurisdiction of the Deputy Chief of Staff/Operations. The Comptroller, in his capacity of Deputy Chief of Staff, is on an equivalent level with the other four Deputy Chiefs of Staff—Personnel, Development, Operations, and Matériel,

---

[28] Lt. Gen. E. W. Rawlings, *Report on Comptrollership Within the Air Force, 1946–1951* (processed).

respectively. He is a lieutenant general. The Headquarters office includes more than 500 positions and there are over 20,000 persons in the comptroller "system," Headquarters and field. A little more than half of these are civilians.

The Office of the Deputy Chief of Staff/Comptroller includes the following organizational elements:

Comptroller of the Air Force—Lieutenant General
Deputy Comptroller—civilian
Assistant for Plans and International Affairs—Brigadier General
Auditor General—Brigadier General

Directorate of Accounting
Directorate of Statistical Services
Directorate of Budget
Directorate of Management Analysis Service
Directorate of Finance

All of the directorates are headed by military personnel, ranging in grade from a colonel in the case of Management Analysis Service to major general in the cases of Budget and Finance. There are civilian deputies in most of the directorates and their subordinate divisions, and civilian and military personnel are interspersed among the staffs.

The principal functions and accomplishments of the various elements of the Comptroller's office are as follows:

Assistant for Plans and International Affairs. This office plans for the organization, personnel needs, training, and careers for the entire comptroller system; it handles problems of the Comptroller in the international field, and performs certain special services.

Perhaps the principal accomplishment of this office and its predecessor organizations has been the extension of the comptroller system to the field, down to the wing and installation level. It has also been responsible for the development and operation of an extensive system for training comptroller personnel for various organizational levels at regular Air Force training institutions and also at private institutions. In both these respects, the Air Force appears to be ahead of its sister services.

The Auditor General. This office, with its field activities, conducts audits of the accounts pertaining to internal operations of the Air Force in the Zone of the Interior; provides technical direction for internal auditing overseas; and conducts audits and surveys of accounts and records of Air Force industrial contractors.

Directorate of Accounting. This directorate maintains the general ledgers of the Air Force and prepares various accounting and financial reports. Its more important functions, however, are in the development of policies and systems for improved and unified accounting control for the Air Force, pursuant to the provisions of Public Law 216. These include development of systems for fiscal, property, and cost accounting and for the operation of the working capital funds.

This directorate has had difficulty in finding and hiring qualified technical personnel for its developmental work. Most of its accomplishments therefore lie in the future rather than the past. The only working capital funds in operation in the Air Force in 1952 were the Clothing Stock Fund, required by law, which began full operations in 1951, and an industrial fund for one printing plant. The installation of a stock fund for petroleum, oil, and lubricants was planned for 1953. The directorate hoped to follow this with stock funds for lumber, commercial hardware, electrical equipment, and other common use items. It also intended to extend the industrial fund idea to the printing plants, and it was tentatively proposing to include laundries and dry cleaning plants, motor pools, lumber yards and the one lumber mill in industrial fund accounts. An interesting experiment has been conducted at the Warner Robbins Depot of the Air Matériel Command, involving the attempted segregation and costing of maintenance operations, distinct from the supply function. While the Comptroller is assuming leadership in these activities, practically all of them fall within the jurisdiction of the matériel offices of the Air Staff and the Air Matériel Command in the field.

The long-range objectives of this directorate include: a simplified, unified accounting system for the entire Air Force; a system of property accounting on a dollar as well as an item basis; central accounting at each base; segregation of maintenance from supply.

Directorate of the Budget. This directorate has responsibility for development and management of the budget system. It prepares and issues the Budget Call, based upon, and including, basic program data furnished it by the Assistant for Programming. It reviews budget estimates for technical correctness and for conformance with policy and program, coordinates and monitors the presentation and defense of the budget before higher authority, and administers the funding program after appropriations are passed.

Its principal accomplishment has undoubtedly been the development and institution of the performance budget system. Its basic budgetary classification was the starting point for the development of the

Department of Defense Cost Category classification, which in turn was the basis upon which the Army developed its new budget structure.

Directorate of Management Analysis Service. This directorate consists of three quite distinct divisions. Its *Progress Analysis Division* makes reports with respect to certain key, critical programs, as assigned —such as Guided Missiles, North African Bases, etc. These are *ad hoc* assignments, and the division is not responsible for following up on the regular Air Force programs. It also occasionally makes summary reports on the status of the Air Force basic missions—strategic, tactical, etc. All its reports are in the nature of informational documents; it makes no recommendations.

The *Planning Research Division* develops techniques for rapid computation of data for use in war planning, and planning of requirements of national resources and industrial production. It is the home of SCOOP (Scientific Computation of Optimum Programs) and operates electronic computers on war planning exercises. Most of this work to date is developmental with respect to computing method, and many of the studies so far made are experimental, applicable to the period after D-Day, and not yet useful for current planning. This division also monitors the development of various planning factors, used in current planning and applicable to both peacetime and wartime.

The *Cost Analysis Division* has in the past been largely responsible for the development and administration of the Air Force costing system, although the developmental aspects were recently transferred to the Directorate of Accounting. The Division receives the cost reports from field installations, analyzes them, develops standard costs for the measurable activities, and publishes and distributes its findings. It also periodically makes intensive cost analyses of particular field activities (such as motor pools or laundries) and also special cost studies on request, such as the cost of a pilot or the cost of training, or the cost of an air defense wing.

The Air Force costing system operated on a world-wide basis from 1948 on. It produced statistical cost data which included cost of military personnel and of matériel, computed at catalogue prices. It was a purely statistical system—i.e. it was not tied in with budget appropriations and obligations and had a different functional classification than the budget projects. The extent to which it was used varied widely among bases and commands, but it does not appear to have been of much value at the Air Staff level. Specifically, the budget people paid no attention to its findings.

Recent joint efforts to improve the system by the Budget, Accounting, Cost Analysis, and Manpower and Organization people led to the adoption in 1952 of a new "Appropriation and Expense Accounting System." A new standard classification of functions and activities was developed, applicable to work measurement reporting, manpower and equipment allocations, cost reports, and, it is hoped, eventually budgeting. The functional chart, however, now differs considerably from the budget project classification. The system is still a "rough-and-ready" one. Military personnel are priced at average rates in each grade; supplies are priced at catalogue prices, which do not include cost of procurement, storage, transportation, etc.; and there is not now contemplated any change in funding, so that the system will still be fundamentally a statistical one.

Directorate of Statistical Services. This directorate plans for and provides technical supervision of the entire Air Force statistical reporting network; it operates the central statistical and reporting services for the Air Staff; and it publishes current statistical analyses of Air Force progress against programs.

Directorate of Finance. Provides Headquarters direction and supervision of the Air Force finance service.

The Comptroller of the Army

Early in the war, General Brehon D. Somerville, Commanding General of the Army Service Forces (originally the Services of Supply) established the Control Division, ASF, as a strong management arm. Its functions included statistics, reports, organization and methods work, and certain others. It was completely divorced from budgetary and fiscal functions, which were under the jurisdiction of the Office of the Fiscal Director, ASF. However, since the major control elements in wartime were nonmonetary, the Control Division became the dominant "staff" organization from a managerial point of view. Counterpart control organizations were established in each of the technical services, in the service commands (now the armies), and at many installations.

Following the close of the war, the Army Service Forces and its Control Division were eliminated though some of the division's functions survived in other units. The control offices of some of the technical services as well as installations remained active, and the divorce between the general management activities of these units and fiscal management persisted. In fact, army regulations until 1952 prescribed the functions of fiscal officers in purely fiscal terms at technical and administrative services, armies, and installations.

The immediate impetus for the establishment of the Office of Army

Comptroller was a series of studies and reports during the war and the early postwar years. The reports during this period by the Senate Special Committee to Investigate the National Defense Program were influential in focusing attention upon the need for more efficient and business-like management and methods.[29]

Secretary of the Army Kenneth Royall, who had served during the war in the Office of Fiscal Director of the Army Service Forces, in 1947 engaged, as a Special Assistant Secretary, Edwin Pauley for the purpose of studying the problem of Army business operations and recommending improvements. Mr. Pauley's findings, which he reported in the fall of 1947, pointed to the need of improved accounting and financial reporting and particularly cost accounting. He recommended that the Secretary employ a high-grade civilian with authority to install improved accounting methods.

At about the same time, another report was submitted to the Chief of Staff by a board of officers, convened to study over-all Army policy and organization. This report, known as the Haislip Report, recommended a comprehensive study of the organization of the Army. It also proposed a permanent unit attached to the Deputy Chief of Staff to carry on a continuing survey of organization and methods. This latter proposal was the impetus for the establishment of the Management Division, later incorporated in the Comptroller's office.

The convergence of the Pauley and Haislip reports led to the establishment a few months later of the Army Comptroller. The functions assigned the new office were those suggested by Mr. Pauley, fiscal and reporting, plus that suggested by the Haislip board, management engineering. The original Comptroller's office in early 1948 was formed by a simple grouping of three existing organizations in these fields: the Budget Division, the Statistics Division, and the Management Division. Subsequently, the Comptroller took over supervision of the Finance Department, the auditing function, and finally the review and analysis aspects of the programming system. But the most significant decision in terms of functional relationships was to bring together under one head the general management activity with the fiscal management activity.

The basic issue at the time of this decision concerned the channel of responsibility of the Army Comptroller. Pauley had proposed a civilian under the immediate jurisdiction of the Secretary of the Army, and

---

[29] This committee, known until 1944 for its chairman, Senator Truman, produced a great volume and considerable variety of reports in the years 1941–48 titled *Investigation of the National Defense Program.*

Secretary Royall endorsed this view. General Eisenhower, then Chief of Staff, preferred that the office be part of the "Army Team," attached to the Office of the Deputy Chief of Staff. (There was then only one deputy.) He felt that if the Comptroller were outside the military family, he would operate more or less as a civilian "commissar," parallel and competitive, and therefore less effective. The issue was settled then, as it was again the following year in connection with Public Law 216, in favor of military control. The Comptroller was made responsible to the Deputy Chief of Staff but with concurrent responsibility to the Assistant Secretary; he was a major general; and he was provided a civilian deputy. Thus was the pattern of civilian-military relations set when the Army Comptroller was first established.

The basic concept in terms of functions, status, and role of the Comptroller has not fundamentally changed since 1948. He was then and is now regarded as a staff arm of the Chief of Staff with a certain responsibility to the Secretary of the Army. To him have been assigned a cluster of the Headquarters functions relating roughly to: fiscal activities—virtually all that have the dollar sign; management and management improvement activities; and reporting and statistical analysis activities. He has command jurisdiction only with respect to the units assigned to him, which now include some of the field activities of the Finance Corps and the Army Audit Agency. The developments of the first four and one-half years have been in the direction of consolidating his position and strengthening his status in Headquarters; of providing him with control over certain new functions; and of extending the concept to the field. The principal incidents in this brief history have been:

November, 1948: *Circular 342* changed the organization of the Army to establish two Deputy Chiefs of Staff, one for Planning, one for Administration, and left the position of the Army Comptroller ambiguous; this circular gave the Army Comptroller supervision and control of the Office, Chief of Finance and the Army Finance Service.

December, 1948: *Circular 394* transferred the supervision of the Army Audit Agency from the Assistant Secretary to the Comptroller.

December, 1948: The Secretary of the Army, by letter, prescribed that all armies, continental and overseas, and the Military District of Washington establish comptrollers.

August, 1949: The National Security Act Amendments of 1949 were approved.

October, 1949: *Circular No. 109*, implementing Public Law 216, changed the Army Comptroller to Comptroller of the Army and established his status as equivalent to that of a Deputy Chief of Staff.

February, 1950: The Program Review and Analysis Division was established.

June, 1950: The Accounting and Financial Policy Division was established.

July, 1951: Manpower authorization and control were transferred *from* the Comptroller of the Army to G-1.

February, 1952: *Army Regulations* No. 10-82 prescribed the establishment of comptrollers by armies, technical and administrative services, installations and major activities "where substantial comptroller functions are performed."

The Office of the Comptroller of the Army is now an organization of more than 400 positions. Its steady growth in size, scope, and importance has been interrupted by one important subtraction of a function, the transfer of manpower authorization and utilization to G-1. This transfer was made following a study by the Comptroller's own Management Division. It meant the loss of one of the Comptroller's original functions and one which would appear to be intimately related to two of his most important responsibilities—budgeting and management improvement. The basic organization of the Office of the Comptroller of the Army in the fall of 1952 was as follows:

Comptroller of the Army—Lieutenant General
Deputy Comptroller of the Army—civilian
Legal Adviser—civilian
Assistant Comptroller of the Army—Operations—Major General
Assistant Comptroller of the Army—Planning Coordination—vacant
Assistant Comptroller of the Army—International Affairs—Colonel

Accounting and Financial Policy Division
Audit Division
Budget Division
Management Division
Program Review and Analysis Division

The Audit Division constitutes the headquarters of the Army Audit Agency, an extensive field auditing organization. In addition, the Comptroller exercises direct supervision over the Chief of Finance and his organization for all statutory functions of the Comptroller.

All of the division chiefs and most of the branch and section chiefs are officers. Many of them have civilian deputies, and civilian and military professional staffs are interspersed at the working level. For example, the Chief of the Budget Division is a major general; his deputy is a civilian; the chiefs of the two branches are colonels; and the chiefs of the various sections are all colonels or lieutenant colonels. As a result of the Army's transfer policy, there is a more or less continual movement in and out of military personnel. Most of the officers are "backed up," however, by one or more technically qualified civilians with permanent tenure and, in some cases, with long experience in their jobs.

The present Comptroller of the Army was promoted to this position from that of Chief of the Budget Division. This is probably a normal line of promotion and reflects the relatively high importance and urgency attached to the budgetary responsibility. The Comptroller was replaced in the Budget Division by a general recalled from a field command for the purpose. The last two heads of the Management Division were likewise recalled from field commands.

The Deputy Comptroller appointed in late 1952 is a man of considerable experience in government organization and management. He came to the Army from an executive position in the management wing of the Bureau of the Budget. He exercises leadership on the development side of the Comptroller program, particularly in the areas of improved accounting, working capital funds, and similar matters. This assignment reflects what appears to be a general design for civilian leadership in the developmental and planning activities of the Comptroller; the operating functions, and particularly the most important one, the budget, are pretty definitely controlled by military personnel.

The achievements of the Office of the Comptroller in half a decade are impressive. Some of the major ones, together with the principal current activities of the various divisions, are described below.

Budget Division. The Budget Division provides leadership and technical direction over the Army budget process. It prepares and issues the budget calls and translates the basic program objectives into budget program guidance. It receives the budget estimates from operating agencies and reviews them, largely from the standpoint of technical correctness and conformance with the guidances. It arranges and supervises the substantive review by the Budget Advisory Committee, of which its chief is chairman, and it supervises the preparation of materials and presentation before higher authorities, including Congress. It recommends funding and allocating programs in the administration of the budget, most of which must be approved by the Budget Advisory Committee.

The most noteworthy achievement of the Budget Division was the performance budget plan, which it developed and instituted in 1951, applicable first to the budget of 1952. Since then, it has worked on perfecting the new classification and has participated in efforts to bring the budget structure in line with the program structure.

Management Division. The Management Division carries on organization surveys and audits, *ad hoc* procedure studies, supervision and stimulation of the Management Improvement Program. It is responsible for development of policies and doctrine with respect to comptrollership throughout the Army, and for planning of training and orientation programs for comptroller personnel.

Among its accomplishments may be included:

1. Several studies of over-all organization of the Army, including preparation of draft legislation leading to the Army Organization Act of 1950.
2. *Ad hoc* studies of organizational problems in Headquarters, leading to organizational changes such as that on manpower, and others on civil affairs and psychological warfare, and the drafting of a special regulation, which lays out the basic responsibilities of army commanders in the field.
3. Extensive surveys, leading to organizational changes, in most of the technical services.
4. Leadership in various programs under the general heading of management improvement, including Cost Consciousness, Supply Economy, Operation Red Tape, Work Simplification, Efficiency Awards. It is now working, through a private contractor, to develop an Army-wide work measurement system.

Accounting and Financial Policy Division. This division has responsibility for the development of objectives, policies, and systems for all Army accounting and for planning and supervising accounting surveys. It has the principal initiative for the renovation of Army accounting along the lines indicated in Public Law 216 and in accord with the current efforts of the General Accounting Office, the Treasury Department, and the Bureau of the Budget. These activities include the planning for fiscal, cost, and property accounting, the working capital funds, and the development of an integrated accounting system.

This division has contributed to a number of the experimental efforts along the lines suggested above. They include tests conducted at Fort Knox and Headquarters, Third Army for an integrated installation accounting system, comprehending all elements of cost; the industrial working capital fund operations at the Picatinny and Rocky Mountain Arsenals, the Manufacturing Division at the Philadelphia Quartermaster Depot, and the printing plants at Ogden and St. Louis; the Stock Fund for Clothing and Equipage; and similar developments now being planned. Although the concrete product of this young division is not yet extensive, it in some respects is in the lead of the rest of the office, indeed of the other departments, in terms of thinking out a well-rounded total plan of fiscal management for the Army.

The Program Review and Analysis Division. In addition to its basic operating function of reviewing Army progress reports against approved program plans, this division is the central staff agency in the general fields of statistics and reporting. It administers a reports control system, prescribes standards for statistics and reporting, conducts special statistical studies, and provides highlighted information for top Army officials as well as outside agencies on request. This division recently undertook to explore and develop methods for basic planning research, the use of mechanical computers, and the development of planning factors, a project comparable to SCOOP in the Air Force.

The program management system is still new and experimental, and the function of this division is in somewhat the same category. The Division has made an impressive showing with respect to reducing reporting requirements and in improving the form and usefulness of progress reports. Work is going forward, under the auspices of the Management Division, to develop further the programming system and particularly to extend it to the field commands.

The Audit Division. This division directs and supervises the Army Audit Agency which has basic responsibility for industrial auditing of Army contracts, and internal auditing of Army accounts in the Zone of the Interior. It also provides technical supervision of auditing overseas.

THE IMPACT OF PUBLIC LAW 216

It is probable that the psychological effect of the National Security Act Amendments, insofar as they concerned comptrollers, was as important as was its legal effect. Certainly the departments concerned already had the legal authority to establish such officers, as both the Air Force and Army had amply demonstrated. Under the act, a civilian Comptroller for the Department of Defense was established with the rank of Assistant Secretary of Defense. This office, backed up by broad statutory powers as well as strong support from its superiors, has gradually assumed a position of tremendous influence in the Department. It is the focus of leadership in the whole field of fiscal management and, through its budgetary review weapons, an important element in military programming. The budget organization of the Defense Comptroller is of special significance in that it is civilian from top to bottom;

it is looked upon by the services as an "outside," civilian group; and, to a considerable extent, its staff members are consciously aware of their role as representatives of civilian interests and civilian control.

Another early result of the act of 1949 was the establishment of a Comptroller of the Navy, which was effected on June 1, 1950, by the designation of the Assistant Secretary of Navy for Air to this title as an additional duty. A naval admiral was named Deputy Comptroller, and the deputy has exercised perhaps the primary responsibility for directing the program. The new organization came into being by a simple grouping of two existing units, the Office of Budgets and Reports and the Office of Accounts and Audit, which were already attached to the Office of the Secretary. The comptroller idea is gradually penetrating to the bureaus of the Navy and the field establishment, but at the time of writing appears to have brought about less disturbance and innovation than in the other services. The functions of the Navy Comptroller's office are pretty definitely in the fiscal fields prescribed by law—budget, accounts, reports, and audit.

In the two departments which already had comptrollers, the act had the effect of fortifying their positions and enhancing their status and prestige. In both cases, the titles were changed, and the effect in the Army was to raise the office a notch in organizational position and in the rank of the incumbents.

But perhaps the most pervasive influence of the law throughout the establishment was the impetus it gave to the improvement of all aspects of fiscal management and the new emphasis it placed upon the functions involved in financial administration, particularly the budget and the accounting systems. The act, in both its wording and its implementation, made the comptrollers the organizational mainsprings and symbols for these drives. The comptrollers have exercised the leadership in each of the departments not only in budgetary improvement but also in the development of new accounting policies and procedures, the installation of revolving funds of the various types provided in the act, and in related fields.

THE COMPTROLLER CONCEPT IN THE MILITARY

Controllers grew up to meet the demands of increasing complexity and bigness in private enterprise. In that realm, they have proven useful. The defense of the United States has often been called the biggest "business" in the country. In fact, each of the military departments is bigger, by almost every measure, than any private enterprise. Therefore, so the logic runs, they should have controllers.

A flaw in this reasoning is that the organization for defense of the United States is not a business in the standard sense of the term. It employs businesses and business practices, and it perhaps should use more of them. But essentially its functions are public and governmental; the processes and the factors entering into decisions concerning it are political; the measurement of performance in terms of objectives in peacetime is political and in wartime rests upon military success or failure, ultimately upon national survival.

The controller epitomizes, in an organizational sense, the supremacy of objective facts and figures in business management, and the recognition, as the ultimate criterion of success, of the profit and loss and balance statements. Where objectives and accomplishments can be *technically measured,* there is reason to juxtapose or even identify the technique with policy and program determination. But where they cannot be, such a relationship may well constitute a triumph of technique *over* purpose. In less cryptic terms, such an application of the controller concept may contribute to: the elevation of subsidiary purposes, which are measurable, over primary purposes, which are not measurable; the emphasis in program and performance upon activities where a "showing" can be demonstrated and proven by "facts and figures"; the application of techniques to situations and problems for which they were not designed and are not suited; the incentive to show short-range economy in lieu of long-range effectiveness.

It is not contended that these tendencies prevail in the military departments nor even that, to the extent that they exist, they are the fault of the comptrollers. It is only that if the business concept of controllership were fully developed and implemented, it would constitute a strong pressure in this direction. While important and tremendously rapid strides have been made toward a faithful translation of the controller concept, concessions have been made to the traditions and to other forces within the services and to the necessities of the times. But there are some who are pressing to go much further. The discussion which follows considers the application of the concept in the military in two basic areas: the position and responsibility of comptrollers in the organization; and the functional grouping within comptroller offices.

The Responsibility of Comptrollers

The controller concept in business envisages a company officer who is part of top management at a level above operating elements of the organization and having direct access to the principal manager. All four Defense Department comptrollers follow this pattern faithfully. All have high level and status; all have access to the principal manager; all are in a coordinative position. Business controllers might approve most enthusiastically the status of the Comptroller of the Army, since his position is above not only the operating units but also the major staff divisions.

The military departments are likewise conforming faithfully to the practice of large business of decentralizing the function by providing subordinate controllers for each major sub-unit of the organization, primarily responsible to their line heads but also having a functional relationship with the central controllers. The military comptroller network, with a comptroller at each echelon down to the installation level, linked together by functional or technical "dotted-lines" and by common orientations and activities, is fast becoming universal.[30]

In a third important respect, however, there is doubt whether the military comptrollerships are in conformity with the business doctrine. This is that they should have a *channel* and a *sense* of responsibility outside the hierarchy of the organization. To be sure, they do have such a channel in law and in form. The comptrollers and deputy comptrollers are appointed and removed by the secretaries of their departments. They "shall be under the direction and supervision of, and directly responsible to, either the Secretary, the Under Secretary, or an Assistant Secretary of the respective military departments: *Provided,* That nothing herein shall preclude the comptroller from having concurrent responsibility to a Chief of Staff or a Chief of Naval Operations, or a Deputy Chief of Staff or a Deputy Chief of Naval Operations, if the Secretary of the military department concerned should so prescribe." [31]

The idea of concurrent or dual responsibility is apparently consistent with the concept of business controllership, involving a mere substitution of the department secretary for the board of directors or its chairman. It has already been noted that the secretaries of both the Army and Air Force chose military men as comptrollers and authorized concurrent responsibility to their respective chiefs of staff. In the Navy, the civilian Assistant Secretary for Air was named Comptroller, but he delegated much of the job to his deputy, a rear admiral. The present Comptroller is the Under Secretary of the Navy.

Regardless of the formal structure, the result in terms of operating relationships appears to be about the same. The "concurrent" channel

---

[30] See Figure 11, p. 132.
[31] P. L. 216, Sec. 402.

is the primary channel. The comptroller (or, in the Navy, the Deputy Comptroller) operates as staff to the chief of staff, not to the secretary. It is probable that the situation and the information of the secretary, particularly in the Army, have improved as a result of collaborative working relationships between his office and that of the comptroller. But it is hardly imaginable that the military comptroller could act as a *checker* or *informer* on his department directly to the secretary—i.e. that he would report anything seriously critical about the command or give advice on change of important policy without clearing it with his military chief. The comptroller is part of the military "team," which is another way of saying that his allegiance to his "command" is undivided.[32]

Public Law 216, it may be recalled, was actually drafted in the Office of the Secretary of Defense under the direction of Ferdinand Eberstadt and W. J. McNeil, who subsequently became the Assistant Secretary of Defense (Comptroller). The draft of the bill initially introduced in Congress provided that all the departmental comptrollers be appointed by and responsible to the secretaries of the departments. The drafters of the bill considered this a most important feature to ensure the secretaries a source and channel of objective information through a loyal and expert force. Thus was the comptroller idea early linked with that of civilian control. The "concurrent responsibility" clause was accepted reluctantly when it appeared that opposition of the military groups would otherwise defeat the whole bill.[33] The compromise accepted the patterns already followed in the Army and Air Force.

A statement made soon after the enactment of Public Law 216 by the (then) Chief of the Management Division of the Office of the Comptroller of the Army is revealing and seems fairly representative of the position of the services on this question:

In conclusion, and on behalf of the Comptroller of the Army, I wish to point out that the principles voiced by General Eisenhower and General Collins when they first considered proposals for an Army Comptrollership are still valid. The Comptrollership must develop as a real *service* to commands—not as a parallel or *competing* commissariat, inspectorate, or duplicate command chain.

We believe that this ideal of service can be realized only if the Comptrollership is married right into the Army team. For if the General Staff

---

[32] Lest the reader conclude that these remarks are intended to be critical or derogatory of this relationship, let me hastily add that I doubt that the military comptroller could operate with any degree of effectiveness in a truly dual capacity.
[33] See above, p. 40.

looks upon the Comptroller as an administrative enemy or an obstacle to be overcome rather than a source of help in achieving the common goal of utmost Army efficiency, the Comptroller device will fail.

In my opinion the intent of the law is clear. If our efforts to render service fail, we can expect the Comptrollership to become a parallel channel which will *police* the Army—whereas I believe that General Eisenhower, General Collins and Mr. Gray were particularly anxious for an organizational design which would permit the Army to *reform itself* from *within*.[34]

Nowhere is this better illustrated than in the process of budget development. The comptrollers, working with the budget advisory committees, review and consolidate the estimates with a primary view to developing and solidifying a defensible service position. Major problems they take to their chief of staff for guidance. Once he has approved the budget, their primary job is to support it against all comers. In these subsequent contests, their principal antagonists include the Comptroller of the Defense Department and the Bureau of the Budget. The department secretary may make important changes in the budget in the few hours he has to deal with it, but he is not assisted by the comptroller and his staff, other than in the furnishing of information he asks for. The first budget review that is critical and objective in an over-all way is that of the Comptroller at the Defense level, since he and his staff are entirely civilian with no career affiliations or allegiances other than the civil service.

As the channel of responsibility is dominantly the military channel, so also is the *sense* or feeling of responsibility predominantly one of military allegiance. The secretaries and assistant secretaries are organizational transients, typically resident a very few years. But the military heads and, more importantly, the system over which they preside, will be here for a long time. The officer, if he is to be successful and happy, must abide by that system and must strive in his work toward its objectives and principles. This is not merely a question of bread and butter, of efficiency ratings, promotions, and important assignments, though they play a role. It is one of continuing effective and productive human relationships with long-time working colleagues; of an indoctrination and orientation going back to the age of eighteen and in some cases almost to birth; and of an organizational doctrine which stresses singleness of purpose, loyalty, and discipline. The very idea of dual or divided responsibility is repugnant to the system and to those strongly indoctrinated in it. The welfare of the sub-organization con-

---

[34] Colonel Kilbourne Johnston in an address to key officers of the Army Staff, October 25, 1949 (processed).

tributes to that of the service, upon which depends the security of the nation, which is an essential to the welfare of the people. They are thus all one, and loyalty to all is expressed through loyalty to the immediate unit and its purposes. Any feelings or expression of direct and personal responsibility to a secretary, a Congress, or the people as a whole is *per se* contradictory to this thesis. High-ranking officers exercising heavy influence over policy decision, it is true, can hardly avoid loyalty contests of this kind. But it would seem unrealistic to inject a system of concurrent or split responsibility as a theme of organizational relationships within a large, unitary establishment operating with a career personnel system, whether or not military.

In one other sense, the responsibility of military comptrollers is not now nor likely soon to become like that sought for business controllers. This is the sense of responsibility to the profession and the standards of controllership as such. None of the services has established a corps or a career of comptrollership, and none has an existing corps or specialism which corresponds to it more closely than the Finance Corps of the Army. Comptroller assignments are temporary and transitory, and present policy is clearly that comptroller officers be furnished from the line and from other specialisms on three- and four-year assignments with complete expectation of return to other types of duty for the balance of their careers.[35] Under such circumstances, it is more than doubtful that any strong sense of comptrollership professionalism could develop among the military personnel, or that it could seriously compete with the existent sense of responsibility to the military profession itself or to the particular military specialism with which the officer is permanently identified.

In summary, the status and position of the comptroller in the military departments is that of staff aid and coordinator to the military commander. This is true not only at the departmental level but at every subordinate echelon where the comptrollers have been set up in strict accordance with the principles of military staff organization. The "consistent" clause of Public Law 216 and the parallelism in comptroller functions in specialisms in the Defense Department, the service departments, and their subordinate echelons have facilitated direct communications among the comptroller offices and provided an authorized

---

[35] The comptroller of one of the departments told the author that one of the worst things that could happen to comptrollership would be to set up a comptroller corps as a permanent military specialty, complete with its own schools and indoctrination. He held that the strength of the idea in the military was the continuous infiltration and out-filtration of officers in comptroller assignments.

channel for "functional" or technical instructions and reports. Pursuant to a directive from the Secretary of Defense,[36] each of the departmental secretaries has designated an under secretary or assistant secretary to be responsible for fiscal matters. These officers and their assistants have worked fairly closely with the departmental comptrollers. As long as the objectives and viewpoints of the military and civilian heads are harmonious, there is no doubt that such working relationships will be effective and constructive. But in the event of important differences, there is little question on whose side the comptroller would and probably should be found. Organizationally and psychologically, it is difficult to see how he could at the same time be a principal staff aid to his commander and a checker on the activities of the command and a reporter to the secretary. A former Comptroller of the Army, who was speaking enthusiastically of the harmonious relationships achieved under the concurrent responsibility system, said of it: "This is where the team is tied together. That's where the civilian authority and the military authority are tied together and the Comptroller becomes a part of the team. As long as these fellows don't get into a fight, it will work fine. If they ever do, I am going to resign! Very fortunately, we have had the closest coordination, the closest sympathy between the Secretary of the Army and the Chief of Staff. That is the way it should be, and I know of no reason whatever why it should ever be otherwise." [37]

The Functions of Comptrollers

Public Law 216 [38] prescribes that ". . . the comptrollers of the military departments shall be responsible for all *budgeting, accounting, progress and statistical reporting,* and *internal audit* in their respective departments and for the *administrative structure* and *managerial procedures relating thereto.*" [39] In his memorandum setting forth "Comptroller Functions and Organization," the Secretary of Defense expanded upon these responsibilities and specified them in more explicit detail. He added the supervisory responsibility with respect to disbursing and receiving cash; the implementation of working capital funds; and statistical and progress reporting including the analysis and interpretation of reports. He specifically referred to various types of accounting—

---

[36] Memorandum to the Secretaries of Army, Navy and Air Force, "Comptroller Functions and Organization," September 27, 1950 (processed).
[37] Lieutenant General Raymond S. McLain (now retired) in a talk before the Army-Wide Comptrollers Conference, May 21, 1951 (processed).
[38] Sec. 402 (b).
[39] Author's italics.

appropriation, property, and cost accounting—as well as to all phases of budget administration.

This prescribed array of activities is almost exactly comparable to the "standard" functions of the business controller, excepting only the inclusion of cash disbursing and receiving which are normally the responsibility of a business treasurer. As has already been noted, the Army has added responsibilities for management studies and management improvement generally, and also the functions of review and analysis in connection with its program system. Its effort has obviously been in the direction of expanding the office to embrace a *general* management role, based upon but broader than its statutory responsibilities for fiscal management. The Air Force has refrained from enlarging the Comptroller's scope in this way, but has rather emphasized service functions in the fields of reporting and statistics, most of which are *non*fiscal in character.[40] Both departments have thus modified the theme and the emphasis of the business controller concept, though in quite different ways.

First, it may be said that there are very substantial advantages in the general pattern of functional groupings under the military comptrollers. Most important is the tremendous impetus and emphasis the grouping of functions under a single head has already given to fiscal management, an area previously neglected or grudgingly accepted as a nuisance. It is more than doubtful that the wide ranging reforms already achieved or underway could have gone as far as they have without the collective force, increased status, and prestige of the comptroller and his divisions.

A second major advantage lies in the possibility of more effective collaboration and coordination among the various functional units. These depend in part upon the relatedness of the purposes and functions themselves, in part upon the willingness and ability of the units concerned to work with each other. A few very solid examples of functional interrelatedness include:

The impact of accounting classifications, policies, and procedures upon budget administration, and *vice versa*.

The relation of financial and program reports and analysis with budget execution.

---

[40] In this discussion, the Navy is not treated. The Navy Comptroller does not appear to have affected functional relationships significantly since the office was established simply by placing a new office over and above two existing ones with no great change in function or scope.

The impact of working capital funds upon organization, budget, and accounting methods.

The relation of work measurement to costing and to program and budget execution.

The relation of budget estimating and review to program review and to organization and management studies.

The potential advantages might be multiplied. To date, however, the comptroller offices have not been conspicuously successful in achieving collaborative effort across divisional lines. The author, in his own explorations in both the Army and Air Force, found in many of his interviews with comptroller personnel a lack of awareness of, or interest in, what their colleagues in other comptroller divisions were doing. Striking examples of failure or absence of coordinative effort were: the failure of the Air Force Budget Directorate to utilize the data derived from the costing system; the simultaneous development of quite conflicting classifications for the performance budget and the program system in the Army; the lack of active participation of either the Management Division or the Budget Division in the Army in the development of working capital funds; the absence in the Air Force of much, if any, relationship between the statistical reporting system and budget execution; the absence of significant participation or co-ordination by the program review, the accounting policy, or the budget people in the planning project in the Management Division of the Army for the development of a work measurement system. In fairness, it should be observed that the organizations are young and in some cases still new; and that concerted efforts are now underway to correct many of these deficiencies. The potential achievements of coordination among these activities are still great.

Disadvantages of the functional arrangement are of three types: grouping of functions that are internally inconsistent; omission of functions that are clearly interdependent; and faulty emphasis.

Internal inconsistencies arise in part from the apparent tendency to consider the dollar as the integrating element in comptroller work. The forecasting and planning of dollar needs, the getting of the dollars, the authorization of them to spending units, the recording and reporting of financial transactions, the disbursement of funds, and the auditing of the accounts and disbursements—these are functions differing in kind, in skills required, in orientation, in the level and nature of discretion. They also differ in the nature of the relationships they entail with the rest of the organization. Some (budget planning) require a close integration and collaboration with the line people; others (accounting, reporting) involve a supervisory and coordinative relationship; still others (disbursing) are almost pure service, detached and nondiscretionary; and finally, auditing establishes an inspectional relationship and demands organizational segregation and objectivity.[41] It may be said that these differing kinds of requirements and relationships need not damage each other if they are segregated within the office. But to the very extent that they are segregated, whatever advantage was sought by putting them together is lost.

Another kind of inconsistency is that between the planning and forecasting—forward-looking—function involved in budgeting and the essentially backward-looking functions involved in almost all the rest of the organization. Accounts, records, audits, management audits, reports, and program analysis all have to do with what *is* and what *was*. They are useful and necessary for management and future planning; but, it may be noted, their use for these purposes is by other offices than that of the comptroller. If the budget is viewed as primarily a historical document, projecting forward past financial experience, and as a tool for the control of dollar expenditures, then it would appear logical that it be located where it is. If, on the other hand, it is primarily a plan, its development should be located at or near offices responsible for planning. Insofar as its location affects the way the budget system operates and develops, the present locus in the comptrollers' offices would appear to be a barrier to the achievement of real program budgeting.

There is one other kind of inconsistency. It is the mixture of operational functions, involving tremendous bodies of detailed and specific information, with generalizing, thinking, and planning functions such as those involved in management and budget planning, in accounting policy development, and in program review and interpretation at the departmental level. It is almost an axiom of administrative organization that the former kinds of activity, when placed in the same organizational setting as the latter, tend to reduce them to their own level. A major need in the budget planning and programming systems in the military and, in fact, in the entire government, is to escape the mass of operational detail, to provide tools and brains for generalizing and

---

[41] I do not share the concern of "purists" in financial management that the functions of disbursement and auditing must for legal and protective purposes be in completely separate offices from each other and from the other financial functions. They are now in fact segregated under the comptrollers to the point where there can be little danger of collusion, and each operates practically as an independent unit.

synthesizing. The combination of functions in the comptrollers' offices may make this more difficult.

Viewed as consolidated offices for fiscal management, the comptrollers' establishments now lack two very important and relevant activities. First is the control and authorization of manpower, now residing in the Deputy Chief of Staff/Operations of the Air Force and in the Assistant Chief of Staff, G-1, of the Army. The significance of manpower authorization to fiscal management is tremendous, partly because of its direct costs and partly because such a great proportion of other costs—supplies, equipment, travel, training, installations, etc.— depend directly upon it. The ability of a budget unit to plan in a comprehensive way, to achieve savings through improved utilization of manpower, to correlate its budget execution with the personnel program, is seriously hindered when another office controls the mechanisms and has the authority for controlling personnel allotments—allotments which the budgeteers must accept as "givens." Furthermore, the correlation of the various systems developed and managed by the comptrollers—work measurement, cost accounting, program and financial reporting—with the manpower reporting and control mechanism is far more difficult and, in fact, has not been fully achieved in either department.

The second major omission is the lack of supervision over, or participation in, the development of the various standard tables of organization, equipment, and allowances which in fact govern such a huge proportion of military expenditures. These tables are, for the most part, developed at subordinate and technical levels, largely upon the basis of military, technical considerations. There is now little systematic method for the introduction and consideration of cost and financial factors. The comptrollers must accept these too as "givens" in their development and review of the budget.

The final question to be raised about comptroller functions is the emphasis placed upon financial and particularly accounting activities. It may be recalled that the business controller grew up from accounting. While some business writers are now tending to subordinate the bookkeeping approach, all seem agreed that accounting remains the core function and the essential qualification of a controller. And budgeting, a late-comer to the business controllers' activities, is looked upon as the development and utilization of accounting information.

The business budget has as yet assumed no such dominant role as the Federal budget for policy decision and for authorization of operations. Even a leading technician in business budgeting states that profitable businesses can and do operate without completely developed or sufficiently long-range budgets.[42] The budget in government agencies, and particularly in the military, is the master "controller" (used in the generic sense) of virtually everything that is done. It is financial, but this aspect is fundamentally instrumental; in fact, in time of war when dollars cease to be the scarce resource, the important budgeting will no longer be in terms of dollars but rather in terms of scarce materials, equipment items, and men. Unquestionably, the most important operation of the military comptrollers' offices is budgeting, and it is becoming so recognized. One military comptroller told the author that the hinge and focus of his entire operation was the budget. The budget heads are ranking officers in the comptroller set-ups. The comptroller himself spends a large proportion of his own time on budgetary problems; and the civilian Deputy Comptrollers of Army and Air Force are both alumni of the Bureau of the Budget.

The military comptrollers have so far changed the accounting-budget relationship to a budget-accounting relationship. To this extent, they have resisted the accounting emphasis of the business controller concept. But the emphasis has had some effect and may in the future have more. Comptroller training for the three service departments has emphasized business-type training, and a considerable part of it has been carried out in university colleges of business. Most of these training programs have included and even stressed courses in accounting. A number of officials within the Defense establishment are pushing in other ways towards a more technically accomplished corps of comptroller personnel, through the placement of qualified civilian accountants in comptroller offices and through the establishment of specialized corps of military comptrollers, qualified as accountants.[43] The impact of the accounting approach is already apparent in the working capital funds, the structures of the budgets, and other recent developments.

The emphases upon accounting and upon independence, implicit in the title and pretty well established in the business concept of the office, constitute now and for the future major problem areas for mili-

---

[42] Walter Rautenstrauch, and Raymond Villers, *Budgetary Control* (New York: Funk and Wagnalls Co. in association with Modern Industry Magazine, 1950), p. 4.

[43] See particularly the various articles by H. W. Bordner, Chief of Accounting Policy for the Department of Defense. The points of view here described with respect to training and to officer specialization are vigorously set forth in his Memorandum to W. J. McNeil on, "Graduate Education and Training for Comptrollership in the Department of Defense," November 24, 1950 (processed).

tary comptrollership and particularly for the relationship of comptrollers with the budget. If the business concept is pushed hard by its supporters within and outside the departments, it could conceivably lead to an outright struggle for power and control between the military specialism and the accounting specialism. In such a struggle, there can be little doubt who in the long run would win. More likely is the gradual emergence of a compromise involving the absorption of a new type of specialism, more or less divorced from military command and planning channels, responsible for dollars, numbers, records, and budgets. Such a situation might lead to the further divorcement of programming from budgeting, each following its own channels and only occasionally linked with the other. And it might thus contribute to a budget less sensitive to program needs and program changes and less responsive to political forces.

chapter VII

conclusions and some proposals

*The man was scrambling around on his hands and knees under a
street lamp. It was late at night. A policeman came by and asked
the man what he was doing. The man said, "I am looking for a
twenty-dollar bill which I lost." The policeman went to his hands
and knees to help in the search. After a few minutes of futile
effort, he was ready to give up. He asked the man: "Are you sure
that you lost the money here?" The man quickly replied: "Oh no,
I lost it up the alley over there but the light is much better
here."*

Origin unknown.

In the first chapter of this study emphasis was placed upon the importance in budgeting and administration of institutions and of accustomed practices. Nowhere in government is the impact of the past
upon the present more pervasive and more significant than in the military organizations, particularly in the older ones such as the Army. In
spite of rapid changes in its environment and in its activities, in spite
of feasts and famines, the basic system of thinking and working together persists. As was pointed out earlier, this is in some respects an
asset and an essential; in others, it is a liability. The drive toward mod-
ernization and rationalization is met and often matched by a stubborn,
silent resistance to change. The recent ideas about the budget have
been and are being grafted on to a system and an organization; they
are not themselves creating a new one. The use of standardization and
of the standard personnel and equipment tables, the free issues of materials and military personnel, and the existence of command responsibility essentially divorced from fiscal responsibility are examples of
long-standing practice, not readily changed from above and outside.
Emphasis upon the status system and the relatively high prestige ac-

corded combat command and staff planning as against fiscal control are others. The primary pattern of Army organization remains, as do the patterns of the technical and administrative services, some of them virtually as old as the Army itself.

The last four years, roughly the years since the passage of Public Law 216, have witnessed tremendous, even remarkable, changes in the management, and particularly the fiscal management, of the military departments. By most administrative standards, a large number of these changes constitute major improvements. They include: the development of comprehensive and forward-looking systems of planning and programming; the installation of new and more comprehensible budget classifications; the modification of the budget process with accompanying shifts in responsibility; the installation of comptrollers at virtually all echelons of the Army and Air Force; and the inauguration, largely under the aegis of the comptrollers, of a substantial body of management improvements of various kinds. Most of these changes were achieved under, and perhaps made possible by, difficult conditions brought about by international as well as national uncertainties, and in a period of rapid growth.

In Chapter I above were set forth certain objectives of public budgeting in a democratic state. They were divided, for analytic purposes at least, between those having to do with program and those having to do with the administration of approved programs. The first category concerned decisions as to what the departments should do—how much or many of what kinds of things and at what costs. The second had to do with how efficiently these things were done or, alternatively, what methods could be utilized to accomplish them at less cost.

The annual military budget has become a most important device, perhaps the most important device, for both program development and program control. And recent years have witnessed significant efforts to relate the budget process with the planning and programming processes. But in certain respects, the budget hinders rather than helps well-balanced program decision-making:

1. The timing of the process requires that fundamental decisions on which budget estimates are based be made from 15 months to, potentially, 30 months before the beginning of the period to which they apply.
2. Basic programmatic decisions are made in advance of the budget, with insufficient reference to their probable costs or to the political and economic support of the nation.
3. The plan becomes solidified in the detail of budgetary computations, reducing flexibility and forcing the defense of initial errors.

4. In part of the review process, at least, each level is more concerned with preparing and presenting a "case" before the next higher echelon than it is in reaching the best possible decisions appropriate to its jurisdiction.
5. The increasing technicality of budgeting tends to center the process, and attendant decisions, upon technically qualified persons—accountants and comptrollers—rather than upon persons qualified and responsible for broad policy and program planning.
6. The detail and itemization attendant upon the present structure of the budget focus attention upon the less important areas of decision and obscure the more important.
7. The distinction between capital and current expenditures, as it has been applied, tends to obscure true program costs and fails to provide a useful classification of expenses by character.

On the other hand, have the budget and its attendant processes helped in the internal management and efficiency of the military departments? Here again there are certain fairly basic shortcomings in the present situation:

1. The budget time-table is out of gear with internal planning needs; it forces pre-planning at a stage too early to be useful for managerial purposes, with the result that operational planning is relatively neglected or is conducted too often on a "crash" basis; the budgets themselves can hardly be related to actual funding when the year begins, and inadequate time is allowed in the field for a real budget estimating job.
2. The classification on the basis of cost categories discourages the merging of budget with program management, as does the technical skill required for budgeting.
3. The budgets and the allotments to users cover only a fraction of the resources actually required and consumed at the user level; the remainder is "free issue."
4. Detailed prescriptions and controls of both a fiscal and nonfiscal nature, imposed by higher authority, severely limit the actual scope of initiative and decision at lower levels; the system inhibits a true delegation of authority and responsibility.
5. Stress on accounting, on legality and propriety in fiscal transactions, on obligations and expenditures, and on detailed record-keeping and reporting, have reduced the budget system's value to management as a device for planning and controlling operations.
6. Except in scattered and largely extra-budgetary instances (and except for the new system now being tried in the Air Force), there is little mechanism or motivation for measuring work and costs in related fashion.

7. Without the mechanics of performance evaluation, there is little budgetary "stake" in doing an efficient job; there is likewise little basis for relating personnel administration with performance and efficiency; commanders by and large have limited acquaintance or concern with budgetary administration.

8. In the Army Class II installations, command and funding channels are both split between the field armies and the administrative and technical services.

ECONOMY, EFFICIENCY, AND THE BUDGET

The shortcomings indicated above have not resulted exclusively either from the innovations of recent years or the practices of the distant past. They are the products of the one imposed upon the other. They represent the outcome of imposing upon a long-existing system first a program approach and second an approach embodied in the phrase, "economy and efficiency." As discussed earlier, the latter approach has from its beginning been associated with the public budget movement. The supporters of Public Law 216 in 1949 identified the basic features of its Title IV—the comptrollers, the performance budget, the working capital funds—with the accomplishment of greater economy and efficiency. In recent months particularly, the public has been led to believe that billions could be saved in the national budget, and especially its military segments, by increasing economy and efficiency without any loss to the functions accomplished. The Sarnoff Committee, after a brief and frustrating experience in the Department of Defense, declared that five billion could be saved in the military departments by more economical practices, though it failed to identify where the savings might be made.[1] Senator Paul H. Douglas, in a book entitled *Economy in the National Government*, in 1952 pointed to "savings" in the military budget "without damage to our armed strength" of from 5.5 to 6 billion dollars.[2] Earlier in the same work, he had declared: "The military authorities are, in fact, probably the greatest wasters of manpower and materials in the country."[3] And he devoted two full chapters to the problem of economy in the military, including a comprehensive chronology of alleged waste.

There appears to be a widely held assumption that the military establishment is wasteful. There is also a general association of budget-

---

[1] The Citizens' Advisory Commission on Utilization of Manpower in the Armed Services, as reported in the *New York Times*, February 19, 1953.

[2] Chicago: the University of Chicago Press, 1952, p. 198. Copyright 1952 by the University of Chicago.

[3] *Ibid.*, p. 146.

ing, more recently performance budgeting, with the goal of economy in government. In fact, some hold this to be the purpose of budgeting, and more particularly the purpose of budgetary reviews. Economy and efficiency are unquestionably laudable objectives, especially in our society. But they are elusive ones, particularly in pursuits such as those of the military agencies. Their broad purposes allow no counterparts with which they may be compared. It would be difficult to prove whether a military department is more or less efficient and economical than another large-scale organization, although comparisons can undoubtedly be made with respect to sectors of its operations. It appears to the author that the significance of the year-to-year budget process to economical and efficient operations has been overstressed, for reasons set forth below.

The first is that the largest potential economies in military operations are indeed budgetary and have to do with basic decisions as to future program and policy. The present programs of building a 120 wing air force, a 20 division army, and several Forrestal-type aircraft carriers may, in part or all, prove to have been "wasteful." Past decisions, like those to attack to the Yalu River, or to "mothball" or not "mothball" our equipment, or to demobilize our forces, or that the defeat of Japan would take a year after the fall of Germany, may have proved "wasteful." It is interesting that this, the biggest kind of "waste," usually appears so only in retrospect, after more complete information is available. At the time such decisions are made they depend largely upon intelligence, used in both its military and its generic sense, and the workings of our political and administrative machinery, both budgetary and nonbudgetary. The attribution of "waste" to past judgments of this order, probably a misnomer, is actually a criticism of intelligence and the way it was applied, rather than of the manner in which money was made available and spent.

A second reason, related to the first, is that a very large part of the "economy" reductions in, for example, the Army appropriations, actually come out of program rather than out of economies in the execution of program. This fact may be disguised to some extent by retaining the basic program but putting off to future years its accomplishment, such as President Truman's determination in his "stretch-out." Or it may be concealed in the Budget Bureau's or the Congress' substitution of their judgment for the military department judgment as to what is needed —as has occurred repeatedly in the case of procurement. But in the vast majority of cases, what is reduced is what is bought and done; it is at least doubtful that reductions usually result in the buying and doing of the same things at less cost.[4]

Third, the vast majority of true "efficiencies" depend upon the internal workings and relationships within the organization. The Defense Department, the Budget Bureau, and committees of Congress may bring about individual economies here and there on the basis of specific studies; they may prod the military agencies into changing their methods of handling individual problems. But the occasional penetration of a few persons into an operation which expends more than 10 billion dollars a year can hardly cover more than a tiny fraction of its processes, and even in that tiny fraction their effect may be very small. The actual saving depends ultimately upon the people responsible within the agency for the use of resources. In other words, the responsibility for doing things more cheaply rests basically upon the people who are responsible for getting them done.

A fourth reason is that the possibility of increasing efficiency within the military departments depends very largely upon the possibility of changing the systems within these departments. Most such changes are systematic, not piecemeal; and most are gradual over several years, not rapid and sudden. It is probable that the most promising principle to govern any such changes is that of authority and responsibility. In the military, this principle, though widely preached, is also widely defective in that the authority and responsibility for the use of resources, whether monetary or expressed in other terms, is not coequal with that for accomplishments. The budget system is relevant to this problem, but it is only part of it. The budget can provide the mechanics whereby achievement and cost are systematically related at every echelon. But the usefulness of such measures depends upon motivations and incentives, themselves intimately related to organizational patterns and to

---

[4] There have, to my knowledge, been no systematic studies of the effects of Budget Bureau and Congressional cuts upon the efficiency of military management. It is my impression that the effect of such reductions upon efficiency is relatively small. One reason is that the reviewing agencies lack the necessary information and time to make an intelligent item-by-item review. A second reason is that their review is—or is intended to be—a review of forecasts and intentions. It is focused upon the future, not the past. The study of Congressional appropriations hearings reveals that a large number of the disagreements reflect differing judgments and predictions of future needs and future costs. And a surprising proportion of the "economy" cuts are of a bookkeeping nature or reflect judgments that money cannot be spent during the budget year even if appropriated. There is, furthermore, some evidence that estimating agencies include in their estimates "insurance" factors in the event of cuts. It is entirely possible that this anticipation of the review process has at times resulted in appropriations higher than they would have been without it.

the system of personnel administration. Ultimately, the hope of greater efficiency in the military departments hinges upon the adaptation to this frame of reference of the career personnel system.

But this consideration must be qualified by a final one: that economy and efficiency are relative terms. They are relative to the purposes of organizations, to the environment within which such organizations operate, and to the time at which they are operating. It is obvious that the American people would not have tolerated the same standards of "economy" for the equipment and supply of our soldiers in Korea as those employed by the Chinese. Likewise we cannot apply in the Army as a whole, for example, the same standards as might be used by a private business engaged in making money for stockholders. Nor would America tolerate the same standards in peace as in war. The standards applicable to different elements of the Army at the same time are different: we would not expect, for example, that guns and ammunition on a hilltop in Korea be "conserved" in the same way as on a target range at Fort Dix, nor that, under either of these situations, they be considered in the same way as they are at an arsenal. We are willing that many thousands of additional dollars be invested in every airplane to provide the individual pilot a perhaps very slight advantage over his potential adversaries. And we are happy and proud that our troops in Korea had turkey for Thanksgiving.

Not least among the problems of military management is the maintenance of a double and perhaps triple and quadruple standard of economy within a personnel system which is by and large unitary. For the qualities and abilities of a successful commander in battle may be quite different and may conflict with those which contribute to success in the management, for example, of a base. The importance and the standards of economy and efficiency applied to the one may be completely inappropriate in the other. The virtues of a "business-like efficiency" which are so applauded in peacetime may prove utterly unacceptable in war. Here again is a basic management problem, beyond the scope of this study. But it may be noted that some amount of "inefficiency" may be a legitimate and "efficient" cost of maintaining and operating a force for war.

The budget, in its rise to near-dominance, has picked up new functions and a greatly enlarged role. It may well be that the single budget process has been overloaded with different kinds of problems, not basically consistent with each other. More specifically, it is doubtful that the dimensions of modern government permit the making of broad policy on the basis of a summation of administrative bits and pieces.

The two purposes of budgeting, the making of program decisions and the provision of an effective system of administration, must be linked; but they should not have to ride the same track at the same time. The present attempt to use the same vehicle for both kinds of purpose is detrimental to both. It is impeding effective policy and purpose determination; it is not facilitating the improvement of administration at the core. Some of the Federal programs considered to be among the most efficient and best administered are those that, through one device or another, have largely escaped the budget process. In fact, in the military, the development of revolving funds, one of the brightest hopes for improved administration, originated partly for the purpose of freeing supply and production operations from the regular appropriating process. The current emphasis upon economy in the budget review process is at once an escape from the real job of making programmatic choices and a screen to conceal the escape.

SOME PROPOSALS

Some of the pages that have gone before suggest the need for rethinking the role of budgeting and perhaps revising its framework and process in the light of the newer demands placed upon it. While the point of reference is the military budget and particularly that of the Army, it is probable that many of these observations have relevance to the organization and operations of other administrative agencies and the Congress. Set forth below are a few proposals growing out of these observations and designed to provide a target for future developments in this field.

A Program Budget

A primary need is a tailoring of budgetary systems and classifications to the requirements of the different purposes they are intended to serve. This means, in effect, two different budget systems: one designed for the development, appraisal, and authorization of future policies and programs at top levels; the other, to facilitate internal programming, management, and control. These we shall refer to respectively as the program budget and the administrative budget.

The program budget should be designed to furnish the most meaningful information for top administrative and for political review. It should facilitate rational choices by the policy decision-makers in the Defense Department, the Executive Office of the President, and the Congress. It should state what the proposed programs are and what they will cost. The classification of programs should be tailored to the respective missions of the departments, but not to categories of cost items.

There are, of course, a variety of ways in which any complex agency's programs may be classified. Perhaps the best guide would be the classification the agency has itself developed for top planning purposes. Usually, this is based on a division of agency mission into its component elements. Those elements may or may not parallel the organization structure. And they may or may not accord with the things money is to be spent for. A program budget is a proposal of things *to be done* and their costs, not of things *to be bought* and their costs. A primary program classification for the Army might include:

> Combat Operations (if any)
> Overseas Noncombat Operations
> Active Defense of the United States
> Operation and Support of Active Forces in the United States
> Training
> Mobilization Reserve
> Research and Development
> Construction
> Services (not directly allocable)

Each of the above could of course be subclassified into its most meaningful elements. In addition, budgetary support information should include other basic data, such as size, type, and readiness of forces; projected requirements of key items of equipment (aircraft, tanks, etc.); and projected personnel strengths. All such estimates, like the estimates of costs for the primary programs, should be over-all, round-number figures. Estimates in dollar detail for budgets that run to billions of dollars are clearly unnecessary, confusing, and suggestive of a nonexistent degree of accuracy.

How would such program budgets be prepared? In the first place, this proposal contemplates a unification of planning and program budgeting. Ideally they should be a single, unified process, developed together. For this purpose, it is suggested that the preparation of the program budget, and its presentation and justification before higher authority, be removed from the comptroller offices and assigned to the appropriate program planning units in the three services.

Secondly, the development of the program budget, like the present development of program objectives, should be a top-level process, centralized in the Headquarters staffs. Program proposals may be invited from the field commands, as they are now, on a year-round basis, and these may, of course, be utilized in developing the program budget.

But the development of the program budget should require no special or annual solicitation of field units. The pricing of budget programs would be done by applying, to basic units of program, cost factors, based on an analysis of previous cost experience. Such factors are well known and frequently used in budget and program offices, and some attain a high degree of accuracy. The development of such cost factors would require a great deal of analysis and some cost information that is not currently available. On the other hand, fairly large sectors of the budgets today are in fact computed in this manner though in considerably greater detail—i.e. by multiplying anticipated program workload by unit average cost factors, calculated on the basis of cost experience. The Air Force has developed and published comprehensive programming factors which might well serve as a starting point for the calculation of costs. Likewise, its current studies in the use of electronic computers for rapid development of program requirements offer great promise for the rapid computation of estimates. In fact, the mechanical problem of developing a program budget would appear to be far simpler than some of the problems now being tackled by the SCOOP project. This method of budgeting would call for essentially statistical, rather than accounting, skills and techniques. It would not necessitate detailed cost accounting data since the cost factors would apply not to specific operations and activities but to basic, broad operations, such as the per man cost of basic training, the cost of equipping a new division, or the cost of supporting a medium bomber wing in combat. Studies on cost factors should proceed within each agency the year around.

Not all of the program budget could be developed in this way. Some activities, by their nature, require a process of building and estimating on a project basis. Major construction and much research and development are of this order. Likewise, new kinds of programs for which there is no relevant cost experience would have to be estimated in much the same way as they are now.

It is not contended that such a system would produce accuracy, in a 10-billion-dollar budget, within plus-or-minus 100 million. If it came within one billion it would probably be more accurate than our recent budgets. As experience is gained in improving the method, the margin of error should decline. Even today, some budget offices can make "flash" budget estimates almost overnight within 3 or 4 per cent of complete accuracy.[5] The method offers promise of greater reliability

[5] "Accuracy," however, is measured in terms of the figures which the budget process itself produces, not actual cost.

than the current budget process, partly because it could be done faster, and therefore later, and would rest upon sounder and more realistic program objectives; partly because it would avoid the cumulative and pyramidal errors that prevail in the present process, particularly in the supply and matériel fields. The present concentration on *item* accuracy may well contribute to total inaccuracy and imbalance.

But the degree of dollar accuracy is, in any case, a secondary consideration. The first aim is that the budget present, in an understandable way, the proposed programs for the next fiscal year, with their approximate costs. The various review agencies, the military and civil heads of the departments, the Office of the Secretary of Defense, the President and his Executive Office, and the Congress, should address themselves primarily to such questions as: should this program be undertaken? should we drop this program? should this one be increased or decreased? Secondly, they should satisfy themselves as to the adequacy of the method of determining cost factors. Increases in cost factors over past experience should certainly be justified, as should decreases.

From the standpoint of agency budgeting, a great potential advantage of a program budget lies in the time factor. The development of the program and the program budget, by one central office, could be a very speedy process, especially since it would be neither necessary nor desirable at this stage to carry the program down to detailed listings of units and objects. It is probable that the entire budgeting process, including intradepartmental review, could be accomplished within two months. Reviews by higher echelons and the Congress would almost necessarily be much briefer, if only because the data to review would be briefer and simpler. With appropriate changes in the law, the time allowance shown in Figure 16 would appear reasonable.

Such a budget calendar would reduce by about one year the time span of the budget and appropriating process. This would mean that the plans and the programs upon which the budget is based would be prepared one year nearer the fiscal year to which they applied. It would mean that budget estimates would be made, from the start, with full knowledge of what was appropriated for the year preceding the budget year; with a firmer basis for predicting the position at the beginning of the fiscal year; with far better knowledge of current progress in procurement, production, personnel, and research; with the benefit of current intelligence about other countries. It would lessen, and in some years eliminate, the necessity of elaborate reprogramming

FIGURE 16

PRESENT AND PROPOSED MILITARY BUDGET CALENDARS
FOR BUDGET YEAR 1955

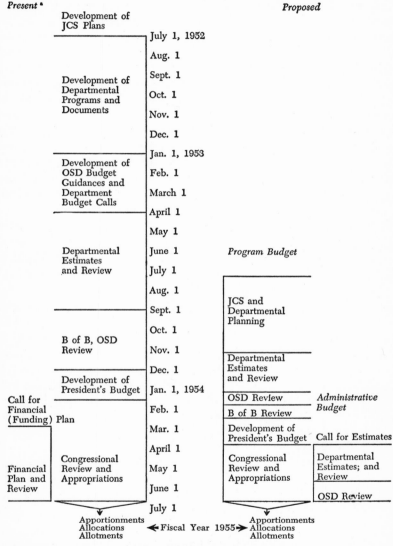

*"Present" practice is based upon an amalgam of the JCS proposal and an approximation of current practice in Army and Air Force.

and rebudgeting between the preparation of initial estimates and the passage of appropriations.

To facilitate intelligent review, the program budget should be accompanied by projections of programs with approximations of costs for the two years following the budget year. Cost estimates for all years should be shown in terms both of obligations and expenditures. Appropriations would, as now, be made in terms of obligating authority. A limited number of lump-sum appropriations should be used, based upon groupings of major programs.

It should be observed, finally, that progress toward a program budget requires cooperation by "all hands." The Army, Navy, and Air Force can do little until the Budget Bureau and the appropriations committees are prepared to review budgets of the kind suggested here. On the other hand, neither the Bureau nor the Congress will act on such budgets until (1) they are satisfied as to the honesty and adequacy of the method, and (2) they are satisfied, through other devices, that the departments can and will administer their appropriated funds wisely, efficiently, and economically. The program budget offers no assurance on these questions.

An Administrative Budget

The administrative budget would furnish the primary vehicle for internal planning and control. It would be based upon the approved program budget, and it would cover the same content, though following different classifications. The administrative budget process would not be basically unlike that of the current budget process; but it would occur about one year later and it would still permit a full three months for internal estimating and review. Unlike the present budget, it would start after the President's budget was known, and it would be based upon firmer program objectives and a reasonably clear knowledge of the funds that would be available. The requesting units would thus have a tangible stake in producing the best case they could for their estimates. In this respect, the process for handling the administrative budget would resemble the present processes involved in the development of financial and funding plans.[6] And, like that process, the administrative budget should culminate in a request to the Bureau of the Budget for apportionments, arriving there shortly after the appropriations are passed.

Unlike the program budget, the administrative budget should pre-

---

[6] See Chapter V.

sent a detailed statement of past, current, and proposed work and costs. Its preparation and review at each level within the service should constitute a searching, thorough, and critical examination of performance and of plans. It could well become an annual spring house-cleaning for management, unencumbered with fuzzy speculation and argument about uncertainties of program in the distant future. It should provide every responsible operating official a "day in court" in which to explain, support, and defend his performance and his plans. It should thus not be a "staff" activity but a process at the very heart of managerial responsibility. The coordination and supervision of this process should not be the responsibility of the program planners who develop the program budget but of the management offices at each echelon—either the comptrollers or such other units as may have jurisdiction of management control. But, of course, the process and the decisions growing out of it must be within the over-all limits of the program budget.

The structure or basic classification of the administrative budget would not be an over-all program classification but an organizational classification. That is, each command, technical service, or bureau would constitute an organic class in the budget; each sub-command, a class at the second level; each installation, a class at the third level; each activity at the installation, a class at the fourth level. A standard classification of functions, service-wide, comparable to that now in use in the Air Force, would constitute the base classes for budgeting and work planning purposes. This classification would likewise be the frame of reference for work measurement, costing, and manpower and equipment allocation. The use of a standard classification would make possible meaningful comparisons among like activities and the development of work and cost standards.

While it is proposed that budget estimates be presented and supported in detail by activity, the allocation and allotment of funds should be in lump sum. Higher authorities in issuing their advices of allotment may properly indicate how they expect the funds to be spent, especially when they have changed the estimates submitted to them. And their allotments should be accompanied by detailed program directives, setting forth what is to be accomplished with the available funds. But the commanding officers at each echelon should have authority to apply the funds in the most effective way possible and to transfer funds as local circumstances require. They should, of course, be held accountable for all such decisions—should report them and, if necessary, defend them. But there should be no question as to their initial authority and responsibility.

Reducing "Free Issue"

There remains the problem that a very large proportion of the resources applied to military programs are "free" to the using and consuming organizations. They are neither costed nor budgeted. The Department of Defense—and before it, the Navy Department—has already
charted the path to correct this situation in part. The present efforts to
put industrial and production-type organizations on working capital
funds are part of the answer. The parallel development of stock funds
for common use items of supply is another part. There appears to be
little reason why the working capital fund idea cannot be extended to
virtually all items of supply and equipment, except in combat zones,
provided that the accounts and inventory records of items purchased
for mobilization reserves are segregated. It would also appear feasible
to apply the working capital system to supply activities at the installation level so that using organizations would purchase their materials
from the local "retail store." Likewise, it might well be extended to
centrally operated service activities, such as hospitals and utilities.

The working capital system is a double-edged weapon. First, it
makes it possible for the consumer organization to budget for, to be
funded for, to purchase, and to be charged for its goods and services
at a price which approximates the total, real cost. As such, it should
encourage wisdom, economy, discretion, and responsibility in the consumption of supplies and services. In the long run, it should contribute
to better accounting, better management, and, incidentally, budget estimates at once more frugal and more accurate. It should discourage the
accumulation of excessive inventories. Not the least of its merits is that
it almost automatically requires property accounting on a dollar as
well as item basis and puts supply accounts on an accrual basis, thus
making possible more nearly accurate determination of activity costs.

The other edge of the working capital fund is that it places the pro-
ducer and supplier activities in a semicorporate status. They are substantially freed from the annual budget process and from appropriation
and obligation accounting. They can plan and budget their operations
flexibly on a monthly, quarterly, and annual basis according to the
needs of their own business management. There appears to be little
reason why a supply depot should not operate along the same lines as
a large-scale wholesaler, or an arsenal along the lines of a munitions
plant. For many military goods there are direct civilian counterparts
and there is thus a possibility of direct competition with private enter-

prise. For many others, direct or "comparative" competition is possible among like units within the services.

A full-fledged working capital fund necessitates the costing of virtually all resources utilized, including: depreciation; personnel, including accrued leave; supplies and equipment; overhead; and transportation. Products are sold to using units at cost. It is possible that, with the development of true cost figures, it will be discovered that many items of supply and equipment can be more economically purchased by using agencies locally than through central supply systems. And, as in civil transactions, the demands of the users for lower prices, prompt service, and quality may well provide direct incentives for improved performance—incentives that do not exist under the free issue system.

It may be noted, also, that one effect of putting the supply and production units on revolving funds would be to eliminate from the annual budget process a substantial proportion of the mass of detail that is now encumbering it. Budget estimates and reviews would be directed to the operating needs of the users, not to the problems of procurement and supply levels. Inspection, audit, and review of operations of the funds could be handled through other and more suitable procedures than that of the annual budget.

The other major area of free issue is the pay and allowances of military personnel. These are now handled through open allotment, budgeted centrally on a world-wide basis, and neither estimated by nor charged to using commanders. Some of the services are now undertaking to "cost" military personnel for limited purposes, but the data are statistical rather than operational in nature. They do not constitute true charges.

This situation necessitates elaborate systems of extra-budgetary manpower authorizations and control. But at the same time it detracts from the effective utilization of manpower by obscuring manpower costs, permitting the "hiding" of military man-hours, and in fact encouraging the use of military personnel on jobs for which civilians would be less expensive.

The obvious way to bring about a real implementation of the stated Defense Department policy—i.e. substitution of civilians for military personnel so as to free the latter for military-type assignments—is to charge military personnel costs to the organizations using their services. Such a practice could be applied to all military personnel in the continental United States except those assigned to tactical units and those in full-time training. Military personnel "spaces" should then be budgeted, and their funds allotted, in exactly the same manner as civilian positions. To be sure, a substantial number of positions of a nontactical nature would and should still be earmarked for military personnel for command, for training and experience, and for career planning purposes. But commanders would be given strong incentives to economize in the utilization of *all* personnel, to substitute civilians for military in assignments for which the former are qualified and less costly, and to free military personnel for tactical assignments.

Modified Roles of the Office, Secretary of Defense, the Bureau of the Budget, and Congress

It is here postulated that the most important functions of higher levels are to review, appraise, and decide on the programs as they are set forth in the program budget. Ideally, each of these reviews, by OSD, the Bureau of the Budget, and Congress, should be separate and independent of each other and each should refrain from detailed inquiries into alleged or suspected inefficiencies in the conduct of the agencies.

Likewise, the administrative budget has been presented as primarily a concern of internal management, not carried forward to Congress and not conceived as a justification of appropriations. What devices can be provided to assure that funds are expended legally, wisely, and efficiently?

The Secretary of Defense in his capacity of managing director of the military establishment should participate in the review of the administrative budget. It is suggested, however, that he not conduct an independent review for this purpose but rather be represented at the top hearings of the three Headquarters and exercise his prerogative of amending the recommended administrative budgets after receipt from the sub-departments.

The Bureau of the Budget should conduct hearings of the administrative budgets in connection with its review of apportionment requests. Where necessary, this examination could proceed after the beginning of the fiscal year, the Bureau retaining its authority to amend apportionments and to reserve funds if necessary. The apportionments, however, should be made only to the level of appropriations and not in terms of the organizational classification of the administrative budget.

The best assurance of Congress and the Bureau of the Budget that moneys are being utilized efficiently is through continuing as well as *ad hoc* investigations of actual practice in the field and through reports and *audits* of past fiscal activity. It is probable, though again not provable, that the studies and inquiries of various of the other Congressional committees have contributed more to the improvement of administrative practices than has the work of the appropriations committees. The mere anticipation of such inquiries is an important stimulus to improved administration. Their sanctions, including cross-examination, suasion, recommendations to agency officials and requests for reports on action taken, published reports, and Congressional attack and publicity, are at least adequate. The effectiveness of such committee work, when based on sound methods of inquiry, is attested in recent years by the work of the watch-dog committees, the Johnson subcommittee, and many others.

The Congress should organize itself to receive and hold hearings on recurrent annual reports by the General Accounting Office covering the regularity of fiscal transactions in each department during the previous fiscal year. It should likewise plan and staff itself for continuing inquiries into operating practices in each department, these scheduled over a period of years so as to assure complete coverage of each agency at least once every four years. Neither of these activities need or should be tied in with the appropriating process.

Control of Tactical Organization and Equipment [7]

From the standpoints both of military effectiveness and of economy and cost, the most important parts of the military budgets are those which relate directly to the internal composition in men and matériel of tactical combat and support units. They have been the object of many recent allegations—unrealistic perfectionism, overspecification, overstandardization, overmechanization, overstaffing, and excessive emphasis upon support and overhead activities.

The extent to which such charges are supportable would be difficult if not impossible to assess, especially by a civilian or lay observer. One reason is that the information is in the main highly classified, difficult

[7] The development and uses of the standardized unit tables have not been discussed in this study except as they are directly related to the budget process. I have, however, suggested that their control in the budget process is fleeting, to put it mildly. That the tables are increasingly becoming central to the concern over military economy is indicated by the book by Senator Paul Douglas referred to above, by the reports of the Johnson Preparedness Investigating Subcommittee of the Senate Committee on Armed Services, and by the inclusion in the defense appropriations of 1953 of Sec. 640, requiring the Secretary of Defense to submit revised tables for all the services to Congress (P. L. 488, 82nd Cong., 2nd sess.). Perhaps most interesting of the Johnson Subcommittee reports in this connection was its "Report on the Utilization of Manpower by the Armed Services: Tables of Organization," Fortieth Report of the *Investigation of the Preparedness Program,* 82nd Cong., 2nd sess.

to uncover, and illegal to reveal. A second is that much of it is extremely technical in both the military and the technological senses. Third, the total content is massive in volume and in intricate detail. A fourth is that there are few if any definitive criteria to apply from either military or civilian spheres of experience. The innumerable decisions which must be made rest heavily upon the exercise of judgment in areas in which uncertainties are very high. Finally, the kinds of knowledge and specialisms which must be brought to bear are exceedingly diverse and are seldom found in a single individual. The primary specialism is undoubtedly military, and, for the most part, the decisions themselves have been controlled by military personnel—and properly so. But other types of factors and knowledges are required—technological, engineering, production, economic, and managerial.

It has already been noted that the annual budget process does not and cannot "get at" these elements, in spite of the fact that they are at the heart of military budgets. Occasionally obvious and absurd errors can be spotted and corrected by budgeteers and by muckrakers from within and without. The requirements of continuity and stability in unit organization would render annual review and modifications of the tables unwise, even if possible. The volume, the detail, the lack of requisite knowledge and information, added to the doubtful prestige of budgeteers in this realm, render it virtually impossible.

A variety of devices are currently employed within the military departments to improve their unit organization and equipment requirements. They include periodic reviews (though still too infrequent) of existing tables and specifications; service tests; reports from combat areas; a variety of reviewing boards; and a considerable layering of coordination and reviews of new or changed requirements. Yet, it appears that many thoughtful military men are dissatisfied with the results, even in terms of combat effectiveness. Over-all, there are increasing charges that the military may be pricing and mechanizing itself out of the "market" of the nation's economy, and out of the field of combat effectiveness. And in this area of dominant national as well as military importance, civilian control is at its weakest. The Office of the Secretary of Defense as well as the offices of the secretaries of Army, Navy, and Air Force have viewed it by and large as "military" and as "operational." They have kept their hands off.

Proposals have been set forth that civilian boards, or committees of lay citizens, be established to look into these problems. Such groups probably have occasional "prodding" effectiveness. But they are not any permanent solution. They are generally not qualified for the job from a military-technical standpoint; even when they are, their opinions lack the force and prestige necessary for acceptance by the military; and they are, by their nature, sporadic and *ad hoc,* not continuing mechanisms.

The Secretary of Defense has a legitimate, even a compelling interest in this area. But the dominant consideration in tactical and organizational decisions should remain military. It is, therefore, proposed that within the Office of the Secretary of Defense there be established a permanent division on tactical organization and equipment. It should be headed by a military officer of high rank, unquestioned prestige among the military personnel, and intellectual independence and initiative. He should be beyond the point in his career where service ambition or loyalty would narrow his judgment or inhibit his decisions. That is, his loyalty should be solely to the Secretary of Defense.

His staff should include both officers and high-grade civilians representing specialized knowledge and reputation in the fields of tactics, technology, production, economics, and management. The functions and powers of this new division would include:

1. Continuing investigation of major items of tactical equipment (ships, planes, tanks, etc.) and of major tactical units of organization, including their authorizations for both manpower and equipment (air wings, divisions, etc.).
2. Participation in intradepartmental reviews of proposed changes or additions of major equipment items and tactical units, with power of veto, subject to appeal.
3. Prescription of standards, criteria, and procedures to be used by the services in the review and authorization of all tactical organizations and equipment and supervision of such systems, including a periodic review of all tables at least once every three years.

The mission of this division would not be economy in the usual narrow sense of the term. It would rather be to assure that the nation is obtaining the maximum combat effectiveness from the manpower, the materials, the production, and the dollars it invests in its present and future combat units. At the Secretary of Defense level, it should work closely with the appropriate agencies to keep currently informed as to strategic plans and needs, production and material feasibilities, and probable developments in weapons and equipment. It would have no part in the annual budget process except in one indirect way. No annual budget should include provision for any tactical units, personnel, or equipment that have not previously been authorized and approved under the procedures prescribed by this division.

index

251